D1544928

THE CONVERSATIONAL FIRM

THE MIDDLE RANGE

Edited by Peter S. Bearman and Shamus R. Khan

The Middle Range, coined and represented by Columbia sociologist Robert Merton, is a style of work that treats theory and observation as a single endeavor. This approach has yielded the most significant advances in the social sciences over the last half century; it is a defining feature of Columbia's department. This book series seeks to capitalize on the impact of approaches of the middle range and to solidify the association between Columbia University and its Press.

The Conversational Firm: Rethinking Bureaucracy in the Age of Social Media, Catherine J. Turco

CATHERINE J. TURCO

THE

CONVERSATIONAL

FIRM

Rethinking Bureaucracy in the
Age of Social Media

Columbia University Press / New York

Columbia University Press
Publishers Since 1893
New York   Chichester, West Sussex
cup.columbia.edu

Library of Congress Cataloging-in-Publication Data
Names: Turco, Catherine, author.
Title: The conversational firm : rethinking bureaucracy
in the age of social media / Catherine Turco.
Description: New York : Columbia University Press, 2016. |
Includes bibliographical references and index.
Identifiers: LCCN 2016002045 | ISBN 9780231178983
(cloth : alk. paper)
Subjects: LCSH: Organizational change. |
Management—Technological innovations. |
Internet—Social aspects. | Bureaucracy.
Classification: LCC HD58.8 .T867 2016 |
DDC 302.3/5—dc23 LC record available at
https://lccn.loc.gov/2016002045

Columbia University Press books are printed on permanent
and durable acid-free paper.

Printed in the United States of America
c 10 9 8 7 6 5 4 3 2 1

Cover design: Fifth Letter
Cover image: © Davide Illini/Stocksy

To Philip

CONTENTS

PREFACE

A T FOUR O'CLOCK one Thursday, more than two hundred of TechCo's employees and most of its senior management team filed into an assembly room just off the company's first floor atrium. TechCo (a pseudonym) is a social media marketing firm that sells software and services to help businesses promote themselves online by using everything from email to YouTube videos, from corporate blogs to Facebook and Twitter. Recently, customer satisfaction with the company's software had declined, and customer churn (i.e., attrition) was on the rise. Folks were heading to an open meeting to discuss the issue.

In fact, the organization had been discussing the spike in customer churn for weeks now on its corporate wiki. TechCo's COO, Keith, had posted over a hundred pages of customer survey and financial performance data online for everyone to see. The results were not pretty. Many corporate executives would shudder to disseminate such information so broadly, but TechCo executives regularly share this level of detail with the entire workforce, and employees typically respond with ideas, opinions, and questions. Ever since Keith's post about churn, they had been doing just that.

To keep the conversation going, the company was now holding one of its "Hack Nights." Hack Nights are voluntary events where employees share their ideas and, along with senior management, collectively hack away at problems they care about. This evening's discussion was being led by three managers, all in their mid- to late twenties. Carolyn from sales, Alexis from consulting services, and Rob from customer support stood before the crowd chatting casually, waiting for the room to settle. After a few minutes, Carolyn stepped forward, greeted everyone with a familiar, "Hey guys," and reminded them why they were there. Then she invited anyone with an idea to come to the front of the room and share it with the group.

The tightly packed room shuffled and shifted as thirty or so TechCoers made their way forward and formed a line. In the queue were a mix of entry-level employees hired in the last year, some longer-tenured employees, and even a few senior executives. Some worked in departments directly affected by the topic of the evening, but others were from departments more removed from the issue such as IT and personnel. One by one, people took the microphone and offered their suggestions.

After the last individual spoke, Rob addressed the crowd. He listed the topics just raised and assigned each to different corners of the room, instructing people to assemble around whichever one they wanted to discuss. At the end of the night, he explained, they would all come back together, and each team would have ten minutes to share its specific recommendations. Pausing for a moment, Rob smiled and said, "Are you all ready for a period of controlled chaos? Go to your corners!"

Almost instantaneously, loud music was piped in, and people began moving about the packed room in a human approximation of bumper cars. At one point, it seemed as if the entire right half of the room was trying to move left, while the left half was trying to move right, leaving everyone stuck in place. Eventually the traffic jam broke and people found their way to their desired corners. The music and sheer number of people talking all at once made brainstorming in larger groups impossible. Employees took to writing their ideas on large flip boards instead and then breaking off into small groups of four or five, pulling chairs together and leaning in to hear one another above the din.

For the next several hours, they worked like this. Pizza arrived at some point and boxes surfed their way around the room, prompting short breaks as team members headed to the kitchen to grab beer from the company's free-beer fridge. Around nine o'clock, after the group had reassembled and then dispersed, a few stragglers collected empty pizza boxes, flipped the assembly room lights off, and headed home.

From the chaos and free beer, to executives sharing information that others might conceal, to lower-level employees weighing in on high-level business issues, this is not what we expect to see in a conventional corporate environment. That is precisely the point.

"The old ways of doing things don't work anymore," TechCo's CEO told me the first time we met. The "old ways" he was referring to were most everything we think of when we think of a conventional bureaucratic firm: vertical hierarchy, centralized decision making, formal rules and guidelines to control employee behavior, corporate communication that follows the rigid lines of the firm's organizational chart, and a staid culture that stifles individual expression. Today more and more firms are questioning these ways as outmoded. At TechCo, the CEO explained, "We're trying to build a postmodern organization that matches the new reality."

That new reality is the social media revolution. Since its inception, social media has profoundly transformed not just how people communicate with one another socially but also how they communicate in and with firms. Inside organizations, employees are increasingly digital natives who grew up with Twitter, Facebook, Instagram, SnapChat, and the like.[1] Born between the early 1980s and the early 2000s, millennials are the fastest growing portion of the labor force and widely noted for their comfort and skill on social media and their preference for newer forms of communication like chat and text over older ones like the phone and email.[2] They are accustomed to more open expression and dialogue than generations past, and they are carrying those expectations into the workplace.[3] Others are too.

In the market, customers are no longer content to just download information about a company's products or services from static corporate websites. They turn to social media to weigh in directly, sharing their opinions and experiences for hundreds, sometimes thousands, to see. When they do, they expect businesses to answer back on those very same platforms. Just like employees, today's customers expect more open, ongoing dialogue from corporations.

Across the corporate landscape, firms are trying to make sense of these cultural and technological changes. They are trying to determine what it all means not only for their business models but also for the very form and structure their organizations take. To investigate this myself, I decided to study TechCo up close, living inside the firm as an ethnographer for ten months. TechCo offers a unique window into the changes being wrought by social media because it has been built in direct response to them. Its software and services are designed specifically to help businesses engage with customers on these new platforms. And, with a median employee age of twenty-six at the time of my study (and a workforce of approximately six hundred at that time), its internal organization has been built with the new generation of workers explicitly in mind. TechCo, in short, is a firm that has taken the spirit and tools of social media and embraced them as organizational philosophy.

Like many these days, TechCo executives talk about this philosophy in terms of "openness." By their own account, they aspire to build a "radically open" organization that matches today's world, and this book follows their attempt to do that. The coming pages take readers on a guided tour of TechCo and its open ways and spaces. We will encounter the organization's open technological platforms, like its wiki and enterprise chat system. We will observe its open gatherings like Hack Nights. We will visit the company's offices, which are open in the physical sense that everyone sits in large workrooms with no walls or cubicles, and also open in the more figurative sense that employees come and go as they please, setting their own work hours and vacation schedules. Along the way, I will analyze what firms like TechCo actually mean by "openness," and we will learn that, just as bureaucracy always has, openness has its own tensions as an organizing philosophy, and some things work better open than others.

Ultimately, I argue that TechCo has achieved its goal of building something new, but openness is not the right metaphor to understand their project, nor does it capture what is truly unique about our technological and cultural moment. At its heart, social media is a platform for voice and conversation, and therein lies its revolutionary potential for firms. By leveraging the spirit and tools of social media, TechCo has succeeded in building something that I call a "conversational firm."

As the description of the Hack Night illustrates, this conversational firm promotes far more employee voice than has been seen before. Across all of its open spaces and platforms, conversations take place that are entirely new to the corporate world. In the process, a more adaptive organization with a more engaged workforce emerges.

The conversational firm is not open in every sense of the word, nor is it entirely postbureaucratic. It does not have open participatory decision making, for one, and certain bureaucratic elements find their way back in, even after having been discarded for more open ones initially. Yet even if TechCo is not as radically open as some may hope or imagine it to be, the changes it has effected are real and powerful. By deconstructing what its project truly is, we will find ourselves deconstructing many long-held notions of the conventional corporate model along the way. In the end, this is the story of how one organization is finding its way to an achievable transformation of the firm in our conversational age. And that is something pretty radical.

THE CONVERSATIONAL FIRM

INTRODUCTION

"**W**E WANT TO rethink everything," Eric said, suddenly shifting forward.

"I have this map in my mind." He extended his left hand to the far end of the table and tapped its white Formica top. "Over here is conventional wisdom—the standard playbook for how you're supposed to run a company." Launching his right hand in the opposite direction, he pounded the table once and smiled. "Our vision is over here."

It was just after noon and Eric and Anil sat across from me in the company kitchen. Several days earlier they had agreed to let me study TechCo, the software company they had founded six years earlier. Over the next ten months I would live inside the organization as its resident ethnographer, observing and documenting its daily practices, routines, and rituals just as anthropologists have long studied remote tribes. Sitting at the table were my tribe's two chieftains, and we were meeting so they could tell me their vision.

That afternoon they explained their driving belief that social media had created new customer and employee expectations in the market. To succeed in this environment, they argued, firms must organize themselves in fundamentally different ways than before. "You can't be that bureaucratic," Eric said. "You have to be more open."

"We shoot for radical openness," Anil added.

As an ethnographer, I was hooked. I wanted to understand what that cherished value meant to the natives and follow their pursuit of it.

* * *

TechCo is a social media marketing firm located in an urban region of the United States. When I met Eric and Anil that day, the firm employed nearly six hundred people, was one of the fastest growing private companies in the country, and had an almost cultlike following among social media marketers and enthusiasts. None of that was what had drawn me there, however. I was interested in studying TechCo because of Eric and Anil's message that the social media revolution was compelling a corporate revolution.

To be sure, they are not the first to suggest that technological developments might spell the death of old approaches to organizing and the birth of new ones. Since the 1950s, scholars in my field have been exploring how technology shapes organizations.[1] Whether it is because the material properties of a given technology demand new work routines and practices, or because technologies are simply objects upon which actors can see and effect new possibilities, scholars have found that technological change is often an occasion for organizational change.[2] Not surprisingly, high-tech companies are often the earliest experimenters when it comes to this.

Social media is also not the first wave of technology to inspire visions of a postbureaucratic world. Starting in the late 1980s and 1990s, academics and practitioners alike began to argue that it might be the beginning of the end of the corporate firm as we knew it. Until that time, the flow of company communication and information had followed the rigid, hierarchical lines of a firm's organizational chart. With the arrival of powerful new network technologies, however, communication within the firm changed dramatically. Innovations like electronic mail, distributed databases, and intranets meant that people could share information more quickly and more broadly than ever before. Work could be distributed, and people could coordinate across time and space in ways previously unimaginable.

Many who studied the firm believed that these new networking technologies would bring new networklike organizational forms.[3] In the firm-as-network, the conventional trappings of bureaucracy would die away. Vertical hierarchy would be replaced by horizontal collaboration. Centralized decision making would give way to distributed authority. The strict division of labor would morph into fluid, project-based teamwork. In our postindustrial information age, we would find our way to the postbureaucratic firm.

Today many people herald social media (including such things as chat, blogs and microblogs, wikis, and social networking sites) for propelling us even further toward that postbureaucratic future. Some point to Wikipedia and open-source software to argue that large-scale production and collaboration can now happen without centralized management or formal structure.[4] Others point to signs of the disaggregation and decline of large, formal bureaucracies and argue that we will see flatter, leaner, and even more transient firms in the future.[5] Meanwhile, companies like Airbnb, Lyft, and Uber are said to be part of a new "sharing economy" in which formal organizations exist merely to coordinate technologically mediated, horizontal exchanges among individuals.

Indeed, one could take Eric and Anil's argument about the transformative effects of social media to be similar to the firm-as-network arguments. Yet even as social media owes its debt to the network technology that preceded it, it is distinct from that earlier technology. The organizational changes it inspires may be distinct as well. Whereas the earlier wave of technological progress suggested bureaucratic firms might be reimagined in the form of a network, today's firms seem to find both a new impetus and a new metaphor in social media: More than a distributed network, social media offers a wide-open platform for communication.[6] It seems only reasonable, then, that Eric and Anil talk of today's corporate revolution in terms of "openness."

They are not the only ones talking that way either. Mark Zuckerberg, CEO of Facebook, has stated that Facebook's mission is to provide services that "make the world more open and connected" and that this "goes for running our company as well." To "be open," he says, is one of the organization's five core values.[7] Google promotes its own "open culture" in which "everyone feels comfortable sharing ideas and opinions."[8] With their open office layouts, their coffee bars and restaurants, volleyball courts and concert spaces, these high-tech giants look little like the tech leaders of a generation ago.[9]

Taking the cue, hundreds of emerging high-tech firms in Silicon Valley and across the country are shooting for openness in everything from their corporate cultures to decision making, from their communication technologies to physical spaces.[10] Even firms we think of as more traditional are joining in the trend. Publishing houses are moving away from private offices to open workspace designs said to facilitate knowledge sharing and collaboration.[11] IBM has adopted blogs and wikilike platforms to promote more open communication among its workforce.[12] General Electric has embraced open innovation practices, going so far as to crowdsource certain design challenges and to bring customers directly into product development projects.[13] All this talk of openness raises important questions, however.

SHOOTING FOR OPENNESS

TechCo and other firms may say they are shooting for openness, but what exactly does that mean? Also, are we sure we even want this?

After all, openness is a complex concept. It is often associated with freedom of expression and democratic forms of governance but also with surveillance and loss of privacy.[14] Past organizational studies have found that corporate rhetoric about open cultures can mask even more oppressive forms of control than bureaucracy.[15] In fact, we need look no further than social media itself—which TechCo and others are using to guide their projects in both spirit and practice—to see the tensions that can emerge in pursuit of openness.

On the one hand, social media's open platforms have served as powerful tools for challenging existing social hierarchies, and they seem to offer inspiring models for how we might build more participatory organizations.[16] Individuals have harnessed blogs, wikis, Facebook, Twitter, and other platforms to destabilize authoritarian regimes in the Arab Spring, challenge the direction of American capitalism with Occupy Wall Street, and organize countless local grassroots efforts. These same tools and platforms have also afforded new opportunities for creative expression and human connection. We use them to connect with old friends and make new ones, to create and share content, to voice our opinions, and to declare our likes and dislikes.

On the other hand, the very same openness that has seemed so liberating has been co-opted by powerful actors to suppress individual autonomy.[17] Twitter may have enabled protesters to organize the 2009 pro-democracy demonstrations in Iran, but it (and other social media used at the time) also enabled the Iranian government to track down and punish dissidents during and after the uprising.[18] The questionable legacies of the Arab Spring and Occupy Wall Street suggest that the open platforms of social media may aid in the initial, heady stages of a revolutionary movement, but also that lasting change demands a sort of sustained commitment and large-scale organization for which these tools are less useful.[19] Finally, for every scholar and pundit who heralds the expressive and connective potential of social media in our personal lives, there are others who point to the potential for bullying or who note that people perform inauthentic versions of themselves on these public platforms.[20]

When a firm embraces the spirit and tools of openness from social media, it imports some of these very same tensions into its organizational fabric. Over the course of this book, we will learn that openness is no panacea as an organizing philosophy. It creates new, exciting possibilities but also brings its own unanticipated consequences that have to be managed. Some things work better open than others, and sometimes the most open practices turn out to be the conventional bureaucratic ones after all.

Across the chapters, I trace the various meanings of openness within TechCo by examining features of the conventional firm that it is trying to discard. I take this approach because whatever else openness might mean, one thing it clearly represents for firms like TechCo is the attempt to transcend conventional bureaucratic approaches to organizing. This, however, raises an even more fundamental question.

TRANSCENDING BUREAUCRACY

Can we actually transcend bureaucracy? Over the years, organizational theory has given us many reasons to think we should want to, but many reasons to think that doing so will be exceedingly difficult, if not impossible.

Writing in 1920s Germany, the father of organizational theory, Max Weber, saw the capitalist firm as a model of rational bureaucratic organization. Its defining features included a strict vertical hierarchy, specialized division of labor, formal written rules and guidelines, selection and promotion of staff on the basis of their technical competence, and separation of personal from corporate affairs. These features combined to make an organizational form so technically superior to any alternative that, by Weber's estimation, the bureaucratic firm was destined to dominate the modern economic landscape.

Weber worried about this development, however. He believed bureaucracy was not just efficient but also dehumanizing, and he feared that it would eventually trap humans in an "iron cage" of their own creation, reducing us all to cogs in an ever-expanding bureaucratic machine. We would seek alternatives, he predicted, but bureaucracy would be too effective a form of control to escape, too efficient a form of coordination to discard. "Revolution in the sense of forceful creation of entirely new formulations of authority" would become "more and more impossible," dreams of breaking out of the cage "more and more Utopian."[21]

Of course, the bureaucratic firm did become the norm, and organizational theorists and cultural critics in the United States eventually began their own explorations of it. Work in the 1930s and 1940s generally built on Weber's notion of its rational, efficient nature.[22] Over time, though, a series of powerful critiques emerged. During the 1950s, organizational scholars and cultural critics began echoing Weber's fear of the dehumanizing aspects of bureaucracy. Works like William H. Whyte's *Organization Man*, C. Wright Mills's *White Collar*, and Sloan Wilson's novel *The Man in the Grey Flannel Suit* characterized life inside the bureaucratic firm as one of oppressive conformity, devoid of opportunities for individual, creative expression.[23]

Around the same time, sociologist Robert Merton hypothesized that bureaucracy might not be as rational and efficient as Weber had imagined.[24] Merton sent his students into the field to test Weber's theory against real organizations, and they returned with evidence of goal displacement and power struggles, red tape and inefficiencies. Yet even as they found Weber to be wrong about bureaucracy's efficiency, they found him to be right about its indestructibility. The now-classic studies of Alvin Gouldner, Philip Selznick, and Peter Blau documented how bureaucratic organizations co-opted interests that threatened to undermine them, adjusted to environmental changes by taking on new missions, and added even more bureaucratic practices to compensate for deficiencies in their existing ones.[25]

Skepticism about the bureaucratic firm only deepened through the 1970s. Inspired by the writings of Karl Marx, a group of scholars proposed what became known as "labor process theory."[26] By their account, the bureaucratic firm was not designed for efficiency; it was designed for the capitalist control and exploitation of workers. Formal rules and job descriptions were ways to divert conflict with management by minimizing direct supervision. The division of labor, as well as new production technologies, were ways of taking knowledge out of the hands of workers and giving it to managers, while also segmenting the workforce so they could not develop a collective class consciousness. Even a firm's informal cultural practices were just tools for pitting workers against each other, obscuring conflict with management, and, ultimately, seducing labor to consent to their own exploitation.

Finally, the "institutionalist" school of organizational theory offered a somewhat less oppressive, albeit still discouraging, view of the bureaucratic firm. Emerging in the late 1970s and early 1980s, but still popular among organizational theorists today, this perspective holds that many of the conventional features of bureaucratic organizations are nothing more than "myth and ceremony."[27] Firms adopt bureaucratic elements such as written rules and policies, standard organizational charts, and human resources departments to conform to long-standing cultural beliefs of what rational, efficient organizations should look like. However, when it comes to their actual internal organization, firms decouple from convention, adopting whatever practices (and organizing in whatever ways) are most efficient.

Powerful normative, coercive, and imitative forces make it difficult for organizational leaders to challenge these myths or even imagine alternatives to them.[28]

Given all these perspectives, it is not surprising to hear talk of wanting to reimagine the bureaucratic firm. Why wouldn't we want to break out of an iron cage that crushes our souls, is of questionable efficiency, and may, at best, be a cultural myth we tell ourselves about how organizations should look or, at worst, a tool for our own exploitation? At the same time, the likelihood of escaping that cage seems low. Whether it is because the bureaucratic firm is a highly effective instrument for coordination and control, or because the cultural environment makes alternatives to it seem impossible, it remains the primary means through which business is organized today, and it does so despite decades of cultural and theoretical critique.

A CONVERSATIONAL FIRM FOR
A CONVERSATIONAL AGE

Despite bureaucracy's apparent indestructibility, this book offers hope that it is possible to pry open the iron cage if we approach things from a new angle. By following what works and what does not work about TechCo's various attempts to transcend bureaucracy with openness—and by examining when and how conventional bureaucracy slips back in along the way—the book provides insight into the opportunities and challenges of shooting for openness as well as the nature and durability of bureaucracy. Ultimately I argue that TechCo has found its way to something quite new and different from the iron cage—a new organizational form I call the "conversational firm."

Such an organization does not do away with all the vestiges of conventional bureaucracy. In particular, it does not become an open, democratic decision-making environment. However, it does maintain a radically more open communication environment than we have ever seen before, and this fosters a more engaged workforce and a more adaptive organization. Using multiple communication channels to promote and sustain an ongoing dialogue with its employees, the firm is able to confront the tradeoffs of openness and bureaucracy directly and to leverage the collective wisdom of its workforce to navigate them. Through its ongoing conversations, the organization finds a way to challenge the market's—and even its own—conventional wisdom, continually iterating and improving upon both the open and bureaucratic practices it adopts as it goes.

In the process, the firm ends up deconstructing our notion of bureaucratic control quite profoundly, and this constitutes a key insight offered by this study. Weber assumed that the elements of the bureaucratic firm he identified were inextricably linked, and an assumption running through organizational theory ever since has been that a firm's formal lines of communication and authority are essentially one and the same.[29] Just consider how an organizational chart is still taken to be a visual mapping of both a firm's formal lines of communication and its lines of decision-making authority.[30] Or how the postbureaucratic rhetoric of the 1980s and 1990s assumed distributed communication would lead to distributed authority.[31] In contrast, the conversational firm that TechCo has built shows us that it is possible to separate a firm's communication structure from its decision-making structure more than we ever thought possible.

In the following pages, we will watch as TechCo distributes information and delegates voice rights both inside and outside the firm quite radically, without discarding, nor particularly destabilizing, its decision-making hierarchy. We will see that communicative empowerment and decision-making empowerment are distinct, that distributing information can be used to improve centralized decision making, that workers do not always want decision rights delegated to them, and that a stable decision-making hierarchy can support the delegation of voice.

Through it all, we will learn that some bars of the iron cage can be pried open more than Weber and others ever anticipated. We will be forced to reconsider our other long-held notions of bureaucracy as well. We will see that corporations can support spaces and platforms for individual expression; that the dysfunctions of bureaucracy (and those of openness too) need not be reflexively absorbed, but can be self-consciously discussed; that labor may demand bureaucratic elements to protect their interests; that technology can bring workers and management together in direct dialogue rather than divide the workforce and divert class conflict; and, finally, that certain myths of organizing can be cast off, and the very question of what is myth and what is efficient organizational practice can become a topic of firmwide debate and conversation.

In the end, the conversational firm that TechCo has built is not entirely postbureaucratic, nor is it radically open in every sense of the term. Just as the horizontal, distributed networks of the 1980s and 1990s failed to translate into the complete dissolution of corporate hierarchy and the end of all bureaucracy as we know it, it is unlikely we will achieve that in the social media age either. But what TechCo has achieved is still a fundamental transformation of the corporate firm and one that is possible in today's world.

Weber believed that bureaucratic organizations necessarily suppressed conversation, both within their ranks and with the outside world, because "any intensive influence on the administration by so called 'public opinion'" would undermine their rational, hierarchical structure.[32] Writing some twenty years later, sociologist Robert Merton said that Weberian bureaucracy was an organizational form that "almost completely avoids public discussion of its techniques."[33] This book will demonstrate that even if we retain certain elements of conventional Weberian bureaucracy (including a hierarchical decision-making structure), it is now quite possible to build firms in which the opinions of employees are heard, firms very much engaged in public discussion of their techniques. In this conversational age, with our new tools and platforms for voice, it is possible to build more conversational firms.

AGENDA

The book is structured as follows. Chapter 1 introduces TechCo's founders and their vision for organizational change, as well the company's millennial workforce whose expectations and habits have inspired the founders' vision. Subsequent chapters each tackle a different feature of the conventional bureaucratic firm that TechCo is trying to reimagine in more open terms. As we watch the firm's experiments with change unfold, the true nature of its organizational project emerges.

Chapter 2 examines TechCo's internal communication environment, asking what happens when a firm rejects the hierarchical control of communication associated with bureaucracy and instead shares information and delegates internal voice rights so that all employees can speak up. Chapter 3 turns to the decision-making environment, asking what happens when a firm tries to reject bureaucratic approaches to control such as centralized decision making and formal rules and guidelines. Chapters 4 and 5 examine TechCo's attempts to rethink conventional bureaucratic approaches to corporate speech and corporate culture. Chapter 6 chronicles how the firm initially rejected a bureaucratic approach to human resources but eventually came to adopt one precisely because of its commitment to employee voice and dialogue. Chapter 7 completes our tour of TechCo with a tour of its very antibureaucratic workspaces. How the firm navigates the challenges of its wide-open physical layout offers a concrete metaphor for how it navigates its wide-open communication environment. Chapter 8 considers the implications that TechCo's conversational model has for past and current theories of the firm. Chapter 9 concludes with a discussion of the future of the conversational firm and its implications for corporate leaders.

The descriptions and analyses presented across all of these chapters are based on ten months of ethnographic observations conducted inside TechCo and over one hundred interviews and reinterviews with individuals at the company. As many corporate ethnographers do, I have changed the names and disguised identifying details of the people I quote, and I have also anonymized TechCo itself. I discuss these methodological decisions and my research process in the appendix. To be sure, this book is not the first to profile one of today's iconoclastic high-tech firms, but its ethnographic method offers something different from most popular portrayals. From sustained observation of an organization's actual practices and with careful attention to what those practices mean both to workers and executives, ethnography is designed to produce a more nuanced and balanced account, grounded in the lived reality of the many people involved.

Nevertheless, no matter how much time an ethnographer spends in the field, no matter how many natives the ethnographer meets and follows around, ethnography is always an incomplete endeavor. The TechCo of today looks different from the one profiled in this book. That is not to say that the organization has lost its commitment to openness or shut down its conversations. Rather, its very commitment means the organization is an ever-evolving entity. For executives and employees at TechCo, I hope this book serves as a timestamp of what was an exciting, challenging, and ultimately very rewarding period for the organization. For other readers, I believe there are general lessons to draw from this deep analysis of a moment in time in one organization's life.

In the pages to come, I try to follow TechCo's lead in embracing the open-ended nature of any complex endeavor. As much as the firm was shooting for a radical revolution, the approach I saw them take seemed more modest at first blush. They were not overthrowing every vestige of bureaucracy in one fell swoop. They were instead deconstructing various elements piece by piece, experimenting with new approaches that, on the surface at least, seemed more appropriate for today's environment. And yet it was through their commitment to open, ongoing conversation and their acceptance of the provisional nature of any given solution that they arrived at something quite transformative in the end. Accordingly, I try to deconstruct their various deconstructions, taking one dimension of organizational life at a time, extracting lessons from their experience as we go. I maintain no delusion that this is the final word. I hope only to join the ongoing conversation about these important issues. More than anything, I hope my chronicle of TechCo's experience sparks insights that inspire the work of future scholars, teachers, and leaders of organizations.

1

THE SOCIAL REVOLUTION

Y FIRST MEETING with TechCo's founders was a casual lunchtime conversation in the company kitchen. Eric and Anil were both wearing jeans and identical gray T-shirts bearing the TechCo logo. Their similarities seemed to end there, however. Eric is tall—a good bit over six feet by my estimate—and he has the lanky, athletic build of a guy who, in his midforties, still likes to shoot a few hoops after work to unwind. With glasses and a thick head of dirty blond hair making its way toward distinguished silver, he has, like many successful CEOs, an executive presence. But he also has an endearing, boyish quality that bucks convention.

"Sometimes I get flak for pushing too hard to rethink things," he admitted with a hint of mischievousness that day, and he remained in a state of nearly perpetual motion throughout our meeting. In one moment, he was leaning back, his chair perched precariously on two legs, one knee bent so his foot could rest comfortably on the table's ledge, the other foot bouncing below. In the next moment, he was lunging forward, draping his tall frame across the table to make a point. It was the body language of someone impatient with the present, searching for a better way.

Anil, by contrast, sat up straight and was nearly motionless. A self-described introvert and the company's chief technologist, he admits to preferring digital communication over face-to-face interaction, computer coding over personal contact, and he remained silent through much of the meeting. Compared to Eric's very physical presence, Anil can seem almost incorporeal, but his quiet contemplativeness has a captivating quality, and employees describe him as a brilliant and kind, if somewhat enigmatic, figure. When he did speak up during lunch, it was to pose a counterintuitive question or to suggest an unconventional take on the topic at hand, as if he were using his distance from the world to rethink it. Despite all the surface differences, I came to see that he and Eric were made of similar stock after all: "It's in their DNA to question things," an employee later put it.

What they questioned, they explained to me that day in the kitchen, were all the conventional ways of organizing a firm. They did not want TechCo to be an "old-school bureaucratic" organization. They wanted it to be a "radically open" one. When I asked what it meant to be more open than bureaucratic, Eric answered, "We just want to give a lot of freedom to people." Then he and Anil elaborated.

Being open meant limiting formal, hierarchical control. Instead of imposing top-down rules to govern employee behavior or having managers supervise a worker's every action, Eric said, "I just want to trust that people will use good judgment and decide for themselves. We don't believe in hierarchy." Instead of centralized decision making by executives, being open meant "radical transparency" and "tons of sharing" of information with the workforce so that employees could participate in the firm's decision process. "We think bad decisions get made when people lock themselves in a room and make a decision in secret," Anil explained. Being open meant a workspace in which managers and employees all sat together instead of being segregated by offices and cubicles. It also meant giving employees free access to company property such as food and lounge areas.

In short, openness meant a lot of different things to TechCo's founders, and almost none of these things were what you would expect to find in a conventional corporate firm. What Eric and Anil defined as "open" directly subverted many elements of Weber's classic bureaucratic model. In fact, what they described sounded more like the open, democratic model to which many antibureaucratic, anticorporate collectives have aspired in the past. I asked if they had a similar ideological or moral agenda, and they were quick to clarify.

"Don't get us wrong," Anil said, "We're red-blooded capitalists. We do this because we think it's good business, because we think it's going to be more profitable in the long run." They explained that social media had created new expectations for openness in the market, and it was their unabashed aspiration to build TechCo into a large, profitable ("billion-dollar-plus," as they put it) corporation. Being open was simply what a firm had to do these days to achieve that level of success.

"It's how you have to run a business today," Eric said, and the two returned to this point several times. Toward the end of lunch, Anil remarked, "Technology has radically changed how people live and work, but most companies haven't caught up." Six years earlier, that very insight was what had inspired them to found TechCo.

The two had met in graduate school in the mid-2000s. Both were captivated by, and early adopters of, social media at the time. They joined all of the then-emerging sites (Twitter, Facebook, LinkedIn, etc.), started their own blogs, and spent countless hours thinking and talking about the implications of these various technologies for individuals and for businesses.

Eric had worked in enterprise software sales before graduate school and left the experience feeling that few companies were adapting their sales and marketing efforts to how customers, especially the younger ones, communicated and behaved online. With the advent of social media, Eric believed that gap would only widen. Meanwhile, Anil was already having success on these new platforms. He may have been an introvert in person, but Anil found it easy to converse on social media. His thoughtful, witty tweets had quickly attracted a large following on Twitter, and his blog took off, gaining thousands of followers in just a matter of months. Both men became increasingly convinced of the tremendous power and reach of social media.

From these experiences, and from their mutual entrepreneurial ambition, a business idea began to emerge. After many late nights and long discussions honing their plan, the two decided to build a company that would sell software tools and consulting services to help businesses market themselves and their products on the Web and through social media. Over the ensuing years, as they sold their vision and TechCo's products to other companies, they came to embrace openness as the organizing philosophy for their own. To understand how they arrived at that philosophy, however, we must look more closely at how they understand the social media revolution and its implications for the corporate world.

CHAMPIONS OF THE SOCIAL REVOLUTION

One hot summer day during my time at TechCo, I stepped from the blistering heat outside into a large conference hall to see Eric and Anil looking cool and relaxed on stage. Before them were more than five thousand corporate marketers, managers, and executives who had gathered for the company's annual user conference.

Over the past few days, a team from TechCo had transformed the city's typically drab convention center into a monument to our hyperconnected age. Massive digital displays now lined the walls. House music was being pumped in from somewhere (or maybe everywhere), and purple-hued black lights illuminated the otherwise dark space, their soft neon glow giving it a distinctly virtual-world feel. Attendees recharged their multiple devices at strategically placed power stations while they recharged themselves with coffee and conversation on nearby sofas. And, at every turn an army of young TechCo employees, marked by their matching T-shirts, stood ready to demo the company's software on slick, flat-screen monitors or to direct people to their next destination.

During the coming week, participants would hear talks on such topics as the future of mobile commerce, how to manage a millennial workforce, and best practices in social media marketing. The conference hashtag would trend high on Twitter as attendees posted thousands of tweets about the presentations they saw, the people they met, and the experience of it all. For the moment, however, everyone's attention was fixed on Eric and Anil. Soon they would unveil three new TechCo applications on the floor-to-ceiling digital screens behind them. But first they began with a reminder of the revolution afoot.

Their message was clear: Social media has radically transformed the market by radically transforming the conversations customers have. In the past, if people were dissatisfied with a product or service, they called or wrote a letter to the company's customer service department. Today they tweet and post their complaints for hundreds, sometimes thousands, of Twitter followers and Facebook friends to see. Individuals also use these platforms to log their pleasure with products and services and to recount positive client service experiences, becoming a sales and marketing channel unto themselves. When prospective buyers want to learn about a product or service these days, they are as apt to turn to one another as to the company itself by scouring online reviews and polling their social network connections for information and opinions. Simply put, through social media customers now direct a whole set of conversations that corporations once controlled.[1]

Addressing the crowd of corporate managers before them, Eric and Anil argued that businesses must meet customers on these new terms and join the conversation on social media. Instead of broadcasting messages through conventional channels like television ads, mass mailings, or telesales, businesses should be active on all of the platforms their customers use. Businesses should respond to comments, share useful product information, and draw people into ongoing dialogue. By speaking and acting as people do on these platforms, firms will become more open, human institutions and less faceless bureaucracies. As Eric and Anil unveiled three new software applications that let companies integrate their sales and marketing activities with a range of social media platforms, they reminded the audience that TechCo products are designed to help do all of this.

In reality, Eric and Anil's vision for corporate change goes one step further than what they articulated in their speech that day. TechCo's founders believe that to respond fully to the profound changes being wrought by social media, firms have to do more than just buy TechCo software and transform their external communication strategies. Firms have to transform themselves internally as well. For starters, Eric and Anil note that traditional bureaucratic practices inside an organization cannot support the speed and volume of external communication necessary to engage with today's customers. Employees need to be given the freedom and the information to converse with customers directly, and that means a more open and less bureaucratic approach to management is required. Furthermore, today's customers are today's employees, and they are carrying their expectations into the workplace, looking for firms to embrace the social media revolution and its associated openness in their internal structure, practices, and culture. This is especially true of millennials, the fastest growing part of the workforce and a group that grew up on social media.[2]

From Eric and Anil's perspective, the millennial generation and its digital natives present an opportunity that corporations must embrace. Firms that accommodate the habits and expectations of this new generation will attract and retain its best workers and gain a competitive advantage. With digitally savvy buyers rendering the conventional ways of doing business dead, TechCo's founders argue that it makes sense to "underrate" experience with those conventional ways and "overrate" experience with the very technologies and modes of conversing that are revolutionizing the marketplace. For these two champions of the social revolution, digital natives are their most skilled and loyal foot soldiers.

Accordingly, our tour of TechCo starts by meeting one of these foot soldiers and observing her at work. Doing so will help us ground Eric and Anil's visionary rhetoric. By stepping away from the founders' words and looking directly inside the firm they have built, we can begin to see the precise nature of the organizational revolution they are enacting and just what sort of change social media is capable of bringing about. This inquiry will continue throughout the book as we discover and deconstruct what exactly openness means at TechCo, what actually is being transformed there, and what all that means for our general understanding of the corporate firm.

FOOT SOLDIERS OF THE REVOLUTION

"I went to an electronic music festival this weekend," Emma said as we walked into one of TechCo's glass-walled conference rooms. She dropped into a chair and adjusted its height for her small frame. "I don't even like that stuff really, but my whole generation is into it so I wanted to check it out."

As she spoke, her eyes shifted momentarily to two TechCo colleagues walking past the room. They glanced in without breaking stride. Returning her gaze to me, she said, "I like learning about different social worlds like that, so it was cool."

In fact, Emma and her whole generation have had an unprecedented ability to create and explore new social worlds. Digital natives, they have been communicating and connecting on social media and networks since childhood.[3] "Facebook came out in high school," the twenty-three-year-old told me that morning, "and I was on chat in middle school." As her attendance at the electronic music festival attests (she had heard about it from a friend's tweet, she told me), these tools have infused her life and those of her generation with a level of communication and information access previously unimaginable.

Until entering the workforce, however, Emma had taken this for granted. A summer internship at an advertising agency opened her eyes: "It was run by a bunch of old fogies and there was just this disconnect between what they were doing and where the world was. . . . Before that, I hadn't thought about things I do naturally as skills I was bringing to a job—like email, social media, social networking, how I consume content all online."

Then she came across TechCo. "I saw on LinkedIn that someone I knew from college had taken a job there. So I went to their website." Then to their blog, their Twitter feed, their Facebook page, their online videos. "I fell in love," Emma recalled.

The company seemed to behave and communicate just as she did. "When they spoke on social media, it was as if it was speaking as a human being. It wasn't like you were talking to a corporation. It made it more human. They were fun. They used slang and referenced memes. They replied to people's comments on Twitter directly. . . . Everything the company did just had a very open, human feel. Any blog post would have a link to the personal profile of whoever wrote it, and people's profiles were just very clearly linked to the company. What the people seemed to be about was what the company was about."

And what the company was about resonated. By providing software and services to help companies connect with customers through social media, Emma believed TechCo was "helping people change how they worked, how whole companies were run." She saw that her ways of communicating and connecting—those things she did so naturally—could be a path to transforming "old fogies" like those at the advertising agency. Most of all, TechCo seemed to embrace these new ways, both externally with its customers and internally with its employees. "It just seemed like a place I had to work."

* * *

Several mornings later, I went to find Emma to observe her daily routine. After she had fallen in love with TechCo online, she had applied for a job and was hired to work in customer support. She had been there for almost a year now, and I was excited about the opportunity to see her generation at work—to observe the supposedly new ways of connecting and communicating they modeled and that TechCo embraced.

Like everyone at the company, including executives, Emma sat out in the open in one of several vast, high-ceilinged workrooms. To this day, the business still operates out of an old, converted furniture factory, with workrooms like this scattered throughout the complex. The rooms hold anywhere from thirty to more than one hundred employees, and all have largely the same layout: exposed brick walls punctuated by drafty steel windows; large, flat, workbench-like desks arranged side by side, forming long, regular aisles; workers sitting shoulder to shoulder and face to face, with no cubicles or walls separating them—a wide-open landscape interrupted by little other than an occasional weathered wood beam.

I had heard the staff talk reflexively of "working out on the floor," and as I walked through the space that morning, it was hard not to recall the nineteenth-century factory once housed there. But something distinctly modern had clearly colonized it since then. Glass-walled conference rooms now lined the workroom's perimeter. Digital displays hung from the lofty ceiling. A sea of laptops and large-screen monitors floated atop the workbenches. And in front of them sat Emma and her peers.

TechCo's fifty or so other "support engineers," as their official title designated them—or "reps," as they were more often called around the company—all sat together in one room. Recent college graduates in their early to midtwenties, reps were staffed in staggered eight-hour shifts and fielded calls from customers with technical questions about TechCo's software. Despite this seemingly conventional setup, what I observed that morning was no ordinary call center.

Apart from everyone's uniform headsets, the vibe was more college-town coffee shop. Everywhere I looked, the reps seemed to be appropriating the open space for shared connection. People moved freely about and, despite the early hour, the room was abuzz with the sound of human conversation. Two reps had pulled their chairs together to talk over bowls of cereal and software documentation. Several others were gathered around a workstation, collectively troubleshooting a problem on the screen. Two more stood chatting by the entrance, coffees in hand.

The space seemed to be a canvas for individual expression. Someone had drawn a massive, colorful dinosaur-scape along one wall, and the staff's visible workstations communicated their distinctive sensibilities. Emma, a psych major from a small liberal arts college, kept a tidy desk and looked preppy in her black skinny jeans, red blouse, and silver ballet flats, although the glitter nail polish she picked at reminded me of her weekend at the electronic music festival. A few seats down sat Anderson, a recent art school graduate and photography buff. With his black Patagonia zipped high and his neck craned in toward his screen, he wore an intense look and was engrossed on a call. Suggesting a capacity for kicking back, however, were a bottle of Wild Turkey Whiskey and an unopened Old Town IPA pushed toward the back of his desk (neither out of place in a company that offers employees free beer anytime they want it). Across from Anderson sat Tory, with his unruly dark hair and large ear gauges. A cold was going around that week—germs "spread like wildfire" through these open offices, I had been told by several people already—and here seemed to be its latest victim. Piled near Tory's keyboard were some discarded orange rinds and next to them a bottle of Nyquil. Tory himself slouched down in his chair and talked hoarsely into a headset, his gray hoodie pulled tightly around his neck.

I pulled a chair up next to Emma and put on a headset of my own. She connected a splitter so I could listen in, then switched her phone to "available." A call immediately rang through.

"Thank you for calling TechCo. This is Emma. How can I help you?" she said brightly. A female caller on the other end of the line explained that the integration between TechCo's software and her email program was not working properly today. "I can help you with that," Emma said. "Can I have your TechCo Customer ID number to get us started?" Like many enterprise programs today, TechCo's software lives on the cloud and is delivered via a SaaS ("software as a service") model. With that ID number, Emma would be able to see directly inside the customer's software system as if she were standing at the woman's desk, peering over her shoulder.

As the customer ticked off her numbered ID, Emma typed it rapidly into a field on one of her two large monitors. Almost instantaneously, she opened six different windows. Her mouse began to fly back and forth across the screens, first clicking on one window, then another, now scrolling down to find a key piece of information and copying it over to a new window, now heading back to retrieve something else. She was checking the program's settings and retracing the customer's steps in hopes of understanding the email problem.

Betraying none of this rapid-fire activity, Emma spoke calmly to the customer. "Oh, are you Jeanette?" she asked warmly as the name flashed by on one screen. "This is Emma. I think we emailed last week about a question you had with the recent upgrade. . . . How's that going for you?" TechCo reps are not held to any scripts or time limits, and over the next few minutes Emma guided the conversation naturally. Meanwhile, she dug deeper and deeper into Jeanette's system, opening more and more windows. By the end of the call, Emma had opened more than twenty windows across her two monitors but to my surprise never once put Jeanette on hold. Displaying both the taste and the knack for multitasking that are often associated with millennials, she continued to converse, all the while scanning rapidly for an answer to Jeanette's email problem.

At a natural lull in the conversation, Emma said, "OK, I can help you with the email issue. But first I see there's an update you've not yet installed.

Can I walk you through that while I start to look into the email problem?" Jeanette agreed, and as Emma walked Jeanette through the first steps of the update, she switched over to her HipChat screen and typed to her colleagues, "Is anyone else experiencing email issues?"

HipChat is TechCo's internal group chat and instant messaging system. While employee voices saturate TechCo's physical workrooms, the workforce is continually engaged in the silent din of digital conversation as well. Each functional group maintains a HipChat "room" that is open to anyone in the company, and most employees keep their own group's room open all day on their computer screens in order to follow, and periodically jump into, the ongoing conversation. Many track conversations unfolding in other rooms as well. Emma, for instance, followed the support group's conversation all day because "it's how I know what's going on," but she also made a point to wander into various product development rooms because so much of her job involved navigating technical features of the software.

Like its physical counterpart, the support team's virtual room was buzzing that morning, and Emma had to wait only seconds for a response to her query. A manager in her group replied on HipChat, "Yes, I sent an email to the [support] team about that this morning." He went on to explain a technical glitch that had taken down some customers' email. For the next few minutes, he, Emma, and several other support reps chatted (virtually) about the issue and how to resolve it while Emma continued to help Jeanette with the update. "In the third field down, type your IP address," she instructed.

"How do I know my IP address?"

Emma smiled and said patiently, "I know it's weird, but if you just Google 'What's my IP address' it will tell you."

The update complete, Emma then guided Jeanette to a part of the system where they could address the email issue. She explained that the problem involved Jeanette's email client and its connection with the TechCo system.

"What's another word for email client?" Jeanette asked hesitantly.

Emma, who by now was controlling Jeannette's computer from afar, waved the mouse over one part of Jeanette's screen, "This."

"Outlook?"

"Yep."

A few minutes later the problem was resolved, Jeanette thanked Emma, and they hung up. Emma began to document the issue in the support group's knowledge management system. While she typed, she said to me, "What you saw there is really typical by the way." I asked what she meant.

"Jeanette," she answered. "Obviously a supersmart woman. She's probably a VP. But I had to translate things for her, help her understand the technology. . . . It's funny. Some of us were recently talking about how to frame support going forward because it's not sustainable to offer everyone unlimited support calls. Someone suggested that we only offer support over chat for customers who just buy the basic product, and I said, 'Hell no.' The customers we talk with, they didn't grow up on chat. I started this when I was eight years old on AOL. HipChat is really just the progression of AIM we all used in middle school. But the customers don't speak the same language."

Having finished her documentation, Emma switched her phone back to "available" and, again, a call immediately rang through. Over the next four hours, she took eighteen calls. It was a study in constant connection and conversation. Navigating her customer's systems, she raced her mouse back and forth across several screens, first maximizing then minimizing one window after another, opening tab after tab on her several open browsers. While doing that, she responded to questions from other support reps on HipChat; and while doing that, she engaged in a witty side conversation over instant message with a friend who pinged her to ask, "Do you watch *Girls* on HBO?"

I found her and her colleagues' ability to maintain so many different streams of conversation impressive and energizing, but I also saw that it brought its own tensions and challenges.[4] With so many people talking to one another in the workroom and to customers on the phone, it was loud, and several times we both had to press our headsets into our ears just to make out a customer's question. At another point during the day, a frustrated support rep took to HipChat to vent about a customer. Almost immediately a manager not previously participating in the chat conversation appeared online and scolded that it was inappropriate to talk that way about customers. Emma turned to me and remarked, "We really should have a private bullshit chat room," referencing HipChat's ability to host private, invitation-only chat rooms, not just those open to the entire company. It was a pointed reminder that not all expression is welcome, and that what is open is open to surveillance too.

I also noticed that constant conversation did not always mean efficient communication. Shortly after Emma had asked her question on HipChat, another support rep joined the chat and asked the very same question, "Is anyone having problems with email?" This time, Emma replied, "Yes, scroll up," instructing him to roll back his screen to locate the earlier conversation that she and others had just had on the topic. This was possible because, unlike verbal chats that exist only in the moment, all HipChats are saved and archived. But I asked Emma about this back and forth, noting that this rep seemed to have missed the manager's original email to the support team, just as Emma had earlier. They were all sitting in the same room, so I wondered why someone did not just stand up and announce, "Customer email is down."

Emma laughed in agreement. "We need to figure out the best way to communicate. We have multiple channels but everyone uses different ones. . . . Even the wiki now, unless you spend a ton of time on it you can miss things." More so even than HipChat, the wiki is TechCo's marquee communication platform, a vehicle through which executives and employees share information and ideas and where the entire company engages in open, ongoing discussions. Earlier in the day a colleague had written a wiki post saying that TechCo should publish a company org chart, and by the time Emma had "liked" it (in the same way one "likes" a friend's post on Facebook), there were already more than forty responses in the post's comment thread. Last week Emma had posted on the wiki herself, sharing some documentation she felt would help new support reps during their training.

The wiki is not a "perfect" platform, Emma told me, but she valued the ability to share her ideas and opinions and to learn from the conversations that unfolded on it: "It's one of my most favorite things on the planet. I hate when I don't have time to check it. You can learn so much about the company, the product, what the executives are thinking. . . . If I have an idea,

I can share it there too. It's a great place to get feedback. . . . It has this great social aspect."

That an open platform might be imperfect but nevertheless enable valuable expression and dialogue would prove to be true of more than just the wiki. Over the course of this book, we will see that TechCo and its workforce are co-constructing a new sort of organizational environment. Employees like Emma carry heightened expectations, and even a unique facility, for a certain type of open participation; and the company, in turn, tries to saturate the workplace with the spaces, tools, and freedom to accommodate those expectations. That said, the day I spent with Emma should raise a number of questions about what sort of "freedom," as Eric put it, openness really implies at TechCo and how far it can ever really go inside a firm. We saw, for instance, the outlines of a fairly conventional hierarchical structure: Emma was assigned to a specific job in a clearly demarcated formal department (support), which was organized by a vertical structure of authority (i.e., frontline employees like Emma were supervised by managers like the one who had appeared on HipChat). We saw that the open platforms and spaces intended to support "radical transparency" also enabled surveillance by managers, and that the environment's physical and virtual openness brought a fair amount of noise, distraction, and inefficiency along with it.

And yet, despite all that, we saw Emma and her colleagues connect and communicate in numerous ways that challenge traditional notions of bureaucratic control. Emma was held to no formal script or time limit in her conversation with Jeanette. In the workroom and on HipChat, she and her colleagues conversed freely with each another, troubleshooting problems together and, sometimes, just blowing off steam. They were free to wander into other rooms (physical or virtual) to follow and join the conversations there, and they offered opinions and participated in company-wide discussions on the wiki.

All this is to say that whatever the social media revolution is bringing about inside firms—whatever openness really means inside TechCo, and however far it can really go inside a firm—my day with Emma made it clear that there was something new and different going on with regard to employee voice and conversation. Just as Eric and Anil understand the social media revolution in the market to be about the new conversations happening among customers, there seem to be a whole new set of conversations happening inside the firm they have built. From this one day with Emma, in fact, we can begin to see the outlines of a conversational firm. What that organizational model is (and what it is not) will become clearer as the book unfolds. For now, it seems only appropriate to continue our tour of TechCo by examining how the firm has organized its internal communication and by turning to that imperfect but valuable social media platform Emma directed us to—the wiki.

2

OPEN COMMUNICATION

S EVERAL WEEKS BEFORE the Hack Night described in the Preface, TechCo's chief operating officer, Keith, wrote a post on the company's internal wiki. TechCo was one of the fastest growing private companies in the country at that time, but Keith's post began on an alarming note. "There are a couple of places where the car is shaking as we hit the accelerator," he wrote.

Keith explained that the company's customer churn rate had spiked up and its customer satisfaction rate had dropped. For a SaaS business like TechCo, high churn can spell disaster because customers pay only small monthly subscription fees for use of the software. If customers cancel their subscriptions too quickly, the company may never recoup the costs it expended to acquire them in the first place, let alone profit from them. Along with his post, Keith attached the 138 pages of detailed business analyses that he and the company's other executives had pored over at a recent meeting. Included were charts comparing TechCo's churn rate to that of its competitors; charts analyzing the impact of different churn rates on TechCo's valuation; detailed profit and loss and cash flow statements; financial projections for the coming months (both the projections that executives shared with the company's board of directors as well as the more ambitious projections they kept to themselves); graphs tracking trends in bookings, customer acquisition costs, and customer satisfaction; and a fine-grained analysis of the recent customer survey that parsed different drivers of their current dissatisfaction.

To frame the data and analyses, Keith had added questions such as "Are we cranking the engine too fast?" and "Are we overheating?" In his notes, he listed thirty "course changes" that he and the other executives had discussed in their meeting, which he phrased in mostly general terms such as "Improve reporting for account managers" and "Fix our model of support." He ended the post by encouraging employees to ask questions and offer their own opinions and comments on the issue.

Following Keith's post, as well as several related ones from other executives in the ensuing days, employees responded with hundreds of specific ideas for those course changes. In a format similar to Facebook, blogs, and many news sites, they shared their ideas in the "Comments" sections of the relevant wiki posts. Suggestions ranged from the small and somewhat trivial (for instance, changing the hold music customers hear when calling tech support) to the more significant (such as developing a new process for onboarding customers onto TechCo's software and redesigning some of the software itself). Employees also asked clarifying questions about the financial analyses and their implications for the business, and executives responded in turn. As the ideas poured in online, Keith decided to hold a Hack Night so that interested employees could come together to work out the details of the suggestions they were making online and to brainstorm new ones. As we saw in the preface, more than two hundred employees attended.

In many firms, detailed information about a weakness in the business would never travel beyond a closed-door meeting of the firm's senior management team, and opening up such an issue for discussion and input from a workforce of six hundred employees would be inconceivable. So why was Keith sharing information that other executives might prefer to conceal? Why were employees taking time away from their own work and personal lives to weigh in on a high-level business issue on the wiki and at a Hack Night? Most important, what, if anything, is all of this informational and communicative openness really accomplishing?

In this chapter, I argue that by embracing the idea of openness from the social media revolution TechCo's leaders have adopted two practices that subvert the conventional hierarchical flow of communication within a firm. First, executives engage in what they call "radical transparency," in which they share detailed, often confidential, information about the business with the entire workforce. Second, executives distribute internal voice rights to everyone in the organization, encouraging employees to share their own information, ideas, and opinions with executives and with one another. The central platform for both practices is the company wiki, but certain meetings such as the Hack Night support these efforts as well.

As the chapter unfolds, we will see how these two practices result in an organization with far greater communicative openness than the conventional bureaucratic firm. However, we will also see that, in leveraging social media as both a tool and a metaphor for organizing, TechCo must now navigate a new set of challenges that are often associated with social media and that paradoxically work to close off some of the very openness the firm seeks.

TRANSPARENCY FROM THE TOP

One morning a few months into my fieldwork, I logged onto the company wiki and saw that TechCo's general counsel had added a post titled "TechCo Equity Summary." I clicked on it and began reading. Laid out in extensive detail was the company's equity structure, including the number of shares and options outstanding, the size of the existing option pool, and the percentage of shares currently owned by employees versus outside investors. The post also detailed the company's full financing history, including the number and price of shares issued to venture capitalists in each round of financing and the company's valuation at each of those rounds. There was a chronological list of option strike prices, spanning all the way back to the company's founding, and a mathematical formula and step-by-step instructions for employees to calculate the value of their own shares at different assumed valuations of the company.

I reread the post, then sat back and tried to decide what to make of it all. My experience with pre-IPO companies when I worked in technology investment banking and my subsequent experience reporting to senior executives at two high-tech companies suggested this was just the sort of information most executives would not want to broadcast. Later in the day, still puzzling over it, I called a venture capitalist I knew and, without disclosing the company's identity, asked if any of his portfolio companies had ever done something like this. "I would fire whoever did," he said brusquely, explaining that it would only distract employees from their jobs as they obsessed over the value of their stock and worried about how that compared to their fellow employees and executives. After hanging up, I dialed a former colleague, now president of a large private technology company. "No way," he answered when I asked if he would consider broadcasting such information to his workforce. "Talk about a monumental distraction," he added.

The general counsel's post betrayed no concern about the information's potential to distract, however. He wrote only that he hoped it would offer greater "transparency" into the organization. From the perspective of organizational and management scholarship, that is an interesting word choice, for "transparency" is often defined in that literature as visibility into the organization's low-level activities.[1] Specifically, it refers to management's ability to observe employee behavior and performance. So defined, transparency at work can turn into surveillance at work, and scholars have long debated its impact on performance and employee satisfaction.[2] Yet when the general counsel wrote "transparency" in his post, and when TechCo executives talk—as they often do—of their desire for "radical transparency" inside the firm, they mean something quite different. They mean visibility into the organization's high-level activities. They mean employees' ability to see what management sees and how management is thinking about it.

Before turning to why TechCo executives might desire this and what it does or does not accomplish for them and for their employees, it is important to understand more fully what such transparency looks like in practice. Keith's decision to share pages of detailed financial analyses and notes from a meeting of TechCo's senior executives was not a rare event; he does this every month after the leadership team meets. He and the finance team also regularly update the company's cash-burn rate and its bank account balance on the wiki. Eric, the company's CEO, uses the wiki to share his quarterly presentations to the board of directors, as well as notes from each board meeting. He and Anil, his cofounder and TechCo's chief technology officer (CTO), use the wiki to share updates on ongoing (often confidential) discussions with potential strategic partners and acquirers, as well as their interpretations of developments in the market such as the acquisition of a key competitor or a competitor's new product announcement. When executives return from conferences, they post notes about what they saw and learned.

The wiki is the primary platform for this sort of top-down transparency, but it is not the only one. Several meetings are designed to support executive openness as well. Each quarter there is an all-hands company meeting during which Keith reviews the business's quarterly financial performance, Eric and Anil discuss strategic issues, and then all three take questions from employees. At the first company meeting I attended, Eric told the five hundred–plus assembled employees about a new product TechCo planned to develop. Almost as an afterthought, Eric told the crowd that this was highly confidential information so not to discuss it outside the company.

To promote transparency at the departmental level, functional groups hold their own all-hands meetings. For instance, there is a monthly meeting for all sales, marketing, and services personnel in which the heads of those groups present detailed performance and productivity analyses of their respective departments and announce any major personnel or operational changes. Finally, during the course of my fieldwork, executives added one additional meeting to aid top-down transparency. Rather than rely on their own instincts as to what information employees might like to have, or to wait until the quarterly company meeting to take questions, they added a biweekly Friday afternoon question-and-answer session. Keith's Wiki announcement of this new meeting read:

> It's getting harder to keep everyone on the same page as we grow. The company meetings are too infrequent to solve this problem and the Q&A time in those meetings is probably inadequate to answer all the questions

and concerns anyway . . . . So, we're going to experiment with an informal, bi-weekly "Ask the Execs" meeting . . . . We'll experiment with the
format but our starting point will be (a) a brief "opening" on what's keeping us up at night these days, and then (b) Q&A, both live and on the
wiki . . . . I hope this helps us keep the lines of communication open and
helps us remain remarkably transparent.

Several questions arise from TechCo's attempt to "keep the lines of
communication open" and to be "remarkably" or "radically" transparent in
this way. First, if theirs constitutes an unusual understanding of workplace
transparency, then from whence that understanding? TechCo executives
talk often about the logic underlying their pursuit of transparency. Quoting
former Supreme Court Justice Louis Brandeis's statement that "sunlight is
the best disinfectant," they argue that sharing information with the entire
workforce holds them as leaders more accountable and leads to better decision making. "We think being closed is corrosive," Anil explained in one
company meeting. "The stupidest decisions happen behind closed doors. If
we do decisions out on wiki where everyone can see them, we're less likely
to do something spectacularly stupid."

This understanding is closely related to definitions of transparency long
associated with democracy and democratic institutions, and most recently
invoked in discussions of the democratizing potential of social media. Transparency there refers to the observability of authorities by citizens and stake-
holders. It is thought to be central to holding the powerful accountable.
Institutions such as a free press, corporate watchdog groups, state monitoring
agencies (e.g., SEC, FDA, OSHA), and newer organizations like WikiLeaks
or the hacker group Anonymous help expose the secrets of those in power
and force disclosure of information that authorities might otherwise conceal.
In doing so, these institutions are believed to play a vital role in democratic
society and to lead to more fair, just outcomes.[3] WikiLeaks, for instance, has
explicitly defined its project of sharing secret corporate and governmental
documents as transparency and justifies it by saying that transparency is central to building "stronger democracies in all of society's institutions, including government, corporations and other organizations."[4]

But this raises its own question: Why would TechCo executives choose to enact this particular understanding of transparency? After all, the democratic discourse explicitly assumes that authorities will not willingly disclose their secrets because doing so could destabilize their powerbase. This is the whole reason third parties who force disclosure are assumed to be requisite. Yet here we see executives volunteering information. To be sure, it can be argued that TechCo's executives could disclose even more than they do (obviously, they only disclose what they want to), but the point remains: They have chosen to share information with their entire workforce that executives at other companies have not historically shared and that many would think foolish to distribute so broadly. So, why do it?

The answer is that TechCo executives do not believe information disclosure destabilizes the firm's or their own hierarchical authority. In the same company meeting in which Anil said that being closed was corrosive, he elaborated on the logic of transparency by noting, "Back in the 1900s, power used to come from hoarding knowledge. It's what drove the hierarchy. [The thought was] 'I have information that other people don't.' We don't think that's true. We think power accrues as a result of sharing knowledge, not hoarding it." The key point is that the power to which Anil refers is that of the firm itself (and presumably the executives who lead it and have large ownership stakes in it).

Recall that TechCo was founded on the observation that social media technologies require a new level of corporate openness to meet the expectations of today's customers and employees and to succeed in the marketplace. One key assumption is that today's corporations need informed employees who can speak and act on the company's behalf on these new platforms. Sharing the organization's knowledge base is consistent with that. Another key assumption is that today's millennial workforce expects greater openness in general. A company whose executives offer just that can gain an edge in the labor market and foster a more committed, contented workforce. By this logic, then, transparency is simply good business. In fact, we saw in chapter 1 that TechCo's founders distance themselves from any political or moral agenda and, instead, directly link their attempt to build an open organization to their capitalist ambition. They are transparent because they are "red-blooded capitalists." They are simply operating with a new theory about the relationship between information and corporate power, one influenced heavily by their understanding of the changes wrought by social media.

But is their theory even valid? Does this sort of transparency advance corporate interests by creating more effective and engaged employees and better firm decisions overall, or is it just an unnecessary distraction? Returning to the churn story can help us answer this question. One evening not long after Keith's wiki post but before the Hack Night, I walked into an Asian fusion restaurant in a different part of town and was led by the hostess to a table where four TechCo workers sat. This was a company "Mystery Dinner," one of about thirty happening in various restaurants around the city that evening. Given TechCo's rapid growth, the company was experimenting with new ways for employees to meet people outside their local work group, and Mystery Dinners, in which groups of employees who did not know one another previously were randomly assigned to dine together, were one such experiment. As the five of us ordered our first round of drinks, we did a round of introductions, and I wondered to myself about the merits of corporate social engineering projects like this. By the end of dinner, however, I was thinking only about executive transparency and the ways in which it seemed to be fostering a uniquely informed and involved workforce.

With three years at TechCo, Steve was the veteran at our table that night. Twenty-eight years old, he was a respected sales manager at the company. Jennifer, a few years younger than Steve, had worked in TechCo's operations group for the last two years. She and Steve had met before, though they seemed only passing acquaintances. Aaron, twenty-three, had started in tech support just three months earlier; and Mike, a customer consultant in his early thirties, had been in a new-hire training class I had observed just a month earlier.

As dinner got under way, Steve, the veteran, asked Aaron how he liked tech support. Aaron answered that he was surprised by how difficult the customers were finding the recent release of TechCo's software. He offered vivid, almost alarmist descriptions of calls coming in over the support line, including forty-five-minute wait times given the huge backlog of callers overwhelmed by the complexity of the software. To these digital natives at the table, the customers' difficulty with new technology was perplexing and even somewhat amusing, but the conversation quickly shifted to the business implications of it.

Mike noted with concern, "In the analysis Keith put up, the number-one reason customers churn is that they think the products are too hard to use." Steve, visibly disturbed by what Aaron had described as well, said, "I knew it was bad, but not this bad. Forty-five minutes is a long time to wait." He asked Aaron what the company should do. Aaron hesitated and responded, "Well, I've only been here three months," but Steve persisted and with a smile said, "That just means you'll be more right than the rest of us." Pausing for a moment, Aaron then offered that perhaps TechCo could provide more direct services through their in-house customer consultants.

Nodding in agreement, Steve said, "I was talking to an executive today, and I think we need to set aside the economics if that's what it takes to solve this. Things that take customers hours to accomplish, we could do for them in five minutes. Maybe we should, if it can solve churn." That would require a larger services arm of the business, he acknowledged, and on that point Mike asked, "The economics are totally different though, right?" Nodding again, Steve explained, "Yeah, totally. If you look at the multiple [the company would] get valued at for software, it's like ten or twelve times revenue; but for services it's like three times. It matters if we IPO. Then again, we can't IPO if churn is out of control."

Jennifer joined in, observing that the way other SaaS businesses had achieved very low churn was by making their products "mission critical, so there's that huge stickiness." She went on, "We're selling something totally new that people haven't done before, but that means they sometimes think they can just keep doing what they've done in the past and ignore us. But that's ignoring the way the world works now." About to take a swig of beer, Steve paused, lowered his bottle for a moment and said, "Right. That's our challenge. We have to bring them forward."

The conversation continued like this for over an hour and a half. I got the impression that these four would stay all night if they believed it would solve the company's churn problem. Without the detailed analysis Keith had provided on the wiki, however, this conversation would never have been possible. Nor, presumably, would the company have been able to incorporate employee suggestions and make rapid changes across the business to solve the churn problem in just a matter of months, as it did. From examples like this, it seems that precisely because the information executives share has the potential to distract—that is, precisely because this sort of transparency gives employees an awareness of issues outside the scope of their specific roles—it creates a workforce capable of adopting a more global perspective on the business. In turn, employees are more willing and able to offer up their own information, ideas, and opinions on important strategic matters. Put simply, the executive transparency practiced at TechCo does seem to foster a deep employee involvement that serves the company's interests.

But what of employees' interests? Critics of social media have written of the so-called unpaid digital labor, and thus exploitation, that takes place when corporations benefit from people's use of social media. For example, we regularly provide free marketing to corporations when we discuss products or share content we like online, tweeting links and "liking" things on Facebook. Some people blog for no pay on sites like Huffington Post that then profit from all the free content.[5] Aren't TechCo's employees engaging in a similar kind of unpaid labor when they read executives' lengthy wiki posts and worry about churn, but only get paid for the work of their day jobs—or when they stay late for a Hack Night, or spend an entire dinner trying to solve the company's churn problem? Isn't it somewhat unfair that when executives share "what's keeping us up at night" (as Keith wrote on the wiki), it probably keeps employees—whose salaries do not reflect that responsibility—up at night too? More to the point, if the power that accrues from all this transparency accrues to the firm and its executives, then how is this any different than what Marxist scholars have been arguing all along? In 1979, sociologist Michael Burawoy argued that managers used cultural enticements to coerce employees to work harder and unwittingly consent to their own exploitation. Is the situation at TechCo today any different?

These concerns should not be dismissed out of hand, but to answer these questions in the affirmative requires an assumption of false consciousness, which the data from TechCo do not support. Later chapters will demonstrate that in my private conversations with employees, they rarely held back criticisms of the company and its executives, and they were not at all blind to when their interests conflicted with management's. However, when it came to executives sharing information, all but one individual cited it as an unambiguous positive. Employees reported deriving both practical and symbolic value from executives' transparency, and they did not interpret the occasional extra or after-hours involvement as exploitative.

For starters, employees noted the educational and instrumental value of it to them personally. According to one of the company's top sales reps, he read the wiki religiously because the information and perspectives executives shared there helped him position the product more effectively, answer prospective customers' questions better, and, ultimately, sell more software. This served the company's interests to be sure, but it also increased this ambitious young man's commissions and helped him advance within the sales organization—two things that, by his own account, he greatly valued. Moreover, he explained that his ambitions extended beyond being just a TechCo sales rep to someday running his own business. Having visibility into the activities and thought processes of company leaders was an invaluable education for that. He explained, "I'll read the wiki for an hour and get so much out of it that I can use [in selling the software]. But the other stuff about the business, it's stuff I couldn't learn at another company." It was that "stuff" he would take with him wherever his career led, he said.

Likewise, an employee in the operations group noted that the ability "to see how [the executives] think about things, what they think about" was "empowering" in her day-to-day work because it helped her to be more effective and to "see how what I'm doing is important." But she too was thinking about the long term, and she believed that what executives shared was a valuable education for "down the road" as well. Top-down transparency may tap into a general human desire to learn, or perhaps educational experiences have some elevated currency for this young workforce.[6] Either way, executive transparency at TechCo was seen by employees as enhancing their human capital and helping to advance their careers not just within the organization but also beyond.

Executive transparency also carried a certain symbolic value for workers. A self-described cynic, Kevin had worked in TechCo's sales department for several years. Though only twenty-six, he carried himself more like a fifty-year-old jaded pro. We met one afternoon in a sun-drenched conference room just off the large Hack Night assembly room. Speaking about the churn issue, Kevin leaned back in his chair, looked out the window, and said indifferently, "I've been here so long, I've seen other ups and downs. Nothing surprises me at this point." Yet when he saw the general counsel's wiki post on the company's equity structure, even he admitted, "I was totally blown away. I stood up at my desk and clapped for the company. That was amazing." For Kevin, that sort of information was not directly relevant to his day-to-day work, but that was the point. It signaled a respect and trust that executives had for employees beyond their specific role. "It means they see us as adults," he explained, dropping the usual hint of cynicism from his tone.

A number of Kevin's peers spoke in generational terms about this and other meanings that transparency had for them. Kylie, twenty-three years old and an outspoken, self-identifying millennial from TechCo's marketing group, drew a direct link between millennials' highly attentive and encouraging parents, on the one hand, and executive transparency, on the other hand, observing, "We've always been told how important we are. That's why we want that sort of access to information and important people, so we feel important ourselves." She further noted that her generation had grown up sharing private details on platforms like the wiki, so executive sharing seemed perfectly designed for them.[7] Comments like these suggest that TechCo executives had read millennial expectations correctly on this score, and their practice of "radical transparency" may tap into, and satisfy, some key elements of that generation's general habitus, or disposition.[8] This, in turn, may lead millennials like Kylie and Kevin to find working at TechCo uniquely rewarding and comfortable relative to other workplaces.

Indeed, many employees interpreted their executives' transparency as a privilege of sorts. They believed it was unique to be trusted in this way and to have such access to high-level business issues, not to mention to work at a company that understood their generation's desire for that. And all of that made them feel important. Interestingly, executives often spoke of transparency as a rare privilege too. That, however, complicates what we might make of the employees' interpretation. In their comments on one another's wiki posts, executives would often commend each other for being so transparent, noting that such information would not be shared at another company. Anil sometimes reminded the workforce that being transparent was not always comfortable for executives, implying that it was a gift bestowed at some cost to the givers. "Not a week goes by where I don't feel like something has stung a bit" to share, he once noted.

There is certainly truth in this framing. Most companies do not share the information on those posts, and to Anil's point, there probably are times when it is uncomfortable for executives to communicate as fully as they do. (At the very least, it takes extra time and effort to do so.) Nevertheless, executives' framing of transparency in this way also serves an important function for them. Beyond the potential to distract, an obvious problem with sharing such extensive, often confidential, information so broadly is the potential for it to leak outside of the organization. In the next two chapters, I explore in detail how controlling an open organization poses some unique challenges, but we can already see one example here: Once executives have disseminated information widely, how can they control its further dissemination? Strong norms against leaking is an obvious answer, and it should not surprise us, then, to see attempts to interpretively frame (or even publicly shame) in service of such norms.

An example of this occurred three years before my study. At the time, Eric and Anil were in talks with a leading venture capital firm about the possibility of another financing round. They shared details of their discussions on the wiki, and the information leaked to the local press. In response, a midlevel executive wrote a wiki post titled, "Why it sucks that information keeps leaking on [a popular business news blog]." The executive admonished the staff, writing, "Transparency relies on trust, don't break the trust. One of the things I like best about TechCo is that we have a transparent company. At most companies people outside the management team wouldn't even know that we were talking with the VC firm." My analysis of wiki posts over the ensuing years suggests that executives did not curtail their sharing because of incidents like this. If anything, they shared more detailed information over time and as the company grew, but they framed transparency as a privilege born of trust more frequently too.

Once that framing entered the company's discourse, it may well have shaped the workforce's own understanding and evaluation of the company's transparency. And yet it would be wrong to cast the executives' transparency in cynical terms. By sharing what they do, TechCo executives display considerably more trust in their employees than do executives at most other companies. And, as we just saw, the workforce derives educational and professional value, as well as personal meaning, from that sharing. Executive transparency also undergirds a second form of communicative openness that these employees value.

EMPLOYEES SPEAKING UP

Whereas "radical transparency" involves executives sharing information down to employees, the second practice that subverts the conventional hierarchical flow of communication within TechCo is letting employees speak up. In conventional bureaucratic firms, the right to address the entire company rests with senior managers, and employee communication generally follows the formal chain of command.[9] At TechCo, by contrast, individuals throughout the firm's hierarchy are given broad voice rights. They are encouraged to share their own information, ideas, and opinions with executives and the entire organization, and to participate in firmwide conversations on important issues. (As the Mystery Dinner showed, executives' transparency undergirds this practice by fostering an informed workforce that is capable of, and genuinely interested in, weighing in on such matters.) The wiki serves as the seminal platform for supporting employee voice rights, and one discussion I watched unfold on it illustrates quite well what is unique about the communication it supports and what is unique about communication within TechCo more generally.

Jacob, a long-time member of TechCo's marketing group, sparked discussion on the wiki one day when he asked, "Should TechCo have an org chart?" Despite the company having more than six hundred people at the time, and despite it having conventional job titles (such as CEO, COO, vice president, director, and manager), executives had thus far refused to publish an organizational chart. They argued that such formalization was unnecessary—a relic of "old school" bureaucratic corporations—and, furthermore, that it would discourage the sort of free-flowing open communication they wanted to promote.

Employees like Jacob disagreed and believed communication in the company was suffering from its lack of an org chart. Since the start of my fieldwork, I had been hearing employees co-opt executives' language of openness and argue that an org chart would offer greater transparency into the company's actual structure and greater ease of communication in it. TechCo was growing quickly and, as Jacob explained in his wiki post, "There are a lot of people at TechCo these days (including myself) who have trouble figuring out who works in which group and what they do." He asked employees to vote on whether they wanted an org chart and to offer their thoughts in the comments section.

Shortly after Jacob's post went live, individuals from across the company began to chime in. In answer to Jacob's question, and consistent with what I had been hearing in my interviews, responses of "Yes," "Yup," "Yes please," and "Absolutely" filled the comments thread. Eventually, a more involved conversation got under way. An employee who had joined TechCo three months earlier wrote, "I hate the idea of really publishing out a hierarchy and reporting structure in the company. I think we do SUCH a great job of treating everyone here as equals whose opinions have equal merit, and I think that throwing everyone into a tree structure undermines that somewhat."

In response, a woman who had been working there for ten months wrote that she did not think having an org chart would change the culture of TechCo. "Let's get real," she wrote, "There IS a hierarchy, as TechCo'y as we want to be. The assumption that having an org chart changes all that is TechCo seems rather absurd to me. Can we please have one?" A long-time member of the sales team responded, "Amen."

The CTO Anil then joined the conversation and seemed to draw it to a close by conceding, "TechCo does have a structure, so we might as well document it and make it accessible." But he added:

Having said that, we should keep in mind that the org structure does not define who you can/should talk to . . . . We can and should break the "chain of command" and talk to whoever we need to in order to move the mission forward. You don't have to go "up and down the org tree" in order to communicate or work with someone.

In fact, discussions on the wiki every single day demonstrated how people at TechCo broke out of the chain of command to communicate. Jacob had sparked this whole conversation by doing just that in his post, and here are three other illustrative Wiki discussions from my time at TechCo:

1. Heather, a junior member of the marketing team, posted an analysis she had done of recent customer wins and losses versus one of TechCo's largest competitors. In the following days, individuals from across the organization and up and down the company hierarchy commented on her post, asking follow-up questions, offering their own perspectives and analyses, and discussing steps the company could take to improve TechCo's win rate. Those who chimed in included TechCo's CEO Eric, the CTO Anil, sales reps and sales managers, product managers and engineers, colleagues of Heather's from marketing, as well as her boss and her boss's boss. Senior sales reps shared their experiences of going head-to-head with this particular competitor in the field, Eric offered his own perspective on how to position TechCo relative to its competitors, and engineers discussed current and future product features being developed to address market demands. By the end of the discussion, folks in marketing had decided to conduct additional customer interviews to collect more information on several of the themes raised by Heather's initial analysis, and a sales rep had offered to beta test a new product feature with two deals in her pipeline.

2. Glenn, an engineer in TechCo's user experience group, had done some recent testing of the effectiveness of TechCo's own website. He had noticed that a particular phrase describing TechCo's products resonated especially well with customers who viewed the site. He wrote a wiki post in which he acknowledged that product positioning was not his area of expertise but suggested that perhaps this phrase be incorporated more broadly into

TechCo's marketing efforts. "At the very least, I think we should test this phrase with our prospects and customers. If we find it resonates, we can push further with it," he wrote. Employees from both marketing and product development commented on Glenn's post, as did the head of engineering, the head of marketing, and Anil. There was widespread agreement that having a conversation to clarify the company's product positioning was important, although a number of commenters believed the specific phrase Glenn proposed was too narrow to describe TechCo's entire product suite. Staff from marketing, as well as Anil and the marketing group's head, offered their thoughts on how Glenn's phrase was "part of the story" but not necessarily the "headline" when it came to positioning TechCo to customers.

3. One morning Anil posted on the wiki that "in keeping with [our] tradition of transparency," senior executives were willing to disclose their compensation to the workforce. The company intended to go public within the next year or two, and Anil explained that this information would be released "to the world" then anyway. In the meantime, he said, this was just another way to demonstrate the organization's commitment to transparency. Anil asked employees to vote "yes" or "no" on whether they thought this was a good idea. Within minutes employees began weighing in with comments. "What's the point of this, really?" someone from sales wrote. Rather than voting yes or no, an employee from the account management team wrote, "There should be a third option for I don't care." What the executives earned was "not relevant" to him or his work, he explained. What was relevant, he said, was that executives continued to make good decisions for the company and to share information with the workforce pertaining to those decisions. He praised the company's regular all-hands meetings as well as executives' practice of sharing notes from their board meetings and senior leadership meetings on the wiki, and he encouraged executives to keep doing things like that instead. A few hours in, an engineer joined the thread to acknowledge that he was torn on whether Anil's proposal was a good idea or not, "but I LOVE the fact that we're discussing it." Many employees said they appreciated the gesture and some voted "yes" to see the executives' compensation. Others were bothered by it and said it would be a distraction from important business issues the company was facing. One wrote bluntly,

"This whole discussion reeks of transparency for the sake of transparency." Offline, a number of individuals approached their managers and other executives directly to say that this was not a necessary or welcome example of transparency. Anil soon rejoined the conversation online to say that people had made some compelling arguments and he was swayed: "We're putting this experiment on hold for now."

These vignettes make it clear that TechCo's wiki is not just a place for executives to post information. It is also a place where employees can step outside the formal chain of command to question their leaders, challenge corporate polices and decisions, and share and discuss their own ideas and opinions in a forum visible to the entire organization. In these ways, social media platforms like the wiki seem to offer a promising new vehicle for employee voice and dialogue.

Past work on employee voice has generally taken one of two approaches. In the field of organizational behavior, scholars have examined the conditions that promote or silence individual expressions of voice inside firms. This literature tends to focus on instances in which individual employees informally speak up to a manager (or in a team setting) to offer opinions and suggestions on local matters of concern.[10] By contrast, in the industrial relations and human resources fields, scholars have generally examined the formal mechanisms through which employees can express their collective interests and grievances to top management, focusing, in particular, on the role of unions.[11] From either perspective, the wiki seems a new and different beast. It is a formal platform, but one on which employees speak as individuals, not as a single collective; where what is said is instantly visible to everyone in the company, not just an individual's manager or work group; and where the topics discussed are often strategic business issues of importance to the entire organization, not just local matters or workplace grievances.

A number of social media scholars and pundits have argued that platforms like the wiki are ideal for enabling voice and dialogue, claiming that they can act as democratizing public spheres for modern society.[12] Like the eighteenth-century salons described by Habermas and the public spheres envisioned by philosophers and political sociologists since then, the open platforms of social media seem to afford a public space in which individuals can transcend social distinctions and come together to share ideas and discuss and debate issues of common concern.[13] The nascent literature on enterprise social media suggests that many for-profit corporations, not just TechCo, see an opportunity to leverage that very potential by using these technologies to promote productive upward communication and employee discourse.

From some vantage points at TechCo, the discussions happening on the wiki really did look like some sort of utopic corporate public sphere. Emma, the tech support rep introduced in chapter 1 who said the wiki "is one of my most favorite things on the planet," praised the egalitarian dialogue she felt it promoted: "It's so cool that if I come up with an idea I can post it on the wiki . . . . It doesn't matter how long I've been here. I can do it now if I want, and if it's a good idea, people will respond." We just saw that Heather, a junior employee, was able to share the results of her analysis with the entire company, have senior executives weigh in on the implications of her work, and then watch as people across the company took action in response to the discussion she had started. For employees so accustomed to sharing their thoughts and ideas on social media, this was a cherished aspect of working at TechCo.

All this open sharing provoked healthy debate within the company too. Whereas Anil commonly said, "We share everything" in reference to the company's practice of transparency, the head of marketing once retorted quite aptly, "We debate everything too!" During my fieldwork, I watched numerous debates unfold on the wiki concerning such topics as how best to demo the company's new product and what the precise methodology should be for training customers on it. Just as a well-functioning public sphere is believed to promote rational, critical debate that eventually leads to enlightened common agreement, these debates often led to productive resolutions.[14] As I was drafting this very chapter, I received an email from a TechCo contact who was excited to tell me that a particularly lengthy, thorny project concerning changes to the sales process had finally been resolved. His email read, "This was a nasty project w/no owner, super-complicated, no good options and super important . . . . Trish and I posted the current plans on the wiki. That created a whole lot of discussion from the masses, and the result was a conversation that got people's attention and ended up solving the problem."

Sometimes the discussions that unfolded and the employee opinions that were shared led directly to the executives changing course, such as Anil's reconsideration of disclosing executives' compensation in light of the discussion on the wiki. Other times, no immediate organizational change came about, but employees were left with a better appreciation for the context in which something had been decided. Glenn's suggestion about product positioning was not taken up, for instance, but it was taken seriously and addressed by both the head of marketing and the CTO.

Perhaps most interesting, the employees' upward communication on the wiki was so startlingly open at times that I found myself wondering if this might be a setting in which employees had finally transcended all the theorized barriers to "speaking up" to hierarchy. Above, we saw employees criticize their leaders quite pointedly for "transparency for the sake of transparency" and challenge an executive decision not to publish an org chart. These were not isolated instances. In response to a post about the company's new HR benefits, an employee wrote that the company's 401(k) match was the worst he had ever seen. In response to a post listing some TechCo company values, another employee wrote, "If I was a new TechCoer coming in and I read [this], I'd probably just roll my eyes and go back to doing what I wanted to do."

Such public voice and dialogue simply have no precedent in past accounts of corporate life. Take, for instance, Robert Jackall's 1988 book *Moral Mazes*. Jackall interviewed managers across a range of firms and found that even though private skepticism of corporate policies was quite common among employees, public criticism of the firm's leaders and their policies was considered a "death wish" in most organizations.[15] Jackall observed, "The hierarchical authority structure that is the linchpin of bureaucracy dominates the way managers think about their world and about themselves," and, consequently, employees tended to engage in strategic silence.[16] The general rule was to "keep one's skepticism to one's self and get on board."[17] Other canonical ethnographies based on observations of corporate life in the 1980s through the early 2000s found the same.[18] Without a doubt, the voices sounding off and the conversations happening on TechCo's wiki (and in related offline public settings like Hack Nights) look wildly different from the discourse we are used to seeing in conventional bureaucratic firms.

LIMITATIONS OF EMPLOYEE VOICE

Greater openness does not mean perfect openness, however, and the picture I have painted is not a complete one of how TechCo's wiki works, nor should we expect it to be. Although new technologies can provide us with powerful new capacities, their potential is always conditioned by how we choose to use them and the specific constraints of our setting.[19] The social and political dynamics that have long suppressed employee voice in corporations remain salient today, and it would be surprising for a new communication platform like the wiki to transcend them all so easily. What is more, recent critiques of the literature on public spheres as well as the emerging literature on social media use within corporations suggest that public platforms of this sort may have certain inherent qualities that prevent them from being as transformative as some scholars and practitioners have idealized (and as we all might like) them to be.[20]

One reason for this is that openness is not inherently democratic. Dynamics on an open platform may well promote more opportunities for dialogue and voice, but they may also suppress certain voices, warp the form and content of what is shared, and even lessen the accountability of central authorities. As positive as TechCo employees were about the opportunity to share their ideas and opinions on the wiki, we will see that they and their executives were acutely aware of these tensions. Reviewing their nuanced understanding of the wiki and how they tried to navigate its limitations offers a first glimpse into the complexity of shooting for openness inside a firm but also the strengths of the conversational environment being fostered at TechCo.

How Noise Silences and Diverts

As any casual observer of the comments section of most blogs or news sites can attest, the "civil society" ostensibly nurtured in these public spaces is not always so civil. This can make the public sphere an uncomfortable place for some and drive them to disengage. At TechCo, employees and executives alike worried about this issue on the wiki. When I asked Jill, a thirty-year-old woman in the marketing group, whether employees felt they could truly speak out on the wiki, she responded, "Yes! Too much. It's borderline inappropriate." She noted a recent instance in which a junior employee in her group responded to an executive's post by commenting, "This sucks." According to Jill, "We say 'Speak up about everything,' but it just incentivizes people to be assholes. It's not fun to participate." So she rarely did.

A main reason it was "not fun" was that aggressive employee responses were not always, or even usually, directed up to executives. Often, they were directed at one another. Two midlevel executives raised this issue on one of my first days of fieldwork. Talking quietly in one of the company's lounge areas, they called me over as I walked by and asked if I had had a chance to look at the wiki yet. One explained, "We were just talking about this. There are some very opinionated people, and their voices overwhelm and drown out others . . . . I worry about all the new people we bring in. They might look at it and say, 'I've got this good idea but I know it will provoke a huge response so I just don't want to get into the fray.'" The other executive added, "You know I'm outspoken, right? It took me three years before I posted on it, and I only did after I was promoted [to his more senior role]. It wasn't so much I felt shy, but it just wasn't worth dealing with the counterargument I knew I'd get."

My daily observations of the wiki suggested that TechCo's own "wiki trolls" were capable of not only driving certain people from the conversation but also redirecting the conversation entirely. When nasty "dustups" (as some employees called them) exploded on the wiki—when one employee "flamed" another and comments flew back and forth in response—it sometimes diverted workers' attention from holding executives accountable in the conversation. For example, in one wiki thread, a sales rep in her late twenties named Maya asked Anil why certain product features customers always asked about had not yet been incorporated into TechCo's software. Almost immediately two engineers responded, criticizing Maya for not acknowledging several features that had been built in direct response to earlier feedback from the sales force. One of the engineer's responses included a mocking picture of a businessman talking into a shoe as if mistaking it for a phone, with a caption implying that Maya did not understand TechCo's product. This, in turn, prompted a third engineer to criticize his colleagues for their tone, and a member of the services team to chime in and remind them, "We're all in this together. Let's act like we're on the same team."

The point is that when the two engineers mocked Maya's question, and then two other employees jumped in to chastise them, the workforce—at least for a moment—stopped thinking about what Anil or another executive's response to Maya's question would be and attended instead to the dramatic dust-up. Eventually, a product manager addressed Maya's comment quite thoughtfully, and the COO and an executive from engineering responded to her question as well. Nevertheless, it was not uncommon for acrimonious dialogue among employees to divide and distract them before the original query was answered.

Beyond the aggressive tone that sometimes drove employees away or diverted the substance of the conversation, the number of voices sounding off could be so overwhelming that it diminished an individual's motivation to participate.[21] As more and more people share more and more information and ideas, public spaces—perhaps especially technologically mediated ones like the wiki—become crowded, and it can begin to seem as if no one comment will be heard above the fray. Explaining why she no longer composed her own posts on the wiki, an employee in TechCo's customer consulting group said it was not worth it. There were so many posts each day, "It's become noise at this point."

She was not alone in this sentiment. As TechCo grew, many worried that the wiki's usefulness as a platform for employee-initiated posts was declining. Its meaning to employees seemed to be changing in the process too. Walking back from lunch one afternoon with Jill, the marketing manager,

I asked a passing question about the strategy behind one of TechCo's new products. She answered, "Someone posted about that on the wiki. You should check it out." Then she stopped walking, turned to me, and we both burst out laughing. She had just told me at lunch that, "The new 'Fuck You' [at TechCo] is to say, 'It's on the wiki.'

* * *

It's like, 'Yeah, go read that encyclopedia to find what you want. Good luck finding it.'" As we stood on the sidewalk laughing, she now apologized, "I think I just told you to go fuck yourself. I'm really sorry!"

The fact that employee voices could so easily overwhelm and crowd the public sphere was why most employee dialogue and voice unfolded in the comments section of executives' posts, and not—as it could have—in the employees' own original posts. Scholars and critics have observed that social media platforms often reinforce existing power asymmetries instead of disrupt them because the voices that can cut through the noise and be heard are those that already have status and resources attached to them (e.g., celebrities and politicians, who have hundreds of thousands of Twitter followers, versus the average user who does not).[22] On TechCo's wiki, however, this dynamic did not necessarily silence conversation in the way scholars have imagined. Because of executives' status and authority, and because employees were genuinely interested in the information executives shared on the wiki, executive voices did rise above the fray, but their posts then became spaces where employee voices convened and sounded off in turn. Even as employees and work groups posted less original content to the wiki over time, most had set up automated alerts to notify them any time the executives they "followed" posted something new. The cross-hierarchical, company-wide conversations that unfolded in the wake of these posts garnered the most participation by the workforce.

And yet, even as executive voices could rise above the din when they spoke (and thus the comments section of their posts could become a space for centralized public discourse), all the wiki's noise sometimes offered executives a cover of sorts. During particularly intense debates, when numerous employees jumped into the conversation to comment one after another, it was unreasonable to expect executives to respond to every single comment. This meant that executives could pick and choose the comments to which they did respond. As Jill explained, "Management gets to hear what they want to hear, and from whom they want."

In short, as powerful as a platform like the wiki is for giving individual employees voice, the number of unique voices that sound off on it (plus the fact that dust-ups often divide, rather than unite, employees) can impede the formation of any one collective employee voice. And this distinguishes it from formal mechanisms for collective voice like unions. Employees reported there was still great value in executives hearing the variety of individual voices, but a few disheartened workers worried. One customer consultant observed, "The wiki now just indexes what people say. There's no mechanism for accountability." Even on a platform designed to support employee voice, the fact is some voices may be silenced or driven away, and it is not always easy to hold executives accountable to those that remain.

All the Wiki's a Stage

A general feature of public spaces like the wiki is that their very openness means visibility, and communications scholars have long noted that visibility shapes what is shared, how it is shared, and by whom it is shared.[23] Because participants constitute not just an engaged community but also an audience to one another's performances, public spaces become a "realm of appearances," and as the sociologist Erving Goffman is famous for noting, individuals manage their public presentations and communications accordingly.[24] At TechCo, I saw these dynamics directly influence both the potential and the limitations of the wiki as a platform for employee voice and dialogue.

On the one hand, the fact that an employee's wiki comments and posts were visible to the entire company—including to an employee's direct manager and the company's top executives—offered a compelling motivation to participate. By sharing ideas and opinions, individuals could differentiate themselves and garner attention from those with authority.[25] Mark, a widely recognized rising star at TechCo, had just been promoted to run a team of fifty employees when I interviewed him. He credited his recent promotion, in part, to the wiki, noting, "For me, it was a good way to do some personal marketing. If you post something and it's seen as thoughtful, it's good for your career . . . . The execs see it and comment." Quiet and contemplative in person, this former English major said he was careful not to post things cavalierly given this visibility; rather, "I do a lot of thinking about things, shopping the ideas around and then eventually writing a post." From this perspective, the wiki's public stage engendered thoughtful performances capable of provoking productive discussion and benefiting both the individual and the common good.

On the other hand, some TechCo employees echoed the academic critique that a public stage makes for a "superficial world."[26] Kevin, the jaded sales manager, said, "The wiki's great for transparency, but it's overused for other things. People use it to promote themselves, get a name. Then it's like, 'Oh, he's saying things on the wiki, he must be legit.' . . . People feel like the only way to show you're doing work these days is on the wiki." Others noted that the wiki's visibility to executives provoked some employees to spend days revising and editing their posts or comments before publishing them, all in an effort to impress. That may well improve the quality of the idea, as Mark noted, but others interpreted the practice as unproductive impression management. Consistent with this, the emerging literature on social media use within corporations has found impression management dynamics to be common on these media.[27] From this perspective, the visibility to executives and peers makes for superficial self-promotion, not productive dialogue.

Concern for one's reputation also provoked concern over intellectual property. When individuals felt they had a particularly good idea, they would sometimes keep it secret until they had posted it on the wiki out of fear of being scooped by a colleague. Angelique, Kevin's colleague on the salesforce, had, by her own admission, used the wiki effectively for "personal branding," but she was attuned to its perverse incentives in this regard. "On the front lines, you have to make a name for yourself to get noticed up," she explained. "So, you can't share [an idea with peers] until it has your name associated with it on the wiki. It would end up on the wiki as 'theirs,' if you did." Although Angelique believed TechCo did "a great job with what the execs share from the top down to us," she felt "transparency is lacking with peers because we need a way to differentiate."

A focus on appearance and differentiation might be particularly acute at a place like TechCo, where the workforce is so similar in age and where most have grown up constructing and managing their online identities. At the same time, though, these digital natives may be uniquely capable, as Angelique seemed to be, of both recognizing a technology's limitations and embracing it for what it is. Emma, our millennial tour guide who heralded the wiki for both its transparency and its participatory nature, said:

> It reminds me of Facebook when it came out. You'd post something and you knew everyone in your high school would see it. So, there's this total narcissism to it, too, where you're sort of showing off, where you want to say something smart or funny. But it's [also] great for letting people know what you're doing . . . . It's a great place to advertise your skills.

Silencing Vulnerable and Dissenting Voices

Visibility on the wiki did not just spur impression management. More worrisome was when it seemed to suppress certain voices and topics of conversation. In particular, some employees hesitated to participate on the wiki for fear of manager reprisal. It turned out that not all TechCo managers liked the wiki: Some worried that their teams' comments would be interpreted as criticisms of them, and others simply thought the wiki distracted people from their real work. Accordingly, employee use of the wiki tended to be correlated with manager views of the platform; entire teams were more or less active on it, depending on their supervisor.[28] For example, employees of Johanna, a manager I was told cultivated a "sense of fear" and actively concealed information from both her staff and senior executives, told me that they were "scared" to post on the wiki. Johanna had made it known that comments on it would not be welcome. She was eventually fired, and her team's wiki use increased thereafter.

Even on teams where wiki use was tolerated or actively encouraged, employees who felt insecure in their role often felt they should not participate.[29] This was especially the case for those on a "performance plan" (employees who had been given formal warning about their job performance and a list of specific improvements required to retain their job). One long-time employee known for his active contributions on the wiki over the years had recently switched teams and found himself clashing with his new manager. When we met at a local coffee shop, he shared with me a copy of his recent performance review and details of his performance plan. He said that even though he disagreed vehemently with some recent wiki posts about churn and felt he had a valid perspective to offer, he did not feel he was in a position to enter into the dialogue. As he explained it, "It depends on who your manager is, whether you can call bullshit on the wiki. It depends on whether they'll protect you. These days, I tend to be very cautious. I read and lurk all the time, but I'm not active. If I had a more secure position, I would be more active . . . . I certainly don't post controversial ideas or plans now." Another employee recently put on a performance plan said she had become similarly "wiki shy."

One could argue that this sort of self-censorship is entirely reasonable and functional. Shouldn't ostensibly subpar employees spend time trying to improve their formal skills rather than engaging in high-level strategic conversations? The difficulty with that logic is that any discomfort with one's local manager, whether performance-based or personality-based, seemed to dissuade wiki participation in this way, and these issues are not always cut and dried, as anyone who has had a difficult manager knows. In short, a platform like the wiki may help subvert the firm's communicative hierarchy in many ways, but it cannot fully transcend it; and as much as executives tried to encourage widespread participation, local power dynamics were often a determining factor for the employees I spoke with and observed.

These findings raise the question of whether other vulnerable groups were also self-censoring. Suggestive evidence for this comes from an analysis of women's activity on the wiki. High-tech companies are often known for their skewed gender demographics and macho cultures. TechCo is less skewed on gender than some of its peers, with women representing close to 40 percent of its workforce at the time of my study. In my interviews, female employees reported fewer gender-specific issues than prior studies of tech firms have revealed. Nevertheless, several told me that they suspected women posted on the wiki less than men, noting that they themselves sometimes felt insecure speaking up on the platform. I explored this issue, and my analysis of the most heated wiki debates—those that garnered the most employee comments—showed that often less than 20 percent of the comments came from women. (However, women seemed to participate in line with their overall representation when it came to less controversial, everyday knowledge sharing on the wiki.)

Beyond individual voices, whole topics could be suppressed at times too. During my fieldwork, TechCo bought tickets for its employees to attend a speech by Sheryl Sandberg, the Facebook COO and author of *Lean In,* a book about gender equality. After the speech, Anil took to the wiki and wrote a post saying that he was inspired by Sandberg's talk and wanted to start a broader conversation about gender at TechCo. In response, about thirty women (and a few men) commented, and out of that discussion, a group of women decided to meet offline and continue the discussion in regular, in-person meetings. One of the organizers invited me to attend these sessions, which were held during business hours in one of TechCo's conference rooms. At the inaugural meeting, she led off by saying to the assembled women that this group— and the broader conversation about gender—was a "long time coming." She told us, "The reason I think it took so long to get this group set up is that at TechCo we do all our communication on the wiki and this is sensitive stuff. What I'll say here, I wasn't going to say it all on the wiki. After Anil started the conversation, I spent two days crafting the post I put up there."

Some employees wondered whether other sensitive issues were being glossed over as well. After a multinational software giant bought one of TechCo's competitors, executives wrote a series of detailed posts analyzing why this development did not threaten TechCo's market position. A number of employees read the posts and accepted the executives' framing of the issue, but others were skeptical. An account manager I interviewed at the time speculated, "The executives are concerned with saying they're worried, saying they're afraid. And people are afraid of saying it themselves because they fear it will be used against them and hurt their own careers at the company." Of another such incident, an employee in the operations group observed that, although there was a "like" button on the wiki, "There's no dislike button on the wiki, and people wouldn't use it if there was. So execs post something and they see the 'likes,' but they don't hear the whispers in the hallway questioning it." Over dinner with a midlevel manager, I asked him about these dynamics. He admitted, "There's definitely a pressure to be positive in public. You can't be too negative, too often, for sure." With disincentives for expressing dissent and positive incentives for dissimulation, a public sphere like the wiki is capable of supporting opinion "bubbles" not dissimilar to market bubbles.[30]

The tension that all of these examples reveals is simply this: What is open and visible is open and visible for surveillance. A tendency for self-suppression emerges from the very same source as the tendency for "personal branding" or impression management; namely, the capacity for surveillance inherent in any open public space. At TechCo, some feared that the wiki was "an accident waiting to happen." Although the staff often lobbed shockingly pointed criticism at the company's management without reprimand, the few instances when employees had been reprimanded were seared in the collective memory.

One particular incident from the past was invoked repeatedly in interviews, almost always in vague but anxious terms. As one employee explained it, "People get in trouble for calling bullshit too much. There was a support rep who was fired for it." In fact, the details of that support rep's firing seem to have been far more complicated than one rogue wiki post, but the incident had symbolic meaning for employees, and not without reason. Even with senior executives who seemed genuinely committed to using the wiki to promote open, honest communication and who seemed uninterested in using it as a vehicle for surveillance and punishment, rational employees knew that in a hierarchical organization management never fully delegated rights. Executives, or their lower-level managers, could decide to rescind employees' voice rights at any time, and that fact alone was enough to distort the conversation and suppress certain voices and topics.[31] Add to that the noise that drove some voices out and the image concerns that warped others, and we can see just how challenging it can be to have truly open voice and dialogue within a firm.

ACHIEVING OPENNESS THROUGH CLOSURE

TechCo's senior executives were aware of these challenges, however, and they experimented with ways to mitigate them and to promote more open dialogue on both the wiki and in general. The significance of this should not be understated. An assumption in most existing literature on employee voice is that managers are largely unaware of the pressures silencing workers (or, if aware, do not care), and that their ignorance limits the effectiveness of any attempt to promote truly open discourse.[32] This assumption did not hold true at TechCo. Concerned that some voices and topics might be getting suppressed on the wiki, Anil often spoke about a "TechCo Bill of Rights," which in his mind was "a list of inalienable rights that every TechCoer has and that no group can take away," first among which was the ability to participate freely on the wiki. Of course, simply saying that rights are inalienable does not necessarily modify the conditions that might be restricting their exercise. More effective, therefore, was when executives introduced anonymous, confidential communication channels so that employees could speak up without the distortions and pressures associated with public dialogue.

Every quarter the company administered an anonymous survey to employees, which was designed to measure employee happiness and to give the entire workforce an opportunity to offer open-ended, anonymous feedback to executives. The hope was that this would raise questions that might otherwise be suppressed on the wiki's public stage. After each quarterly survey was collected, one executive—usually a vice president from TechCo's people operations group—posted the raw data from the survey, as well as a detailed analysis of trends in employee happiness over time and the key themes that had emerged from employees' confidential comments. At the next company meeting and in posts on the wiki, Keith reviewed the steps he and other executives were taking to address any "hot button" issues that had been raised.

Compared to conventional accounts of corporate communication, this is quite remarkable. A key assumption in labor process theories of organization is that executives have an interest in segregating workers so they cannot develop a collective consciousness, and, further, that managers often harness new technologies to effect that segmentation. Yet here we have executives leveraging new tools and communication platforms to create common knowledge of employees' private sentiments, sentiments that are often directly critical of company policies and practices.

No solution is perfect, certainly, but the limitations of TechCo's various attempts to be more open were often discussed, and that again is unusual. In a comment on Keith's post about the new biweekly "Ask the Execs" Q&A meeting, one employee wrote of his own department:

> The sales team has the lowest [employee satisfaction rating on the quarterly survey] and I'd bet, has the most questions/concerns about our future here, but when we are given the chance to talk to the executives, none are asked. I'd say this is due to the fact that you cannot ask anonymous questions and nobody wants to be tagged. Can we think of a way to do this?

In other words, one thing the open dialogue on the wiki encouraged was discussion of the limits of open dialogue and how to address them.

In response to the employee's question, a widely respected midlevel manager jumped into the wiki conversation and offered to collect any questions confidentially offline and pose the questions herself at the meeting. Though still not a perfect solution, it was a workable one for the time being, and Eric, the CEO, quickly responded, "[This is] a good idea for two reasons. One, some people are shy. Two, some questions are hard to ask. Sunshine's the best disinfectant—let's let it come in via you."

Toward the very end of my fieldwork, TechCo adopted an additional anonymous feedback channel. Through a new software application, managers could now send weekly, one-question surveys to employees. The questions varied, depending on what topic managers and executives were interested in polling that week, but the point was to assess employee happiness and solicit direct feedback on any issues surfacing at the time. The technology itself maintained employee anonymity and then displayed the anonymized survey results not only to executives but also to the entire workforce. Affording both voice and transparency, the tool seemed to be an instant hit with employees and executives.

Finally, my very presence at TechCo was a testament to executives' and employees' joint desire to promote open, uncensored sharing and their joint recognition that such radical openness might require a bit of closure at times. Both groups repeatedly noted that my fieldwork was valuable precisely because I was promising employees anonymity. By their account, this would allow me to capture an even more honest, accurate representation of people's experiences within the company. Employees and executives alike seemed keenly interested to see how the image revealed by my research would align, or not, with the image presented in public spaces like the wiki.[33]

THE MEANINGS OF OPENNESS

To summarize, TechCo executives have used the company wiki, as well as several other vehicles, including company-wide meetings and employee surveys, to crack open the conventional vertical control of communication within a corporation. Executives engage in what they call "radical transparency," where they share detailed, often confidential information with the entire workforce, and they distribute internal voice rights so that employees share and debate ideas and opinions with executives and with one another. At the time of my study, the radical transparency seemed to be working quite effectively. Promoting employee voice within a corporate environment was not without its challenges, in part because openness itself can unleash dynamics that preclude its full realization. However, the imperfection of TechCo's attempt should not blind us to what it has achieved.

For all the ways in which discussion and voice could be suppressed on the wiki, recall that the section on the limitations of employee voice began by describing participation so active and open that its unvarnished tone was off-putting to some. That itself can be considered an accomplishment when compared to the more formal, stilted dialogue of many bureaucratic organizations. Even if the company has not achieved a fully egalitarian utopic ideal of totally open communication, the level of debate and engagement occurring on the TechCo wiki and in the company's large, open meetings is unlike anything found in past ethnographies of corporate life. The fact that employees and executives seem to recognize the limitations of their own attempt—and that their discussions are open enough to surface these challenges—is also unusual and significant. It allows them to confront the limitations as they arise, and, as exemplified by their increasing adoption of additional anonymous channels, continually iterate in the direction of greater communicative openness.

Such communicative openness raises an obvious follow-on question: what does subverting the hierarchical control of communication mean for other forms of hierarchical control within the firm? Returning to the org chart debate, we can begin to see some of the profound complexity of this question. In response to Jacob's post about whether TechCo should have an org chart, TechCo's CEO Eric wrote, "If we do it [have an org chart], it should be upside down w/the employees at the top and me at the bottom." Anil entered that same discussion to remind employees, "You don't have to go up and down the org tree in order to communicate." Therein lay the tension.

Org charts have historically been taken to be a visual representation of the firm, with the lines of the chart representing both the hierarchical structure of authority and communication.[34] Eric and Anil were not crazy to think that an org chart was an awkward, not entirely appropriate thing for TechCo to have. We need only consider the fact that the organization was having a firmwide, nonhierarchical conversation about whether to have an org chart depicting its hierarchy.

From my private interviews, however, it seemed clear that having an org chart was not a threat to how most employees understood TechCo. A member of TechCo's marketing group told me that the company had a clear chain of command, so she did not understand resistance to a visual representation of it: "We have these structures. Why not put it on paper?" A veteran account manager said that just because the company had a wiki and open dialogue, "no one here is under the illusion that if you get thirty 'likes' to your post, it becomes policy." TechCo was not "some sort of socialist leadership where decisions are made, I don't know, by critical mass, or collective will."

And yet, ironically, Jacob's wiki post had asked employees to vote on whether they wanted an org chart or not. Over the course of several days, 117 people voted in favor, and zero voted against. Between the vote tally and the consensus expressed in comments on the wiki, it was clear what the workforce wanted, and Anil's apparent concession to the collective will appeased employees that there would now be an org chart. However, when my study ended months later, executives still had not published an org chart, and I was, once again, hearing employee rumblings about the issue.

In the end, TechCo never did get a conventional org chart, but executives did not just ignore employees' voices on the subject either. They decided instead to implement a new software program that, in their opinion, would give employees the information they wanted in a slightly different form. The rollout was still under way when I left the field, but I followed up with the most ardent org chart advocates over the coming year to learn their perspectives. They were pleased.

"It includes org-chart-like views, and provides the transparency of an org chart, but it doesn't have the same top-down feel," one told me. The software allowed employees to browse the organization and see who worked for whom, he explained, but instead of a traditional org chart that would have been "presented to us on a slide" by executives, "this is something we interact with on our own" and employees had "some measure of control" over how they were personally displayed in it (e.g., by writing their own profile and biography). He valued those features, and despite being one of the most vocal org chart proponents initially, he said of the final resolution, "We got to a better place."

The path to that resolution is telling. Employees had been given voice, and one thing their voices communicated was recognition that TechCo was a hierarchical firm not a democracy governed by collective will. But then they voted anyway, and while their votes seemed to have some sway, they did not exactly carry the day. At the same time, executives feared that highlighting the organization's hierarchical structure would close off the open flow of communication, but then they activated their own hierarchical authority to override employees' voices and votes. They did not distribute a conventional org chart as the staff had requested, but they did find an alternative way to be responsive. Open voice was not vote, open dialogue was not democracy, but a conversation had been had, and it may just have led to a better place overall. Such is life inside a conversational firm. In the next chapter, we will continue to unravel the relationship between communication and control at TechCo by examining how the firm shoots for openness in its approach to decision making.

3

OPEN CONTROL

TOWARD THE END of the customer churn Hack Night described in the preface, employees reassembled as one large collective to vote. Four teams were selected to present their ideas at the next "Experiments Meeting," a monthly venue where employees can propose new project ideas to executives (called "experiments" to signal their provisional status) and where executives monitor the progress of ongoing experiments. Experiments Meetings are yet another TechCo practice designed to support employee voice rights.

In the days following the Hack Night, members of the four teams worked diligently to prepare for the upcoming meeting. Huddled in corners of the company lounge and over lunch tables in the kitchen, they honed their ideas as well as their plans for communicating them. Shortly after one such huddle, I caught up with Jessie. Twenty-five years old and relatively new to TechCo's services group, Jessie was exhilarated by the prospect that the company's senior executives would soon be giving her team audience. "It's empowering, this opportunity," she said. "It's not about having to apply to be in some 'Experiments [Department]' after you've worked for so many years or something. If you've got a good idea, they'll hear it."

A week or so later I sat in the company's largest conference room waiting for the Experiments Meeting to begin and for ideas like Jessie's to be heard.

Pizza had just arrived, and the seven or so executives in attendance were now congregated around the cardboard boxes stacked on the back counter. They talked and joked with one another with ease. "How long you planning to keep that?" one vice president kidded another, nodding at the new full beard his colleague was sporting while handing him a paper plate. They both laughed and helped themselves to some slices. "I saw Nick's email about the [user conference] budget. Let's catch up after this if you have a sec," Keith said to the head of marketing while lifting the lid on a box to inspect its contents.

Making their way to the conference table, the executives continued their casual exchanges as they ate. After a while, Rob, Alexis, and Carolyn—the three young managers who had run the Hack Night and who were there today to keep the meeting on track and record its decisions—signaled that it was time to start.

Over the next several hours, teams of two or three employees entered the room and presented their ideas. If the executives were a study in relaxed ease that afternoon, the presenters were one of contradictions. On the one hand, they embraced the spirit of informality with their casual dress, sometimes surprisingly so for a meeting with the company's senior leadership team. One young male presenter wore a wrinkled and questionably laundered flannel shirt. Another donned an oversized hockey jersey, backwards baseball cap, and several days' stubble. On the other hand, subtle clues suggested the presenters were all highly attuned to the formal power structure before them. There was nothing sloppy about their carefully prepared slides and well-rehearsed presentations, and the hands of several shook when they spoke. Two even seemed to freeze when Eric cracked a joke. As the executives burst naturally into laughter, the two employees held themselves back for a moment, glanced at one another as if to confirm the joke was not on them, and then smiled tentatively. Later in my fieldwork I would learn that employees generally perceived these meetings to be stressful, high-stakes affairs.

That day, each presentation unfolded in a similar way. Employees walked through their slides, and executives lobbed questions at them casually but persistently to better understand the proposal: "Remind me what the current onboarding process is." "What's the average time between a sale closing and the customer getting set up on the software?" "Didn't we try something like this two years ago?" "Why wouldn't you do it [this way] instead?" Inevitably such questions led executives to start debating the proposal's merits among themselves or even to hash out an alternative project they seemed to prefer. When this happened, they reoriented their attention away from the presenters at the front of the room and toward one another around the conference table. Meanwhile, the presenters stood by quietly and tracked the conversation, ready for whenever the room's attention might suddenly shift back to them.

Despite such digressions, the final resolution was always the same, and always in support of employee autonomy. Eric or Anil would eventually commend the employees on their good work and offer words of encouragement that suggested no explicit managerial intervention was being made. "Don't let us talk you into an uninspired middle ground," Anil said to one presenter in reference to a particularly long sidebar during which the VP of services had adamantly opposed the proposed project and the VP of sales had proposed an entirely different structure for it. "So what's the next step?" Eric asked another team as they packed up their laptop and notes to leave. "Great job guys . . . . Just do your thing!" he said to two others. Executives had given these workers the voice rights to share their ideas, and now they seemed to be delegating the decision rights to run with those ideas.

This was a conscious strategy on the part of the executives. At the end of chapter 2, we saw Eric and Anil worry that displaying the organization's hierarchical reporting structure would undermine its open communication environment. Likewise, here the executives intentionally restrained themselves from exercising decision-making control over employee experiments because they worried that doing so would erode confidence in the free, open communication environment they hoped to encourage. Research on employee empowerment suggests they were doing exactly the right thing.

A notable case in this regard is Oticon, the hearing aid manufacturer whose attempt to encourage employee-driven experimentation and innovation failed miserably when executives could not help but "selectively intervene" and micromanage their employees' proposed projects in an equivalent venue to TechCo's Experiments Meeting (what Oticon called its

"New Projects and Products Meeting").[1] Manufacturing plants have also seen numerous "team empowerment" and "workplace democracy" initiatives falter when management stepped in to exercise direct control after explicitly or implicitly promising not to do so.[2] The issue is that once executives have signaled a commitment to support employee participation, employees will perceive managerial intervention as reneging on that commitment, and they will withdraw their own commitment to participate in turn.[3]

By all accounts, then, the fact that TechCo executives held themselves back from exerting direct control over employees' projects during this meeting was a positive step in their quest for promoting employee voice. This did not, however, prevent executives from forming opinions on the merits and viability of the ideas they heard, something that became quite apparent to me during a break in the meeting. After the four teams delivered their presentations, they headed back to their day jobs. Soon more employees would arrive to deliver updates on the company's other ongoing experiments, but for now the executives were alone. They stood and stretched, checked email on their phones and laptops, and chatted among themselves. "What'd you think so far?" Keith turned to Eric and asked. Dropping himself into his chair, Eric leaned back and after a moment's reflection said, "The second and the last were great. The other two need work before they can fly. Not so sure on those." "Agreed," Keith said.

Until that point I had been under the impression that all four proposals had received their support without modification. Now I wondered whether some of those experiments were doomed, or at least moving in a direction the executives did not fully endorse. I questioned the merits of not being more direct with the staff, and as I sat through numerous Experiments Meetings over the coming months, I would learn that the executives themselves struggled with this same question. At one point or another, each of them expressed concern that they were failing to give clear direction because they did not want to discourage employees from sharing their ideas. During a break in another meeting when once again no presenters were in the room, Keith looked down at his notes from the presentations he had just seen, shook his head, and said, "No one wants to say no. We're not good at killing things."

Even though employees were not privy to these private ruminations, they too sensed the tension at hand. Coming out of one Experiments Meeting, a veteran presenter said to me: "People are encouraged to have all sorts of ideas, and then no one wants to be the one stamping out an idea or championing it. But it can be maddening at times." Executives had spent much of that day's meeting debating the merits of her proposal, so she knew they had concerns, she told me. Yet they had left its direction up to her, and now she was not sure where to go with it. This was what always happened in the meetings, she said, "You go back to your small group [after your presentation] and someone says, 'What decision got made?' and you say, 'There really wasn't one.'"

Her sentiment was shared by others. The very same employees who told me they valued being heard in these meetings described their executives' management style in them to be "frustrating," "maddening," and even "a waste of my time." Being heard was valued, it seemed, but not receiving clear direction was another matter. In the days following the Hack Night Experiments Meeting, for example, a number of the presenters complained to Rob, Carolyn, and Alexis that they were at a loss for how to proceed. On their behalf, Rob sent an email to the executive team that read, "Last Monday's meeting didn't leave us with a ton of direction on how to drive each experiment forward." He suggested that they hold the meeting again, but that this time the executives either assign an "executive sponsor" to a project who would work with the team to develop their idea or suspend the project if no sponsor was forthcoming. His email ended by saying that he hoped this format would "serve as a platform to provide honest feedback and next steps."

To be fair, some of the issue here is that experimentation is, by definition, an uncertain process. The executives themselves could not know which path would yield optimal results, so it often made sense to leave things open-ended and see what might emerge from employees' efforts. However, much of the time employees sensed that the executives were simply restraining from giving direction they wanted to give or holding back decisions they had already made, and this frustrated the staff. In one instance, an individual who had been working on an experiment for over a year had come to the conclusion that his project posed too much risk to the business and should be shuttered. He told me that he was sure the executives agreed with him, and he just wanted them to kill it so he could turn his attention back to other matters. But after two Experiments Meetings during which he voiced concerns and the management team continued to support his work on the project, he finally decided to present such a doomsday scenario at the next meeting that they would have no option but to end it. I observed that meeting, and afterward he said to me, "I got a definitive no. I am thrilled to get a definitive no!"

Experiments Meetings were not the only settings in which employees wanted to see more direct managerial control. In fact, one of the most consistent findings of my study was that even though the executives seemed genuinely committed to giving employees voice and to limiting centralized decision making, employees across the organization repeatedly—and quite explicitly—called for greater hierarchical control. This is particularly striking when we consider that one of the central tenets of modern economic sociology is the alienating nature of hierarchical control for workers: Marx taught us about the alienation of labor, Durkheim about the anomie arising from the modern division of labor, and Weber about the iron cage of rationality in which bureaucracy ensnares workers. What then do we make of Kylie, a twenty-three-year-old entry-level employee who said, "The 'no hierarchy' thing drives me nuts"? Or her twenty-five-year-old colleague who complained, "I wish management would just exert a bit more control sometimes"?

We can begin to formulate an answer by recognizing that past scholarship and managerial practice have often overlooked a crucial distinction in the nature of hierarchy. Sociologists Bob Freeland and Ezra Zuckerman have recently theorized that the firm is both a hierarchy of decision rights (who gets to decide what) *and* a hierarchy of voice rights (who gets to speak up and have their opinions heard), and that we must treat these as analytically distinct concepts.[4] In practice, most attempts to build postbureaucratic firms—cases like Oticon as well as team empowerment and workplace democracy initiatives in general—have involved commitments by executives to delegate both sets of rights (either explicitly or implicitly) hand in hand.[5] When executives later intervene in the decision-making process, they renege on their commitment to employees, and the foundation of trust on which these postbureaucratic projects depend crumbles.

But do voice and decision rights always go hand in hand, or should we treat them more discretely as Freeland and Zuckerman suggest? TechCo's executives have quite clearly delegated internal voice rights in their quest for communicative openness. Employees are encouraged to share their ideas and opinions openly on the wiki and in venues like the Hack Night and Experiments Meetings. But does this mean that employees expect the executives to delegate decision rights too? The company's founders define openness as giving "a lot of freedom to people," but does a promise of open communication necessarily imply one of open decision making? Does subverting the hierarchical control of communication mean the hierarchical structure of decision making must fall as well? If not, what does this mean for the nature of employee empowerment at TechCo?

TechCo executives grappled with these very questions, if not in these exact terms. When they curtailed their own decision-making authority in Experiments Meetings for fear of signaling lack of commitment to open voice, they implicitly assumed that the workforce was conflating the two sets of rights. At the same time, they tried continually to decipher and manage the workforce's expectations about which rights were being delegated and which were not. One morning in a meeting of just the senior leadership team, an executive thumbed through the results of the latest employee survey and asked the group, "Did you notice in some of the comments, it felt like [openness] was getting co-opted to mean democracy?" Eric and Anil nodded, then after a pause Anil said, "They're orthogonal concepts. They don't necessarily go together . . . . Opinions can be heard but that doesn't mean decisions are by popular vote." Several weeks later, I would watch as Anil tried to convey that message to the workforce in a companywide presentation. That morning, however, Eric countered, "The trouble is millennials think they're the same thing."

Consistent with popular portrayals of the millennial workforce, Eric and other executives often noted that this generation was uniquely averse to any form of corporate control. "Millennials don't like rules," Eric said on more than one occasion.[6] Were that true, it would not be unreasonable to assume that employees' heightened expectations for freedom and autonomy at work included expectations for more open decision making. This was why executives felt they had to be so careful in settings like the Experiments Meetings. Yet the executives also seemed to recognize that employee expectations were not entirely straightforward. In that same morning meeting, a VP suggested, "I think millennials want to be vocal, but they know I don't run a democratic organization." They were "OK" with that, he thought: "They want voice, but they don't have to have a vote."

As it turns out, that was exactly what employees suggested in my conversations with them. When I asked Angelique, a sales rep, whether she felt the company had struck the right balance between flatness and hierarchy, she replied:

> Honestly, I don't think anyone here wants a flat company . . . . I'd like a place where you can challenge the hierarchy; that's hugely important to me. But Eric is the boss, and I should know how many steps there are between him and me . . . . Ideally, I want a decision to come from the top down but with input having been encouraged and elicited from throughout the chain and a culture of challenging decisions to be embraced.

My interviews further revealed (as did the org chart debate discussed previously) that employees generally maintained no delusion that executives were forfeiting their formal decision-making authority when they threw open the organization's communication structure. Like those presenters at the Experiments Meeting who dressed casually but whose hands shook when they spoke, employees seemed quite capable of embracing and valuing the company's informal expressive environment while also accepting and orienting to its formal authority structure. A twenty-four-year-old sales rep explained, "Despite the fact that I wear flip flops and have a beer at my desk, it's a corporate place. That's a good thing in my mind." A customer support rep commented, "We have a chain of command. We don't always use it, and I sometimes wish we did more. But we have one." In short, my observations suggested that executives had less to worry about than they thought. Most everyone, executives and employees alike, seemed in agreement that the company's open expressive environment did not imply the end of all hierarchy inside the firm.

But why would TechCo employees accept that bargain? Why didn't they expect—or even seem to want—the executives' promise of openness to mean open decision making in addition to open communication? One answer is that perhaps their youth and inexperience make them especially open to direction from authority because of the learning that might come with it. It could also be that TechCo's millennial workforce carry specific expectations and habits from their past, which make them uniquely capable of distinguishing (and accepting) the distinction between voice rights and decision rights.[7] Most of these employees developed their habits of open expression and voice in the context of a highly structured upbringing designed to advance their personal and professional development. Scholars have documented the distinctive styles of "intensive parenting" and "concerted cultivation" by which millennials and surrounding generations were raised, observing that middle- and upper-middle-class childhoods are now organized around structured activities with clear milestones and levels for progression.[8] It is interesting to consider employee calls for more managerial direction and hierarchy in light of this, and some employees directly linked those demands to their upbringing.

When I asked Kylie why the "no hierarchy thing" drove her so "nuts," she thought for a moment and then shifted to speaking about her generation, explaining: "We were raised by helicopter parents. They shepherded us from one structured activity to another . . . . We need structure. I need structure at least! We've always been given concrete things to do and known how to move to the next level." In the absence of clear direction, they did not know what it would take to get to the next level; and in the absence of hierarchy, there were no levels to get to.[9]

Over the course of my fieldwork, as the executives tried to make sense of employee calls for more hierarchy and managerial control, they began increasingly to appreciate this aspect of their workforce. One executive, who had initially been concerned that employees were confusing openness with democracy, eventually concluded that perhaps he and the other "gen X" executives had projected their own sensibility onto a millennial workforce who "might be totally different on that dimension." Whereas gen Xers like himself "hate structure and being told what to do," he said he now recognized that millennials' "entire existence has been structured, and it's what they're used to. All their time has been booked and scheduled by authority figures. They've been led into every activity they do, and maybe they just expect it."

With a growing appreciation for employees' perspective, some executives began building in more formal levels of hierarchy, with more rigidly defined job responsibilities and criteria for advancement. For example, the head of marketing, who had previously run his group with a hands-off style and a flat structure, responded to employee discontent by rolling out two specific career tracks in his group. One track had five levels of hierarchy and promotion, the other had three; and along each were more clearly defined lines of authority and scope for decision making as well as clear criteria for advancement. In an anonymous survey of the marketing team after this new structure was announced, the response was overwhelmingly positive, with 96 percent of the marketing staff supporting the changes. A number of employees heralded it as an act of "transparency" because, as one put it, "now [the staff] have a better sense of what is expected of them." (In this we hear echoes of the org chart debate, where formal structure and authority were equated with openness, not its opposite.)

Another explanation for why the workforce expected voice rights but not decision rights is that perhaps this was simply the organizing metaphor they had in mind when they joined TechCo in the first place. Prior research suggests that employee expectations are often set by the metaphors available to them.[10] In contrast to postbureaucratic projects of the 1990s that were built around metaphors of horizontal, distributed networks, the metaphor around which TechCo organizes itself is one of social media. Whereas the 1990s network metaphors implied horizontal collaboration and distributed authority (and thus suggested the fluid, project-based heterarchies written about at the time), social media suggests above all a platform for voice and conversation.[11] As Emma explained earlier, the company's wiki "reminded me of Facebook, when it came out in high school"; HipChat was "the progression of AIM we all used in middle school." Her experience at the company was a continuation, and an organizational instantiation, of what she and other digital natives had come to love and expect from social media—an informal, expressive environment in which every individual, regardless of status or social distinction, could share his or her ideas and opinions. Maybe that was all they expected and wanted.

Generational dispositions and organizing metaphors aside, however, perhaps there is an even more compelling explanation for the workforce's reaction: It could simply be that an organizational model in which voice and dialogue are open but decision making is not works well once we understand that these two concepts can be disentangled. Studies of "procedural justice" in the legal system and inside firms have found that the process by which decisions are made is often as important to feelings of fairness and justice as are the decisions themselves. In particular, having the opportunity to express one's opinion—having voice in a decision-making process—is valued, even when the final decision is out of one's control.[12] It is possible that voice rights are even more important than decision rights.

Returning to Kylie and her distaste for the "no hierarchy thing," perhaps millennials like her are not so unusual after all. They may simply be offering us the analytical leverage of an extreme case: From their unique habitus that seems to value radically open communication while also expecting a certain degree of hierarchy, we can see that it is quite possible for people to expect and value voice rights while not expecting (nor even wanting, in some cases) decision rights. We can see, in other words, that communicative empowerment is distinct from decision-making empowerment, and the former can be valued in its own right.

THE DIFFICULTY OF DELEGATING DECISION RIGHTS

Even with employees calling for more hierarchy, everyone (Kylie included) agreed that some decision rights should be distributed broadly throughout the company. In this section, I describe how executives and employees jointly struggled to make this happen. Their experiences reveal just how challenging and complex an endeavor it is to delegate decision rights.

In conventional Weberian bureaucracy, employees are given minimal decision-making authority over most of their daily activities. Their use of corporate property is strictly controlled; formal rules govern how they spend their time, including what hours they must work and when they can take breaks; and job tasks are so clearly defined that there is often little room for individual discretion in the performance of one's duties. TechCo's leaders do not want a conventional bureaucracy, however, and they believe that giving employees freedom over just these matters is elemental to the sort of open organization they are trying to build. Instead of elaborate bureaucratic controls, they have adopted a single overarching policy designed to give employees broad freedoms in these areas. That policy is called "use good judgment" (UGJ), and to understand its meaning and evolution at TechCo, we must begin in the company's kitchen.

In the kitchen stands a large, commercial refrigerator with a stainless steel frame and two glass-paned doors that reveal its contents: beer, stocked top to bottom. The beer is free to employees, and they can drink it whenever and wherever they want. The only instruction they are given is to "use good judgment." First adopted during TechCo's startup days to deal just with the free provision of beer, those three words were meant as a simple reminder that freedom was a privilege and, thus, not to be abused with irresponsible use.

As the company grew, its menu of perks—and the application of the UGJ policy to them—grew as well. By the time of my study, "good judgment" was the only condition placed on employees' otherwise unrestricted, open access to free food in the kitchen, to using the company's common lounge areas and the ping pong and foosball tables therein, to purchasing books through its free books program, even to bringing pets to work. Whereas the workforce balked at the idea of management delegating authority over certain decisions (like the approval and management of strategic projects in Experiments Meetings), they celebrated these freedoms. Through them, executives seemed to be signaling a desire to open up and share the organization and its property with employees. Just as the executives' willingness to share confidential information on the business was read by the workforce as sign of "trust" and "respect," so too was this act of openness and sharing. It was the executives' way of treating employees "like adults," a sales rep told me; "a way of saying they hire responsible people who don't need to be micromanaged," a colleague of his said. According to Emma in customer support, "It means I'm trusted. There's no one hawking over me."

Over time, the executives took UGJ beyond workplace perks and applied it to additional domains. First was control over employees' time. Several years after TechCo's founding, Eric and Anil concluded that millennial preferences for flexibility, as well as the constant connectivity enabled by mobile devices and broadband in the home, rendered nine-to-five work hours and formal vacation policies "a relic of the past." Going forward, TechCo employees were told they could come and go from work on their own schedule so long as they used good judgment, and that they could take as much vacation as they wished, whenever they wished, so long as they used good judgment. Not surprisingly, employees loved the idea of having this control, and the company began touting this application of UGJ in its recruitment activities.

As the policy expanded to cover more and more perks and then employees' control over their own time, UGJ seeped even more deeply into the fabric of TechCo, and its meaning expanded one step further. It came to represent the company's overall approach to management. Where employees might otherwise have been given formal instruction on how to carry out their daily work or how to perform specific tasks of their job, they were told simply to use good judgment. Customer support reps were given no formal script to follow and could take themselves out of the phone queue when they deemed it appropriate, sales reps could approve their own discounts, engineers could decide when a bug was problematic enough to freeze other work on the product and pull resources onto addressing the issue, and so on.

By the time of my study, use good judgment had become a mantra of sorts throughout the company. It was the company's "default policy," Anil said, and it was meant to signal executives' desire to dispense with formal bureaucratic practices and embrace a spirit of informal openness instead. Employees embraced the spirit and intent of it, and many reported that it was the reason they had chosen to work at TechCo. Yet despite such enthusiasm for all that UGJ signified, both employees and executives had begun to question the policy's overall effectiveness on the ground.

On one of my first days in the field, an executive confided in me that he feared UGJ was a "grandiose statement" that was not working as envisioned. Expressing hope that my research might shed light on this, he pressed, "I want to know how it's really working. Does it work? Is that what people even want?" Given the desire to build a radically open organization, the temptation had been to continue expanding the scope of delegation over time, but problems were now arising. Another executive admitted that he had recently begun to think UGJ might reflect a "love affair" with the idea of an open, informal environment more than a practical approach to governance and control. Drawing on a second analogy, he explained, "It's like the Republicans saying we should privatize Social Security. It's fine and good to say it, but when you really think about it, you realize it could be a complete disaster."

TechCoers from all levels shared these concerns, and an employee in the services department captured the sentiments of many when he said simply, "It's great in principle. I don't know if it works in practice." It appeared that the open-ended approach to workplace control, which they all supported in spirit and had seen work fairly well for the delegation of voice rights and perks like beer and food, was encountering unforeseen obstacles when extended to other domains. In examining two of these challenges—one that surfaced when UGJ was extended to employees' control over their time, and a second that became evident when UGJ was stretched further to control of employees' daily work—we will see that the delegation of decision rights is difficult to accomplish even when all parties support it. It is perhaps especially difficult in an organization pursuing "radical openness" along other dimensions.

OPEN INEQUALITY

One challenge with delegating decision rights is that executives cannot always delegate rights equally, and this may diminish employee morale. The contrasting experiences of Nick and Oliver are illustrative here. Both in their early twenties and recent graduates of well-regarded universities, Nick had majored in computer science and now worked on TechCo's engineering team; Oliver, a political science major with an interest in marketing, worked in customer support. On the morning I was scheduled to meet with Nick, he texted to say that he had gotten a slow start and would not arrive at the office for another half hour or so. A bit before 10 A.M. he joined me in the conference room, where I had been waiting, and apologized: "I don't normally come in at 9, so I should have known not to schedule something for then." Mind you, Nick was no slacker. Over the next hour, his comments revealed an intensely driven young man who worked long hours and who had chosen TechCo over another software firm because he believed it would offer him greater learning opportunities and because "I loved the culture of 'Use Good Judgment.'" He explained that the flexibility implied by UGJ had signaled to him that TechCo "put a lot of trust in employees" and so would likely offer a more developmental and fulfilling work environment. When he joined, he found that to be the case.

Oliver and I met over dinner one evening. His workday had started at 11 A.M., but not because he had gotten a slow start. To offer consistent coverage of TechCo's phone lines, TechCo assigned customer support reps like him to staggered shifts, with scheduled, mandatory breaks. During his recruitment and training, Oliver too had liked TechCo's promise of use good judgment, but after he started work, he learned it meant something different than he had anticipated: He learned that it would not apply to his work hours. "I had no idea. I started, and they said you'll work 11 to 8. I thought that sucked, but I'd already taken the job," he explained. Use good judgment still meant something quite real to Oliver and his fellow customer support reps (as noted, they were given no formal call scripts and told simply to use good judgment in their customer communications, which was a freedom they embraced and valued). However, that cherished control over one's schedule, which most employees expected upon joining TechCo because it was promoted in the company's recruiting and which others in the company actually enjoyed, was not available to these workers.

In fact, it was not available to a number of employees in the company. Entry-level sales reps, who were responsible for cold-calling prospects, were expected to be at their desks during normal business hours. Sales reps in general could not take vacation whenever they pleased because managers reasoned that the team would miss its monthly sales targets during popular vacation months like July or December if scores of reps headed off all at once. Across the organization, employees observed that TechCo's intense work hour norms often rendered the implied flexibility of UGJ moot, especially for junior employees; and a not infrequent joke was that having no vacation policy meant having "a no vacation policy," depending on the demands of one's job and one's specific manager.

A consistent employee criticism was that the company was "talking the talk" of UGJ but not always "walking the walk." Noting how TechCo touted UGJ in recruiting activities and marketing but then failed to deliver on it, Nicole, a member of the sales team, complained, "We market ourselves one way but we act differently." She felt UGJ and the flexibility it implied "need to come with a big caveat or an asterisk next to them" so as not to mislead employees like Oliver.

TechCo's experience in this regard is not unique. The company is neither the first organization to adopt an open-ended policy like UGJ (executives originally got the idea from Nordstrom, the national retailer known for its amusingly short "employee handbook" that reads: "Rule #1. Use good judgment. There will be no other rules."), nor is it the first to struggle with its implementation and face employee morale issues in the process.[13] Organizational economists refer to such open-ended policies as "relational contracts," and they observe that many corporations rely on relational contracts of one sort or another to get things done, but just as many struggle to make them work as promised.[14] The challenge is that such policies rest on informal, implicit agreements of trust between managers and employees, and trust is quite fragile. In the case of policies like UGJ, management promises to give employees discretion over certain areas of their work life (like their work hours) in exchange for employees promising to adopt a particular standard of behavior in exercise of that discretion. If executives break their side of the promise by failing to allow such discretion, they encounter a major "credibility problem."[15]

A closer look at TechCo's experience, however, suggests an important nuance on the commonly understood credibility problem of relational contracts, and one that may be particularly salient in a firm pursuing other forms of organizational openness. As much as customer support reps and sales reps wished UGJ meant they could have more control over their schedules, they generally understood the practical reasons for why it did not, and few employees ascribed the policy's practical failure to any ill-intent on the part of executives. More often, employees echoed Nicole when she said that despite her frustration with the gap between TechCo's marketing of UGJ and its use in practice, "I understand their [executives'] intentions are in the right place."

In this way, TechCo's workforce had a sophisticated understanding of the realities of organizational life. Scholars have noted that the credibility problem of relational contracts often stems less from ill-intent on the part of management and more from the inherent nature of the firm in which decision rights can only ever really be "loaned" to employees (rather than "owned" by them) because certain exigencies may lead management to take them back.[16] TechCo's employees seemed to intuit this fact of organizational life. For them, the issue was less that executives had promised certain rights and then retracted them, and more that those rights were not universal and that this was clear to all. In short, TechCo had a problem of open and visible inequality more than one of credibility.[17]

Throughout the company, it was widely recognized that some groups "lived" UGJ more than others, and when I asked employees to explain their assertions that UGJ was not working in practice when it came to control of employees' time, this was what they spoke about. To a person, everyone seemed to know and be in total agreement about where the policy did and did not apply in this regard. One after another, employees offered up the same hierarchy of privilege that they felt existed in the company and that, in their eyes, undermined the legitimacy of UGJ. At the bottom of this hierarchy sat customer support and entry-level sales reps, universally recognized to be "second-class citizens" (as several put it) when it came to control over their time and schedules. Enjoying slightly more control were senior sales reps and sales managers, as well as those in TechCo's services group. Always sitting uppermost in the hierarchy were those in engineering and marketing, the "first-class citizens" for whom UGJ was most relevant on this issue.

Interestingly, this inequality seemed salient to both first- and second-class citizens. When I asked Nick, the engineer, what UGJ meant to him, he paused before answering and drew a comparison to other groups by observing, "Engineering has a privileged position in the company." Although UGJ "works great" for him and although he was grateful for the flexibility it offered, he said he felt bad for his peers in other groups. "I've sat in on support calls. It was a hellish week for them [when I did], and I know that what they do is valuable," So the fact that peers like Oliver were not afforded all the same rights left him feeling uncomfortable. Executives too were aware of this issue and its impact on morale. Explaining that UGJ was "more true in some places and less true in others," one executive told me that he worried about the "blue collar, white collar divide" it exposed.

The general challenge is that in a complex, differentiated organization, the rights that can be delegated to different roles will undoubtedly vary. Consequently, the public delegation of ostensibly universal rights is bound to encounter problems. What is more, even though employees at TechCo understood the practical bases for such distinctions (rooted in the nature of different jobs), these distinctions were constantly visible to them and therefore difficult to ignore. When Nick wandered in late for our meeting, windbreaker on and still damp from the morning drizzle outside, he walked past the desks of entry-level sales reps who had been working since 8 A.M. and who could not help but notice when other employees arrived and left. Nick knew the support team worked in shifts because he had often wandered by their workstations and even sat in on some of their calls. Everyone in the company could see that sales reps were not able to take vacation whenever they wanted because reps made their formal requests for vacation on the wiki, posting which weeks they hoped to take off on a public calendar; and sales reps could see other employees discuss their vacations in HipChat's public chat rooms and overhear conversations about them in the common lounge areas. In short, with no offices, and people's comings and goings visible to all, and with corporate communication about work policies appearing on an open platform like the wiki, there was just no missing this sort of inequality.

Because TechCo's workforce is so homogenous in age, this inequality was likely all the more visible and jarring. Were inequality in rights aligned with a distinction in age or seniority, perhaps it would have seemed less awkward or noteworthy. Moreover, some studies of millennials suggest that distinctions for this generation were minimized during their upbringing as grades were inflated and awards and recognition granted broadly for purposes of building self-esteem.[18] If that characterization has any truth, then TechCo's millennial workforce may be especially likely to note, and uncomfortable to confront, such distinctions now. Either way, the result is the same: A policy intended to distribute decision rights (UGJ) created a new hierarchy of privilege in its place because those rights could not be delegated equally. Where this new status hierarchy was directly visible to employees, it undermined the legitimacy of the policy and the whole distribution of rights that policy signified.

OPEN CONFUSION

Tellingly, where distinctions existed but were less transparent, employees did not raise the issue of inequality. Instead, they identified a different, and even larger, challenge to implementing UGJ: They expressed "confusion" and an overall "lack of clarity" on what good judgment even meant. This issue surfaced most dramatically when the policy was extended to employees' control over their actual work. Although everyone supported the idea of an open environment in principle, it often felt like "bowling without gutters," as one individual put it, to receive no more formal guidelines than the words "use good judgment." "You don't always know what the parameters are that you should be working in. It's too loose," this same individual explained. Recent research on relational contracts has found that implementation of these sorts of open-ended policies can depend as much on issues of "clarity" as on those of "credibility"; and for many employees at TechCo, it was clarity that was sorely lacking.[19] Conveying the challenge succinctly in a wiki thread on UGJ, a twenty-six-year-old woman on the services team wrote, "Sometimes I think I am using good judgment but find that others disagree."

Those who had been at TechCo since its early days drew comparisons to a time when UGJ had worked well precisely because there had been agreement on this score. One long-tenured sales rep suggested that as the company had grown so, too, had the number and variety of opinions being voiced, and this undermined the common agreement that once had made UGJ practicable. He explained, "When the company was small and the culture homogenous, UGJ worked really well because everyone had the same definition of good judgment. Now it's harder to agree on that." Others noted that the company's young workforce, in which many employees lacked prior corporate experience, made this definitional issue even more salient. "We hire people who don't have the experience to know what good judgment even means," said a human resources employee involved in the company's recruitment and training activities. She worried that UGJ was "a utopian view" that assumed all employees being hired knew what good judgment meant. In her opinion, that assumption was "not necessarily true."

Just as social scientists have theorized, employees observed that in the absence of a "common definition of the situation" the sort of informal coordination implied by UGJ was difficult to achieve.[20] Heather, a veteran of TechCo's marketing group who felt UGJ had worked when the company was smaller but no longer did, said simply, "It's a shit show now. If you don't have people who agree with what good judgment is or people who are so young they don't know what it is, how can [you] use it?" She recounted a recent meeting in which her manager had instructed his assembled team to "use good judgment" in devising new marketing campaigns that could help them meet their monthly quota of leads. "What does that even mean?" Heather asked me rhetorically, adding, "They talk in these vague, ambiguous ways. They're not taking the time to define things."

Yet executives faced a paradox in this. They had committed to giving employees voice rights, which meant a commitment to letting people express their own opinions about how things should be defined. This, however, led to just the sort of confusion that was making the delegation of decision rights with UGJ so challenging. The paradox becomes clear when we examine the one part of TechCo that had less of a commitment to open communication but more success delegating decision rights with UGJ than the rest of the organization—the engineering group.

In stark contrast to others at TechCo—and offering a valuable counterfactual as a result—the company's engineers believed UGJ worked quite well when it came to their daily work, and none reported the clarity problem that Heather and so many others raised. Nick, for instance, explained that, beyond control over his time, UGJ "is really the official policy for everything in our group," and in his opinion, "It works very well. It's empowering." He offered the specific example of declaring "crit sits" (i.e., critical situations in which a problem with the product is determined to be so significant that other developers must stop work until it is resolved). Rather than being given formal guidelines or told to seek manager approval, TechCo engineers were told simply to use good judgment when deciding whether a bug constituted a crit sit or not. "It's just a matter of doing what makes sense," Nick explained, and he expressed no uncertainty about "what makes sense" in those instances.

Likewise, Daniel, a soft-spoken but articulate programmer I met over Thai food one afternoon, said that UGJ worked well even for "major decisions about the product." He and several colleagues were building a new product that would integrate with customers' other social media tools, and on this "it's really up to us to decide what to do. It's not like you present your plan [for the product] and have to get approval." The team just used their own judgment, he said, and because he was confident they knew what good judgment meant in this circumstance, he felt no need for further direction. He explained, "There's no strict mandate to do things in a certain way, but there's social pressure. Not some formal rule, but it's in our heads like a lot of different cultural norms and stuff. We know what the expectation is basically."

In short, the same three words that were "vague" and "ambiguous" in most parts of the company carried clear expectations in engineering. When a manager said use good judgment, engineers knew "what the expectation is," as Daniel put it, or "what makes sense," as Nick put it. But why did that consensus emerge in engineering and not elsewhere? What was so different here?

For starters, in contrast to employees in marketing, services, or sales (groups that hired people with a broad range of educational and professional experiences), TechCo engineers entered the company with more training in common. The company recruited engineers who had taken certain computer science classes and who knew specific coding languages, so TechCo engineers started out with at least some shared knowledge base and expectations. More important, though, was that engineering did not have as radically open a communication environment as the rest of the company, and because of this, the heads of the group could more easily convey their own definition of what UGJ meant.

At the time of my study, engineering was less communicatively open than the rest of TechCo in a variety of ways. At the most basic level, the group was positioned largely outside of the open, public spaces in which everyone else at the company convened and conversed. Engineers had their own private kitchen, and the group maintained private, invitation-only chat rooms on HipChat. People across the organization noted that the engineering group was managed as "its own island" with little connection to or communication with the rest of the organization, and engineers themselves noted this separation, often with some sense of regret. An engineer who had worked at the company for less than a year said he initially had been surprised by how little contact he had with nonengineers: "I have very little interaction with the rest of the company. It feels really separate and isolated to me." A colleague of his described engineering as "cordoned off and insulated from the rest of the company" with "not a lot of communication" with other groups.

According to the engineers with whom I spoke, this came from the top. Whereas executives in other groups were known for their radical transparency, the heads of engineering were known for not sharing much high-level information with their staff. "They don't go out of their way to share," one engineer reported. "They aren't as transparent as others at the company," said another. Nor did they tolerate extensive discussion and debate. Several engineers noted that they were discouraged by their department's leaders from participating on the wiki because those executives believed that the extensive debates and numerous voices on the platform offered more distracting noise than productive dialogue. One explained, "If a big debate breaks out [on the wiki], they'll just pull [the people debating] into a conference room and say 'let's resolve this.'" Another said, they often "shut down conversations you try to have around issues. There's one message, and that's it."

That "one message" is crucial. Employees in other parts of TechCo reported a lack of clarity around UGJ. They noted that the number and variety of voices precluded any consensus on what "good judgment" meant. The delegation of voice rights seemed to work against the successful delegation of decision rights with UGJ, in other words. But here in engineering, the group's leaders had essentially consolidated voice rights at the top in a way that enabled the delegation of decision rights with UGJ.[21] By allowing for just "one message," these executives effectively silenced the engineers' voices, but by the engineers' own accounts, this afforded "one clear vision" to coordinate around and guide their decision making. "The top of the engineering group is not at all living the open, transparent TechCo culture thing. But the group is really well-run to the degree there are really clearly defined paths for what we're working on," said one member of the group.

Furthermore, although the group's leaders were not transparent on many issues, several employees noted that the leaders were actually quite transparent on one issue that directly clarified what good judgment (and bad judgment) meant in practice: Any time an engineer was fired, the executives explained the decision to the entire team. According to the engineers with whom I spoke, this was invaluable in terms of clearly conveying their managers' expectations. As one junior engineer put it, he was "not a part of any higher-level dialogue" and didn't "have access to [the engineering executives] or their thinking" on many matters, but he felt he knew precisely what was expected when he was granted "huge control over lower-level things like how to build a feature or when to deploy it to customers."

Outside of engineering, TechCo executives were not unaware of the clarity problem they had with UGJ. However, they often struggled to overcome it because of their commitment to employee voice rights and the challenge of delineating those from decision rights. A story relayed to me by one member of the senior leadership team demonstrates this. Toward the end of my study, Eric and others on the leadership team decided that the sales team should be restructured. They devised a new organizational and reporting structure and decided that Eric would take over management of the group until a new head of sales could be hired. Describing the announcement of this restructuring to the sales team, an executive recounted:

> We gathered all the sales managers together to make the announcement. That was great, totally the right idea. But after we told them all about the changes and that Eric would be their new head of sales until someone else is hired, one of the managers asked, "How should we tell our teams this?" Totally reasonable question, right? So, we tell them, "use good judgment." But it turns out now there's massive confusion on the sales force as to what's going on because some managers went back and explained the changes one way, and others said something different. We missed an opportunity to provide some clarity. There was no clear messaging from the top.

Yet, as noted, lack of "clear messaging from the top" was basically inherent to this organization given its commitment to voice rights. In a space so thick with open dialogue, where hundreds of voices might chime in on the wiki on any given issue, it was challenging to arrive at consensus. And, in the absence of clarity, it was difficult to settle on the precise meaning of UGJ in any given situation. Confused themselves, some managers hesitated to interpret it for their employees at all. When asked for specific direction or guidance by their teams, they just echoed executives, saying "use good judgment" and leaving it at that. For many employees, those three words came to mean "a cop-out used in place of management," and this fueled the workforce's already fevered calls for more and better managerial direction.

Managers themselves understood the frustration. As one manager in the services group acknowledged, "UGJ is a way for people at my level to avoid making decisions." Speaking of the alleged empowerment that came with UGJ, a manager from sales said bluntly, "Empowerment is bullshit. It's much harder for me—much more work for me as the manager—to structure things for someone [on my team] to be successful than to just say 'Go do it. Go use good judgment.'" But managers like her struggled to find clarity.

When they did try to interpret good judgment on the ground, its meaning was frequently contested. A consistent point of contention was *whose* (definition of) good judgment should apply when disagreements arose. Both managers and their employees believed they had been granted broad discretion to act as they felt appropriate, but this did not mean they would interpret every situation in the same way. When Nicole had concerns about the work ethic of a new sales rep on her team, she wanted to convey this to the rep and offer him clearer guidance on her expectations for appropriate behavior and job performance. She quickly learned that doing so would not be so straightforward. Not only did her employee's definition of good judgment differ from hers, but Nicole's own manager had a different definition than she did. Nicole explained, "My manager felt I shouldn't say anything. But I felt it was unacceptable, so I had a sit down with the individual." Later that sales rep complained that Nicole had failed to live up to UGJ and grant the staff their promised freedom.

Despite all these challenges, UGJ was by no means a total policy failure. Because of the company's open communication environment, concern over UGJ became a topic of firmwide conversation and thus something that could be confronted head on. Comments such as "the Use Good Judgment philosophy is not scalable" were voiced in the employee survey and on the wiki, and employees began calling for more training to clarify what "good judgment" meant in particular circumstances. Executives proved a receptive audience. Still committed to minimizing formal controls as much as possible and not ready to give up on UGJ, they were thoughtful students of both their own successes and failures with the policy, as well as the experiences of other companies with similar policies. After researching Nordstrom's success with UGJ, one executive said he realized, "When you actually dig into it, they have a lot more there. There are all these institutional things that support it like guidelines and training." [22]

Consistent with prior research on relational contracts, executives came to see that within TechCo itself UGJ was working better in areas where it was reinforced and supported by complementary practices that clarified what good judgment meant. In particular, just the sort of job-specific training that employees were calling for seemed to help instill clear expectations for appropriate behavior and task performance. Consequently, the company began investing more heavily in the development of training programs throughout the organization. A respected member of the company's people operations team was pulled off his day job and tasked with developing a program for training new managers, and various departments began developing more formal, job-specific training for their staffs.

As programs like this got up and running, UGJ began to work better. For example, support reps greatly valued having no call scripts and having the discretion to take themselves out of the phone queue to address complicated customer issues (instead of always escalating them to a manager); and based on my observations, this worked well in practice. However, those who had worked in that group for a while explained that this had not been possible in the past. It only worked now, they explained, because by the time a rep was faced with these decisions, he or she had spent an entire month in intensive training, taking calls alongside experienced reps who had offered guidance and feedback on their every call. Training like this offered clarity without having to abandon the firm's commitment to voice rights.

CONCLUSION

TechCo's experience with UGJ suggests that delegating decision rights in an open organization is not impossible, but it certainly is not easy. In chapter 2, we saw that delegating voice rights has its own complications but that, in general, TechCo has succeeded in creating an open communication environment for its workforce. Here, we have seen that creating an open decision-making environment is a far more complicated affair. There may be some decisions employees do not even want delegated. For those they do want delegated, the organization encounters challenging credibility and clarity problems, and these obstacles may surface even more starkly in the open physical and discursive spaces of a firm like TechCo. In such an environment, it is transparent when not all rights are equally delegated, and voices reign so freely that clarity proves especially evasive. Next, we look at what happens to corporate control when employee voices reign free not just inside the company but also outside of it.

4

OPENNESS CONTROLS

WHEN EMPLOYEES SPEAK freely within the firm, it can complicate executive attempts to delegate decision making. But what
happens when employees can speak freely not just inside the
firm but also outside it? For an organization attempting radical openness,
employees' external speech poses a whole new set of problems. To understand why, let's step away from TechCo for a moment.

On Sunday March 17, 2013, Adria Richards sat in a packed conference
hall in Santa Clara, California, surrounded by hundreds of technology
enthusiasts and software developers. She was at Pycon, the annual user conference for the open-source coding language Python. For almost a year now,
Adria had worked as a "developer evangelist" for the Colorado-based company SendGrid, promoting and marketing SendGrid's email management
service to developers across the country. With a popular personal blog and
more than nine thousand followers on Twitter, Adria was well known in the
tech community and well positioned for this sort of work. Pycon was a great
venue for her to meet even more developers and spread the SendGrid word,
but Adria had been on the road for nearly a month now and was tired. This
was her fifth and final conference before she would head back home.[1]

As Adria sat listening to one of the day's final sessions, she overheard the
men behind her make a few sexual jokes about "big dongles" and "forking

someone's repo." Technically, a "dongle" is a piece of hardware, often a cable, that plugs into a computer;[2] and in open-source projects, "forking a repo" means to copy someone's software repository so you can continue development work on the software yourself.[3] Tired and irritated by the sexual innuendo, Adria turned in her seat, took a picture of the men with her smartphone and tweeted it from her personal Twitter account along with the message, "Not cool. Jokes about forking repos in a sexual way and 'big' dongles. Right behind me #pycon."[4]

Within minutes, Pycon staff, who followed Adria on Twitter and had seen her tweet, approached her in the conference hall, asked what had happened, and then spoke with the men involved. According to the chair of the conference, who was quoted several days later by various media outlets covering the then-unraveling saga, the situation was resolved quite straightforwardly at the time: "We pulled the individuals aside. We got all sides of the story. They said she was right, and they were very apologetic."[5]

As it turned out, the situation was far from resolved, and by the end, little about it would be straightforward. What happened was this: The photo Adria had tweeted identified the men to their employers. Within a day of the incident, one of the men had been fired for it. That individual then took to social media himself. Identifying his former employer as the mobile gaming company PlayHaven, he publicly disclosed his termination on Hacker News, a social news website popular with software developers and entrepreneurs. There he apologized for his offensive comments but suggested that Adria herself had acted irresponsibly in light of her visibility on social media. He wrote, "Adria has an audience and is a successful person of the media . . . . With that great power and reach come responsibility. As a result of the picture she took, I was let go from my job today. Which sucks because I have 3 kids and I really liked that job."[6] Shortly after this, the CEO of PlayHaven posted on the company's blog, confirming that the developer had been fired and distancing PlayHaven from his offensive comments, writing that the company was "dedicated to gender equality and values honorable behavior."[7]

News of the developer's termination spread quickly on social media, and it outraged some members of the broader developer and hacker community.

In a matter of hours, Adria's personal website as well as her employer Send-Grid's corporate website were hit by a flood of DDOS (distributed denial of service) attacks. Eventually, both sites were taken offline by the hackers' assault.[8] Individuals claiming to be associated with the hacker group Anonymous threatened to harass SendGrid's customers next, and Adria received bitter personal attacks on Facebook and Twitter, including calls for her termination and even death and rape threats.[9]

The following morning, SendGrid announced on its Facebook page, Twitter account, and corporate blog that it had fired Adria. The company's Facebook post read, "Effective immediately, SendGrid has terminated the employment of Adria Richards. While we generally are sensitive and confidential with respect to employee matters, the situation has taken on a public nature. We have taken action that we believe is in the overall best interests of SendGrid, its employees, and our customers."[10] In its tweet, the company reiterated that Adria had been fired and included a link to the corporate blog, where, in a post titled "A Difficult Situation," SendGrid's CEO explained, "Her decision to tweet the comments and photographs of the people who made the comments crossed the line. Publicly shaming the offenders—and bystanders—was not the appropriate way to handle the situation." The post went on to say that in the wake of Adria's tweet "a heated public debate ensued" and "quickly spiraled into extreme vitriol."[11]

Spiraled is right. But what of SendGrid's own reaction? Why did they fire Adria and then publicly shame her on social media (for publicly shaming someone on social media)? What too of PlayHaven? Why did they fire the developer, then blog about firing him? After all, the incident occurred on a Sunday evening outside of either company's corporate offices, and it was originally communicated over a personal Twitter account. When we consider that SendGrid was attacked for Adria's tweet and that PlayHaven felt compelled to note its support for gender equality, however, the companies' motives become clear: Each organization was trying to distance itself from the employee in question and ensure that no one would mistake the individual's comments and actions for those of the firm.

The issue confronting these organizations is that social media has rendered the connections between employers and their employees readily transparent.

In the process, these new open platforms have eroded the boundary between personal and corporate communication. When people list their employers on their personal Twitter and Facebook accounts, or when a quick search on Google or LinkedIn reveals their employer regardless—and, especially, when people use their personal social media accounts to promote the company's products or services as Adria did and as many corporations actively encourage their employees to do—then an individual's personal identity and speech become difficult to disentangle from those of the corporation.

The fact that employee speech might be mistaken for the firm's constitutes a major disruption to conventional bureaucratic notions of corporate control. In the past, it was generally accepted that only the CEO or specially designated top executives could speak for a company. Public statements that might affect the firm's reputation had to be run up the chain of command for approval and often required review by the organization's legal and public relations departments. In other words, external voice rights (the right to speak on behalf of the corporation) were strictly and hierarchically controlled.[12] But such control seems lost in a world where any employee voice on social media can bear on the firm's reputation.

To address this issue and avoid experiences like that of SendGrid and PlayHaven, corporations have generally responded in one of two ways. Some have tried to maintain control over the firm's external voice by imposing formal rules and restrictions over what their employees can say on social media. Others, like TechCo, have seemingly embraced the erosion of control by explicitly delegating external voice rights to their workforce.

For firms embracing the formal approach, detailed social media policies are now common. A central element of nearly all of these policies is the requirement that employees distinguish their personal communications on social media from those made on behalf of the firm.[13] For instance, IBM's policy tells employees to "make it clear that you are speaking for yourself and not on behalf of IBM" and always to "use a disclaimer such as this: 'The postings on this site are my own and don't necessarily represent IBM's positions, strategies, or opinions.'"[14] Best Buy's policy instructs employees to "State That It's YOUR Opinion . . . . Unless authorized to speak on behalf of Best Buy, you must state that the views expressed are your own."[15]

The policies of Apple, Oracle, and many others include similar disclaimer requirements.[16]

In addition to disclaimers, another typical requirement of corporate social media policies is that employees "be respectful" to others online. The firms just mentioned include such admonitions in their policies, as does software maker SAP, which requires its workforce to "carry the professional norms and standards of any SAP office onto the social computing platforms" they use.[17] Finally, most social media policies include an explicit prohibition against disclosing information that is considered confidential or proprietary to the firm, including details about its customers. Consider again IBM's policy, which proscribes the release of such things as: client details; IBM's own "internal reports, policies, procedures, or other internal business-related confidential communications"; and any "other sensitive inside information" including personal commentary by employees on the company's performance or business plans.[18] In short, formal social media polices like this are designed to make it clear that the firm maintains hierarchical control over its external communication and that only its officially designated spokespeople have the authority to speak on its behalf.

In contrast to this approach, TechCo has no social media policy beyond the three (by now familiar) words: use good judgment. That is, employees are told they can tweet, blog, comment, or post whatever they want so long as they just use good judgment. Despite the growing popularity of formal social media policies, TechCo is not alone in forgoing them. The online shoe retailer Zappos, for instance, has a policy only slightly longer but no more specific than TechCo's, which reads, "Be real and use your best judgment."[19]

Companies that embrace this approach do so because they believe restrictions come at too great a cost. Consistent with TechCo's broader philosophy about the impact of social media, these organizations want their employees to connect and communicate with customers on social media as the market now seems to demand. They rely on their staffs to sustain and participate in the many online conversations that bear on the business; so, rather than circumscribe employees' online speech, these companies seek to distribute external voice rights throughout the workforce.

Social media pundits promote this strategy. Andy Beal, author of *Radical Transparency*, has said, "The more restrictions that you place on employees [on social media], the less room you give them to be a real asset to your online reputation . . . . If you have an employee blogging policy with hundreds of restrictions, you're stifling the ability for those employees to be ambassadors for the company."[20] In short, firms like TechCo and Zappos want employees to speak for the firm, and they embrace the very lack of separation between personal and corporate communication that firms with more formal controls seem to fear. Recall from chapter 1 that Emma was attracted to TechCo precisely because the company's voice was so clearly linked to those of its employees. She said, "When [TechCo] spoke on social media, it was as if it was speaking as a human being . . . . Any blog post would have a link to the personal profile of whoever wrote it, and people's profiles were just very clearly linked to the company. What the people seemed to be about was what the company was about."

Yet even if one agrees that TechCo's approach is better suited to today's market, it does not solve the problem of control. As noted in chapter 2, confidential information (e.g., about an upcoming round of venture capital financing) does sometimes leak outside of TechCo and cause problems for the organization. This risk would seem only to be heightened by letting employees say whatever they want on social media. Moreover, even if a firm like TechCo can sometimes leverage employee voices to good marketing effect, it cannot easily pick and choose when those voices will be taken to represent it. Consequently, organizations that do not formally restrict social media use must worry about what their employees say on those platforms every bit as much as, if not more than, other organizations.

Indeed, the fact that TechCo executives feel the need to tell employees to "use good judgment" on social media is indicative of the dilemma the firm faces. Consider that in chapter 2 TechCo executives did not instruct employees to "use good judgment" when it came to personal speech on the internal wiki. Inside the firm, executives seemed to want truly unrestricted voice in service of open dialogue. However, executives did invoke UGJ when delegating decision rights in chapter 3, suggesting at least an implicit recognition that some sort of minimal control or guidance is necessary when employee decisions can affect firm performance. Their instinct to apply UGJ to social media use makes sense because it is not just a voice right being delegated here. Because employees are transparently and publicly linked to their firms these days, every time they speak on social media they are effectively making a decision that has implications for the firm and its reputation. Employees must make a judgment call, in other words, about what to say publicly; and what they decide to say can affect the organization. Thus, even as firms like TechCo reject formal controls over employee use of social media, they still actively try to influence the judgment those employees exercise on it.

INFLUENCING JUDGMENT

Brian Cassidy is a young, driven TechCo sales rep. His story demonstrates how TechCo tries to influence employees' social media use through open internal conversation and collective education on what constitutes appropriate speech. Through Brian, we will see how social media has fundamentally transformed, but not necessarily eroded, corporate control of external voice and a firm's ability to direct the conversations happening outside its four walls.

One day at work Brian came across an online news article about a local event. A heated debate was unfolding on the comments thread that accompanied the article, and Brian jumped into the fray. Brian disagreed with the comments of a poster named Scott and ended his comment with a lewd reference directed at him. (The irony of promising anonymity to an open organization in the social media era is that I cannot offer too many specifics of the incident without a simple Google search then revealing the parties.)

As Brian later recounted, when he hit "submit" on his comment, "here's where things went sideways." It turned out that the comments thread was powered by Facebook, and this meant that when Brian logged in to post his comment, the website pulled identifying information from his Facebook account to go alongside what he wrote.[21] When his comment appeared, its author was revealed to be not just "Brian Cassidy" but "Brian Cassidy—Works at TechCo."

As fate would have it, the target of Brian's comment, Scott, knew about TechCo and about the freedom it gave employees on social media. Scott immediately tweeted about the incident, criticizing TechCo for not having more control over its employees' public communications. He then wrote about the incident on his own blog and submitted the same post to several widely read social news sites. Because TechCo's own software alerts a company when it is being mentioned on social media, TechCo executives learned of the issue within hours. Speaking about the incident months later, one executive reflected, "The ironic thing is, Scott knew us. He was just doing what we advise our own customers to do—to be out on social media, to take advantage of interesting events and publish content about it on social media to get attention."

In the coming days and over a series of intense phone calls and meetings, the senior management team debated what to do. They realized that "the knee jerk reaction is to fire him," as one put it, and they felt confident that they did not need a formal social media policy to do that. Although formal policies presumably offer even greater legal cover to fire employees in cases like this (e.g., if their speech directly violates an explicit guideline), TechCo had told its employees to use good judgment, and Brian's comment did not reflect good judgment according to the executives. As one executive observed, if a company could legally fire an employee for offensive comments overheard in person, then it could presumably fire an employee for the same online.[22]

Yet TechCo's executives did not fire Brian. In the end, they let him keep his job but required him to write a wiki post on the incident for the entire company to see and, for one year, to recount the incident in each of Tech-Co's monthly new-hire training sessions so that incoming employees could learn from his experience. Brian's wiki post was titled "Social Media and Good Judgment: A Cautionary Tale." He began it by describing the incident with Scott and writing of his own behavior, "This is what I would call bad judgment." In his presentation to the training class I observed, he told TechCo's new employees, "I fucked up, and I give you this talk so you don't fuck up."[23]

The point of all this was not to publicly shame Brian; it was to reinforce the use good judgment policy. In effect, TechCo's executives seized this as an opportunity to address both the credibility and clarity problems noted in chapter 3. Writing on the wiki at the time, executives reiterated their support for UGJ and acknowledged that in the wake of incidents like Brian's, there was clearly a need to better define what good judgment meant with regard to social media use and in other domains where UGJ applied. Executives announced that they would begin using the wiki to provide "concrete and engaging examples of real world situations where either good judgment or bad judgment was used" so that a common "knowledge base" could develop. In the months that followed, they did just that, and Brian's post became the first in what was ultimately known as the "Bad Judgment" section of the wiki. Over time, as various incidents arose on one issue or another, additional posts were added there (including one about an insensitive tweet made from TechCo's corporate Twitter account in the wake of a natural disaster, and even one by Eric, the company's CEO, after a joke he made misfired and offended some employees).

These bad judgment posts served as a starting point for conversation as the workforce collectively processed the meaning and lessons from each incident. Brian's in particular sparked a lengthy discussion. He had concluded his bad judgment post by noting:

What I should have realized when I wrote that post [to Scott] is that I am *always a representative of TechCo* regardless of the time of day, where I am, or where I'm commenting. Even though I might not be on a sales call or wearing [the company logo], that doesn't mean I'm not a TechCoer . . . . What I should have realized is that *with the way social media works, I am never just 'Brian Cassidy'; I am 'Brian Cassidy from TechCo.'* (emphasis added)

In responses on the wiki and in their conversations offline in the days, weeks, and months that followed, employees came back to this point again and again, as if they were all slowly working out what it meant to be "always a representative of TechCo." In the comments thread to Brian's post, a woman from marketing wrote, "I feel strongly that people's Facebook stuff is their personal stuff," but she said the reality is that communication is so transparent today that whatever one posts can reverberate through one's professional life as well. A respected member of TechCo's sales team wrote that he used to post his personal opinions online all the time but no longer did. Because his comments were visible to both his professional connections and his family members, he had come to realize that "I have more to lose than to gain."

That was the point. Through Brian's post and the firmwide conversation around it, TechCo was tacitly influencing employee judgment by getting them to see that they personally had more to lose than to gain by speaking out of turn on social media. TechCo's reputation was not the only thing on the line after all. When the Adria Richards scandal broke out some months later, an executive posted about it in the Bad Judgment section of the wiki, reiterating the lesson they had all learned from Brian's incident and that was once again on view. All because of an off-color joke and one tweet, the executive noted, people had lost their jobs and Adria now feared for her safety. "Remember there is no longer much of a separation between work and personal," he wrote.

SELF-DISCIPLINED VOICE

With their required disclaimers and proscribed speech, formal social media policies maintain control by reminding people that they are always at risk of being taken for a company spokesperson and that they must police and mark that boundary. The more informal approach taken by TechCo and companies like it accomplishes something rather similar: When the workforce read and collectively processed Brian's post on the wiki, they were reminded that they would always be held accountable for what they said on social media and that it was up to them to regulate their speech accordingly. Yet the nature of corporate control in this case is actually quite different and new. It rests on self-discipline by employees, not formal direction and discipline by the firm.

The TechCo sales rep who said that he no longer posted his personal opinions on social media because he had more to lose than to gain claimed that he alone was responsible for this decision. He explained, "If my 20-something me heard me say this, he'd call me a sellout. But I've made this decision. It's more of a personal decision for me, though. Not something I do because someone told me to do it." Once employees like him recognized that they were always at risk of being identified on social media (i.e., once they realized that, whether they liked it or not, they would always be "Brian Cassidy—Works at TechCo"), the firm did not need to exert much explicit control beyond that. Social media in all its radical openness did the self-disciplining for it.

In the wake of Brian's incident, the words "use good judgment" became a pervasive shorthand expression for the transparency inherent in social media and the corresponding need to remain ever-vigilant of one's own speech. When a young woman in marketing excitedly shared that she was going to be interviewed by a magazine, another woman at our lunch table congratulated her but cautioned, "Just remember to use good judgment in whatever you say, you know?" When I asked a woman in TechCo's customer support group what UGJ meant to her, she recalled the Brian incident, many months past at that point, and said she kept the policy in mind "for everything I do these days," explaining that, "I want to make sure I never say anything out of line."

TechCo certainly could have fired Brian as SendGrid did Adria. It could also have had a more explicit formal policy in place that said comments like his were inappropriate. But what more would that have accomplished? When the workforce watched the incident with Brian unfold in real time on social media (as many did), and when they later read and collectively processed his post on the wiki, the lesson could not have been more clear: It was up to them to make sure they did not say anything inappropriate.

FREE SPEECH OR FALSE FREEDOM?

If employees are self-censoring, the question naturally arises: What, if any, freedom are they actually gaining in all this? That is, if individuals restrict their own speech in ways that serve the firm, aren't we witnessing the suppression of employee voice, not its delegation? Is it a farce to say that TechCo has given its workforce external voice rights?

After all, even though TechCo executives sought collective education not public shaming with the bad judgment posts, they were using them as examples in much the same way authoritarian regimes make public examples of people to generate common understanding of appropriate behavior and fear of transgression.[24] What is more, after Brian's bad judgment post employees told me that if another individual did something similar on social media, that person probably would be fired this time. Not firing Brian had seemed appropriate in that first instance, but, as one individual put it, "Of course, it all depends on the circumstances." Brian's situation had been an opportunity for learning, but it was not a precedent, in other words. Employees knew that their external voice rights were merely "loaned, not owned;"[25] and, as their wiki discussion demonstrated, they knew that social media made their exercise of those rights transparent to the executives who had lent them.

In this light, we can see that the sales rep who said it was "a personal decision" to stop posting his opinions on social media had more likely come to that decision because of the implicit control that the firm—aided by social media acting as its surveillance arm—commanded over him. Even if TechCo said that it was giving the workforce broad freedom on social media, employees understood that that freedom was circumscribed. They knew they would never be completely free of their professional identity and that their speech would always be accountable to the company, so they had better manage their voices accordingly or face the professional consequences.

From this perspective, it is tempting to conclude that all of this is just some new form of oppressive corporate control—tempting even to draw the analogy to authoritarian regimes in which fear of punishment suppresses free expression and promotes public conformity with the regime's interests. Yet even though TechCo clearly retains certain controls over its workforce here, that analogy falls short in the end.

In contrast to the dynamics in an authoritarian regime, there was no widespread private dissent among employees about how TechCo had handled Brian's situation, nor were there private complaints that their voices were being unfairly suppressed on social media. (In the next chapter, we will see that TechCo's workforce is quite ready to complain about the suppression of voice if they believe it is warranted.) Instead, in their conversations with one another and in their confidential interviews with me, employees celebrated both the executives' handling of the Brian situation and the company's overall approach to social media.

Far from being put off by the public nature of Brian's punishment, the staff generally saw it as a testament to executives' commitment to open communication that Brian had not been fired but was rather allowed to stay and learn from the mistake. They also appreciated that the organization as a whole had been able to have a conversation about the incident. The truth was, employees agreed with executives that Brian had exercised bad judgment. In their opinion, what he did was "pretty embarrassing." "We can't have a catastrophe like [he] almost caused for the company," one individual said, reflecting a sentiment I heard from many. So long as they worked at TechCo, their professional fates were tied to the firm's, and they did not want the company's reputation tarnished any more than their executives did. (The erosion of boundaries between corporate and personal identities runs both ways.)

Of course, this perspective may well have been influenced by the firm and the bad judgment posts, but the workforce was not blind to the firm's influence in that regard. They knew that TechCo was trying to influence their judgment about what was appropriate on social media—executives never hid that fact; they had said it was the whole point of having the bad judgment posts in the first place. And yet, by employees' own accounts, this did not necessarily mean the firm's influence ran counter to their own interests or that good judgment for the firm was not also good judgment for them. It is not always false consciousness when employees agree with their employer.

As one sales rep explained it to me, he had a reputation to protect beyond TechCo, and "I don't have two Twitter handles, I just have one." He thought carefully about what he said online and how it might affect his singular "personal brand." The importance of this had been reinforced to him in graduate school seminars and presentations on how to use social media to build one's professional reputation. "I don't think [managing what you say] is unique to TechCo," he said. "In this day and age, I think it's just huge. People don't work at one company for too long so when you hop around, you have to take something with you, and what you take is your personal brand." He knew that speaking out of turn on social media would impair his brand, not just TechCo's, and he knew that monitoring what he said on social media thus served his own interests, not just the firm's.

The more general point is that for digital natives who grew up managing their presentations of self on social media (and being warned by teachers and parents about the dangers of being too open), self-monitoring on these platforms was simply not that new or disconcerting. According to a woman in product management, TechCo's use good judgment policy made sense, and formal social media policies were "stupid," because she and her colleagues were well schooled on what speaking "freely" on social media really meant in practice. They understood the score, she seemed to say, and they appreciated that TechCo trusted its staff to behave accordingly.

Not every firm displays that level of trust. Even with all the forces for employee self-discipline in today's social media age, many companies have chosen to adopt formal policies that explicitly prohibit employees from saying certain things and that disassociate the organization from its staff through disclaimers. When TechCo's social media policy was introduced in a training class I observed, the trainer said to the room of new employees, "You're all adults. We'd like you to use good judgment," and nothing more. Embedded in that short statement was more trust for employees than can be found in other firms' lengthy formal guidelines and restrictions.

Speaking to the whole company once, Anil acknowledged that mistakes were bound to happen on social media and in any other area where use good judgment applied. But he said that TechCo would prefer to live with some mistakes than to adopt rigid requirements that try to correct for every past misstep and preempt future ones, "punishing the many for the few and the hypothetical." He continued, "We don't do that. We trust ourselves." When it came to employee speech on social media, the company's leadership was once again choosing to "put their trust in the people," one employee told me. And this was no small matter. "If you treat people like adults, they generally act like adults," another individual said about the firm's social media policy. Indeed, when trusted with freedom, people tend to become more trustworthy, and that tends to ensure more genuine freedom from control in the end.

THE NEW REGIME

By trusting employees to monitor themselves, TechCo is also forging a new organizational model, a more conversational or communicative one than we have seen before. According to recent theoretical work by sociologist Ezra Zuckerman, the very existence of firms has historically depended on "the right to speak on behalf of the organization" being "always strictly controlled."[26] Zuckerman argues that firms must consolidate external voice rights at the top of the hierarchy. Otherwise, if every employee can speak publicly on behalf of the organization, "suddenly, the organization reverts to being a collection of individuals rather than a coherent actor," and its ability to manage the internal coordination and external commitments necessary for survival "evaporates."[27] By this logic, the fact that companies like TechCo embrace the blurring of personal versus corporate speech and explicitly delegate external voice rights should have profound implications. And yet at TechCo external voice rights are no longer strictly controlled in the manner they were previously or as envisioned by Zuckerman, and the firm is not evaporating. Why?

The reason, as we just saw, is that those voice rights are still being policed, only by a new regime. Firms like TechCo can live with the widespread distribution of external voice rights wrought by social media precisely because their employees know that (a) the firm still retains the ultimate control to fire them if they speak out of turn, and (b) social media's transparency will immediately reveal any transgressions. The social media age might look like one in which open firms like TechCo are completely ceding control over external voice, but it is actually one in which they can afford to delegate external voice rights quite broadly because of the control they still retain and the disciplining nature of social media's own radical openness.

Just because the firm retains a certain form of control, however, does not mean employees receive no more freedom under this new regime than under past ones. Once again, TechCo and social media are challenging our understanding of the relationship between communication and control. Whereas conventional bureaucratic firms retain formal hierarchical control over their external voice, TechCo has released formal hierarchical control over it by leveraging a different form of implicit control made possible by social media. This does not result in complete freedom of speech for employees, but it supports a form of open communication that they nevertheless understand and value, both outside the four walls of the firm and in the conversations happening inside them.

Reflecting on his time at TechCo, an individual who had worked at the company for several years before leaving to join another tech firm said:

> I think the [UGJ] social media policy was one of many things that made you feel like an adult. [You felt] that the company valued the creativity that [giving employees] agency unleashed, and that the company trusted you to be a wise agent. And, yes there were limits, but they were reasonable limits.

Employees like him knew their speech was not entirely free and open on social media, just like it never really was inside the firm on the wiki either. They were not deluded about any of that, yet they valued the freedom they did have and the trust it signified.

5

OPEN CULTURE

I HAD NEVER heard of a culture deck before. One day a busy midlevel executive said in passing that I should read the draft Anil was writing. Before I could ask the executive to clarify, his cell phone rang. I jotted "Culture deck? Figure out what that is" in my notebook and left him to his call.

Several days later, in a small, dimly lit conference room tucked into a back corridor, I met with Anil, TechCo's CTO and cofounder. He had brought his laptop to show me what he was drafting, but first he shared some history. Anil explained that for the first few years after TechCo's founding "no one talked about culture." In fact, the word "culture" did not appear on the wiki or in company emails until the company began administering its quarterly employee survey. When Eric and Anil read employees' positive comments in the first survey, however, "We realized we had a culture and that it was a pretty good one," Anil recalled. Sensing that a good culture was an asset worth preserving, the founders began to focus on it. Like the wiki, executive transparency, and use good judgment (UGJ), culture seemed as if it might be another tool for supporting the open revolution they were trying to effect inside the firm.

As it turned out, the question of corporate culture proved to be a complex one for a firm as committed to employee voice as TechCo is. The challenges were not unlike those faced with UGJ. In an environment that prized individual expression, how could a coherent, unifying culture even emerge? And what role should executives play in shaping it? Almost as soon as Eric and Anil decided that corporate culture might be a useful tool for managing and organizing the workforce, employee voices weighed in on their effort and critiqued it.

Eric and Anil's first instinct had been to hire a consultant to document and formalize the company's existing culture. Thinking back to that time, Anil smiled and with the tone of a bemused but proud parent recalled how that had gone over with employees: "People thought it was awful. They thought it was the beginning of the end that we were bringing in an outside consultant to tell us what our culture was. Debate on the wiki exploded overnight." Accustomed to voicing their opinions and hashing things out internally, employees rejected the notion that someone from outside TechCo could define their collective experience for them.

Unlike the consultant, Anil had the workforce's trust and respect, though; with Eric's prodding, he stepped in to "lead the culture charge." About three years before my study, he wrote what he now calls "the original culture deck," or "version 1.0." Version 1.0 was a short slide deck that enumerated a set of qualities TechCo employees tended to have and Eric and Anil valued—qualities like being digitally savvy, marketing focused, and comfortable sharing information and voicing one's opinions. Less controversial than the idea of an outside consultant, this effort was noted but largely ignored by the workforce at the time.

Now that he was drafting version 2.0, Anil reflected back on that original experience. Writing version 1.0 had been like "a coding exercise" for him, he explained when we met: "I'm a programmer, so I think about things in terms of coding. It was like writing an algorithm to get the sort of people and behavior we want in the company." To organizational scholars, these words invoke a familiar perspective on corporate culture. In his 1992 book, *Engineering Culture: Control and Commitment in a High-Tech Company,* Gideon Kunda argued that companies—especially the cutting-edge technology companies of that time—were explicitly "engineering" corporate cultures for purposes of workplace control, instilling values and beliefs in employees to elicit desired behavior from them.[1] Although two decades had passed since Kunda's book, what could sound more like engineering culture than Anil's talk of computer coding and versions 1.0 and 2.0?

Yet Anil and TechCo's eventual approach to culture turned out to be quite different from what Kunda found in those 1990s tech companies. The companies Kunda studied wrote culture documents to socialize existing employees into the proper "member role."[2] They used those documents in intensive employee training sessions and prominently displayed them throughout the corporate offices for all the workforce to see. Sometimes those documents and the culture behind them garnered public recognition or press, but for the most part, culture remained an overwhelmingly internal affair for these firms.

In contrast, by the time I arrived at TechCo, culture was becoming an external affair for the firm. Version 2.0 of the culture deck would never be deeply incorporated into the company's training sessions, but it would be actively disseminated on social media to audiences far beyond the existing workforce. The day we met in the conference room Anil was clear about its purpose: He was writing version 2.0 in a way that could be understood and appreciated by an outside audience because this document was to be "both a guidepost for our people *and* something for us to put out publicly." He wanted version 2.0 to "resonate" externally in a way version 1.0 had not. Some days later another executive explained to me that TechCo had publicized version 1.0 but it had not "taken off" with the public as hoped, and this was a major impetus for version 2.0. As my time at the company unfolded, I heard from both employees and executives alike that culture was something to be shared publicly. But why?

Why was culture something to be shared with the outside world and not just the company's workforce? Why did TechCo seem more intent on marketing its culture externally than on engineering it internally? And what role did employee voice play in all of this?

CULTURE FOR RECRUITING

In 2004, the organizational scholar James Baron observed that an organization's internal employment model and personnel practices could be used to establish an external identity in the labor market.[3] This academic insight gained significant momentum among tech companies in 2009, when the video streaming company Netflix publicized a 126-slide Powerpoint presentation known as the "Netflix Culture Document." Written by Netflix's CEO Reed Hastings and its then head of HR Patty McCord, the document laid out the company's employment model, detailing its approach to management, pay, and promotion.[4] Bullet-point slides declared that instead of controlling employees, Netflix's culture was about "freedom and responsibility"; instead of deep employee commitment, Netflix neither expected nor conferred "loyalty." One slide detailed how the firm operated like "a pro sports team . . . not a family," paying its "stars" top dollar and cutting individuals who delivered only adequate performance. The overall image conveyed by the document was one of a modern, high-performance work culture. That image proved so appealing to people in the notoriously tight Silicon Valley labor market that the document was a boon for Netflix recruiting.

TechCo and others took note. The idea that workplace culture might help retain talented employees was not new, but the Web and social media now enabled companies to disseminate images and descriptions of themselves to prospective employees too. In labor markets where the demand for specific workers outpaced the supply, such as the Silicon Valley market for computer programmers or TechCo's own competitive market, an appealing culture that was promoted effectively could be a powerful weapon in the battle for sought-after talent.

As Anil opened his laptop to show me his working draft of version 2.0, he explained that he had come to see culture as seminal for recruiting. This was clear from the deck he then walked me through. One of its very first slides stated that the reason TechCo cared about culture was that it cared about recruiting talented workers. Its final slide included a link to the company's job website where prospective applicants would find a list of current openings. The slides in between enumerated various things likely to appeal to today's young tech-savvy worker, such as the company's general aversion to strict rules and guidelines; its unlimited vacation policy and open offices; and perks such as free beer, a free books program, and the company speaker series.[5] (Because the deck is publicly available, quoting slides directly would reveal the company's identity. To avoid this, I summarize its content when necessary.)

Like its earlier incarnation, this deck also listed qualities that TechCo employees ideally embody. This too was for recruiting purposes because, as Anil explained, "we only want to attract good fits." Culture was not about attracting just any talented employee, in other words; it was about attracting those most suited to TechCo's specific environment and needs. Recent sociological research has found that employers often prefer to hire people who are culturally similar to them, and marketing culture promotes that objective by drawing similar applicants to the organization in the first place.[6] Much as Match.com or other dating sites allow you to present an (appealing) image of yourself to attract a compatible partner, TechCo's logic was that by putting a clear (appealing) description of its culture out there, the company could attract individuals most likely to thrive in it.[7]

There was an even deeper logic at work, though. Whereas Kunda found that firms in the 1990s saw culture as a supplement to hierarchical, bureaucratic control, TechCo's founders hoped that by attracting cultural fits who would naturally behave in ways the firm desired, they might minimize the need for formal hierarchical controls entirely. As one executive put it to me, recruiting cultural fits with this deck was an attempt "to manage by culture instead of by hierarchy," and doing that, he said, was consistent with the firm's overall attempt to be more open than conventional firms. Similar, then, to what we saw in chapter 4 regarding employee speech on social media, culture for TechCo was not about the elimination of all corporate control but about leveraging a new form of control that might somehow permit greater openness. And whereas Kunda found that corporate culture in the 1990s worked to suppress open communication inside firms, we will see that the key question TechCo has had to confront about its new approach to culture is what it means for the firm's commitment to open voice and dialogue.

For now, though, the key point to note is simply how different the two approaches to culture are. Over the coming months, TechCo did not use its culture document as the basis for some new, intensive training program as the tech companies Kunda studied had done. Instead, TechCo incorporated the document heavily into its recruiting activities. Beyond promoting it on social media, executives presented it at recruiting events I attended, and managers and recruiters used it as a conversation piece in the job interviews I observed. Simply put, while the tech companies Kunda described used culture to create right-minded individuals through socialization, TechCo was using culture to attract talented, like-minded individuals through selection.

MARKETING CULTURE

Beyond the usefulness of culture for recruiting, Netflix's experience had offered a second lesson that TechCo executives could not help but note. Shortly after Netflix released its document online, it caught fire on social media. Millions of people, and not just prospective employees, viewed it. Thousands posted and blogged about it and tweeted and retweeted links to it. The technology trade press published numerous articles about it, profiling both its content and the public response it was receiving. In the years following its release, the deck garnered more than eight million views on the slide-sharing website Slideshare.net, and Sheryl Sandberg, the COO of Facebook, was quoted as saying, "It may well be the most important document to come out of Silicon Valley."[8] With all this publicity, the Netflix deck suggested that corporate culture was a way to reach not only prospective employees but also the wider public. Marketing culture was not just good for recruiting; it was good marketing period.

With this in mind, Anil told me he was now writing version 2.0 for an even-broader audience than the labor market. As he walked me through the deck that day, I saw that it did not just list the perks of working at TechCo and the attributes of individuals who fit well there. It also carefully laid out his and Eric's vision of the social media revolution and the postmodern organization that they believe the era demands and TechCo represents. Essentially, it put into writing the ideas and themes they had been promoting for years and that readers of this book are quite familiar with by now:

that TechCo's mission is to help other companies harness the Internet and social media to market and sell to customers; that these technologies have transformed how customers and employees live and work and, as a result, the conventional bureaucratic organization is obsolete and a new, more open organization is required; and that TechCo is a model of just that with its radical transparency from executives, open dialogue and debate among employees, and minimalist controls like UGJ. It may have been called a culture deck, but it was really a manifesto for a new type of firm and an identity claim that TechCo was it.

Several weeks after Anil shared this deck with me, he shared it with the entire company, and shortly after that with the rest of the world. In a social media blitz, he put the deck online and wrote a post about it on both his personal blog and TechCo's corporate blog. He tweeted a link to the slides through his widely followed personal Twitter account, and TechCo's marketing team shared news of it on the company's Twitter, LinkedIn, and Facebook accounts while employees did the same through their own.

This time, it resonated. In fact, it went viral. In a matter of days, the deck was already amassing tens of thousands of "views" online, prominent technology news sites and bloggers were writing about it, and Eric and Anil were fielding requests to speak about corporate culture at major industry conferences. In the ensuing weeks and months, Anil obsessively tracked the number of "views," "mentions," and "shares" the deck received on various social media platforms. Standing before a packed room of industry analysts a few months after its release, he proudly reported that the deck had been viewed online more than half a million times so far and declared, "from a marketing perspective, it has been a huge success."

The buzz seemed to generate new interest in TechCo's products and services, and the company received a record number of inbound sales leads in the months after the deck was released. The momentum continued, and a year later an executive would tell me that it was all because of the culture deck that TechCo was now "mentioned in the same breath with Google, Facebook, and Zappos" when it came to corporate culture. "And that's been huge for name recognition, not just with job candidates, but customers, prospects, potential investors, you name it," he said.

If the 1990s was the era of engineering culture, the experiences of TechCo, Netflix, and others suggest that this is the era of marketing culture. It should come as no surprise, really. Social media offers companies a low-cost marketing channel with enormous reach. Furthermore, it seems almost to call for the very declarations of self that marketing a culture entails. Technology scholar Sherry Turkle has observed that social media use is all about the construction and performance of identity.[9] As individuals on those platforms, we create public profiles and manage our identities by sharing internal thoughts and beliefs, revealing details about our daily lives, and identifying our likes and dislikes for all to see. Marketing culture is like that, only for corporations: TechCo made a powerful identity claim with its culture deck by revealing its beliefs and thoughts about how organizations should be run, sharing details about its internal life and activities, and identifying what it valued (and distancing itself from what it did not).

Today individuals and corporations speak on the same platforms and communicate through the same channels. Is it any surprise that they have begun to perform their identities in a similar manner? Individuals who construct an appealing online identity can attract attention, friends, and followers. Corporations that do that can attract customers, job applicants, perhaps even investors, press coverage, and more. So why wouldn't they? As we have seen, marketing culture is just good marketing these days.

Finally, if any company was going to embrace this potential in social media, TechCo was it. With employees allowed to say anything they wanted on social media (so long as they used good judgment), TechCo perhaps more than other firms needed some way to ensure it still had a consistent identity in the marketplace. Moreover, disclosing details about internal culture could be seen as "an act of transparency and openness," as Anil once put it. In that sense, marketing their culture was consistent with building an open organization.

Beyond that, marketing their culture was actually core to TechCo's business model. One day not long after my meeting with Anil, I met with the company's head of marketing. He explained that companies would only buy TechCo's software and services if they saw the value in social media and were willing to transform their sales and marketing activities to leverage it. Because TechCo's own operations were optimized for social media, he said it was often "its own best case study" for selling others on that vision, and marketing TechCo's culture was particularly ideal for this. By revealing some of the values and practices underlying TechCo's own open, social media–enabled organization, the company could offer a road map for others; and by disclosing those details through savvy social media marketing (like a popular culture deck), TechCo could demonstrate the power of social media and its own status as an expert on it.

"I think we are about the future, about a whole new way of thinking about business and questioning rules and conventional wisdom, and so this is another way to prove we are really about that," said the head of marketing. "It gets really recursive, but we market to companies about marketing themselves on social media, so we damn well better be good at marketing ourselves on social media." The culture deck had been a smashing success by that measure.

OPEN EMBRACE

As it took off on social media, TechCo's executives were obviously thrilled with the external reception. Employees were as well. They seemed to embrace the logic of marketing culture unproblematically. For these digital natives, sharing aspects of one's internal life to present an appealing external face on social media was second nature—they had been doing it for most of their lives. Like their executives, the workforce also believed culture was crucial to recruiting. They valued the company's ability to attract smart, like-minded coworkers, and most noted that they themselves had been drawn to TechCo because of its image and "positive buzz" in the labor market.

For many, the culture deck and its popular reception also offered the thrill of status and prestige. Employees recounted with pleasure how friends and parents had called them after seeing the culture deck online or mentioned in a news article, and they repeatedly spoke about the "pride" they felt to be working for a company receiving such positive attention. Leah, a twenty-five-year-old woman in sales, explained to me, "TechCo does a great job making itself out to be the cool company to work for, and the culture deck is really smart in that regard. I tell people I work here, and they're jealous because of what they've heard." Like a witty Twitter feed or a thoughtful blog, she said, the culture deck made TechCo sound cool, and "it's cool to work for a cool company."

For employees who were focused on building their own personal brand online, the culture deck was especially valuable. Celia, a twenty-four-year-old woman in TechCo's services group, said of herself, "I'm very conscious of my brand on Twitter, LinkedIn, and Facebook. I don't do anything unless I know how it's going to impact my brand, and I want my brand to fit with the company's—the tone, the spirit, the external communication." Because the culture deck communicated such a "cool" identity for the company, and because it did so through such an attractive piece of marketing collateral, she and those like her leveraged the deck by linking to it on their own websites, sharing it through their personal social media accounts, and writing personal blog posts about it.

Employee excitement about the deck's public reception was about more than just looking cool, though. In many ways, the response it was receiving validated these young workers, their habits, and their beliefs. The deck stated that today's digitally savvy workers and consumers (and the technologies they grew up with) were forcing a revolutionary shift in how corporations did business. That the public was responding so positively to this message suggested there was truth in it, and employees considered themselves lucky to be working for a company that got this, and got them. Also, their work and TechCo's entire business were predicated on an assumption about the value of social media marketing. The fact that the company was receiving so much positive attention on social media validated that assumption and gave them added confidence in their employer and its executives.

Thirty years old, Sean had been working in TechCo's marketing group for a few years when I caught up with him over lunch one day. He referred to the deck as a "great, great marketing tool," and like many of his peers I interviewed, he credited TechCo's executives for being "very smart" in having understood that marketing culture on social media could be a powerful way to stand out. In fact, Sean saw the deck as such great marketing that he judged it only by that standard. Although he would eventually read it more closely, when it first came out his immediate reaction had been to distribute it, not digest it: "I tweeted it. I shared the link. To be honest, I went to ten minutes of the presentation [where Anil presented it to employees]. I had a busy day. But I quickly clicked through the deck. It was really well put together, so I shared it."

OPEN REVOLT

Like Sean, nearly all TechCo employees supported the external marketing of culture. However, many gave its content deeper consideration, and when they did, they often had questions about its internal meaning. Two issues in particular surfaced. One had to do with perceived gaps between the culture that was being articulated by executives and the culture employees felt they experienced each day. The other concerned the fact that executives alone were defining and articulating the culture.

LIVED VERSUS MARKETED CULTURE

As ethnographers know well, any articulation of a group's culture is necessarily a simplification, and just like UGJ did not apply to every employee in the way executives tended to talk about it, most employees could recall an instance in which their day-to-day experience at TechCo had diverged from something stated in the culture deck. For a period of time, this seemed to erode workforce morale quite dramatically.

Immediately after the culture deck's public release, the nature and tone of employee comments shifted markedly in my interviews and conversations. The overwhelmingly positive statements about TechCo's culture that I had heard in earlier interviews were now replaced with overwhelmingly negative comments about how the culture deck was a misrepresentation of the company's "real" culture. In contrast to their positive expressions about the culture deck's marketing value outside the company, when I asked what the culture deck meant inside TechCo I received answers like these:

> "It works better outside than inside."
> "Techco is like the overzealous Christian that talks about his faith but isn't really that devout in practice."
> "The culture deck is a joke. . . . Everything they said is great, and if it were true, it would be great, but it's not."
> "I think we need to start assessing what we are doing and how it's different than what we are preaching. . . . The culture deck is so far off. . . . It's just completely wrong."
> "It's different looking in versus working here. . . . I'm not sure everything in [the deck] really holds. We say these things about ourselves, but they're not true."
> "I often wonder if culture is important for marketing but not in reality."

With more than one hundred slides claiming to describe TechCo's culture, the deck offered considerable fodder for scrupulous employees. Yet the nature of the criticisms puzzled me at first. For one, they were consistently phrased in the relatively general, almost vague, terms of the previous quotes. Only when I pressed would I receive an example or two of where the interviewee felt the deck misrepresented real life inside the company, and those examples were inevitably specific to that individual's experience (e.g., an employee who felt his manager was rather inaccessible said the company was not as informal and transparent as it claimed to be; an employee whose meeting schedule prevented him from working at home in the mornings complained that the company was not as flexible as marketed; and so on).

To be sure, some common themes emerged from those critiques. The deck said TechCo was transparent, open, and informal, and employees generally felt the company could be even more so in places. I understood these critiques, but at an aggregate level, I was still puzzled by the employee response. Generally a skeptic of such corporate pronouncements myself,

I was on the lookout for gaps between the culture TechCo touted and that which I observed, but the more time I spent at the company and the more deeply I became embedded there, the more TechCo seemed to be genuinely atypical in the extent of its openness, transparency, and informality. All the things the culture deck said TechCo was, in other words, TechCo seemed to be, or at least seemed to be more than any other company I had encountered. As I probed employees for a better understanding of their point of view, I came to see that their responses were less about specific accuracies or inaccuracies in the culture deck than about competing definitions of culture held by them and their executives.

Anil and TechCo's other executives saw culture as a coherent set of ideas and beliefs that could be articulated and set down on paper (and, thus, marketed). Employees embraced this definition when it came to the external uses of culture. However, when it came to daily life inside the company, they invoked a different definition. Culture inside the company was not something written but something lived—not a list of ideal, even if generally accurate, beliefs and values set out on flashy slides, but the inexorably messier way in which things really got done on the ground. Leah, the sales rep who praised the deck for making TechCo seem cool, said she did not look to it as a description of TechCo's real culture. When it came to that, she explained, "I work here. I'm here all the fucking time. I know what it's like." Dave, a veteran of TechCo's administrative staff, put it this way, "We can say whatever we want in the culture deck. That's not culture. Culture is what we're really doing."

A colleague of Dave's complained of a "disconnect between management's thoughts [on culture] at a theoretical, academic level versus what the everyday employees see and think." Scholars have long grappled with a similar disconnect. For decades, sociologists of culture have debated whether culture operates as a coherent system of shared beliefs and values, or as something less coherent and more practical, grounded in everyday life.[10] Orlando Patterson calls this the difference between "cultural knowledge" and "cultural pragmatics."[11] Cultural knowledge includes the widely recognized and explicitly espoused values, norms, and beliefs around which people coordinate, whereas cultural pragmatics are the ways in which people actually enact those values, norms, and beliefs on the ground. Patterson argues that it is not a matter of one or the other definition being right or wrong. Both are elements of a group's culture. What is more, there are nearly always gaps between the two.

From this vantage point, it is clear that no slide deck could ever fully capture a group's pragmatic culture, even if it does a fairly good job of inscribing the group's general cultural knowledge. The anthropologist Clifford Geertz fell into the camp of scholars who believed culture was a coherent system of meaning, so much so that he believed a group's culture could be read like a text.[12] With the culture deck, TechCo's executives literally provided a text from which to read their company's cultural knowledge. This enabled outsiders to appreciate TechCo's orienting values and beliefs like readers of an ethnographic text, but it also highlighted all the gaps to employees familiar with its internal pragmatics.

This is not to say that all employees found the gaps problematic. Those in marketing were most likely to be copacetic with the deck. It was not that they felt the deck represented internal life perfectly; it was that they did not care so much whether it did because they saw the deck as a marketing document, not a cultural one. As Sean, the marketing employee who tweeted the deck before reading it, told me, "Whether or not it's true today doesn't matter." For him, having a message that resonated outside the company "matters even more than what the culture really is." He trusted TechCo's executives to come up with an appealing external message, and it was enough for him to know that the message "represented the spirit of the company." Anything beyond that was not particularly relevant.

A thirty-one-year-old woman who had worked in marketing for several years before recently transferring to another department expressed a similar sentiment. Over lunch one day, she explained to me:

> Even if all the employees knew that it wasn't [true], it still would be good to have that brand externally. It reminds me of Range Rover ads where they show people off-roading. How many Range Rover drivers do you know who actually off-road? They're all soccer moms who are driving through manicured suburban streets!

The comments of most employees, however, suggested that, at least initially, it was deeply alienating to encounter a description of TechCo's culture that did not exactly mirror their own experiences. Because employees were (understandably) not differentiating between cultural knowledge and cultural pragmatics, any gaps between the executives' characterization and employees' own daily work lives felt inauthentic. The culture deck was good marketing, but was it also false advertising, they seemed to be wondering. Angelique, a sales rep we met in previous chapters, said that as much as she appreciated the marketing value of the deck for recruiting and branding, "My fear is that we're like that couple that's on the rocks but they post pictures of themselves on Facebook kissing on the beach and all their friends get jealous of what a great relationship they have. I don't want that. I don't want us out there bragging about our great culture when some stuff is broken inside. It feels fake."

To Anil's credit, he had introduced the deck as "part description, part aspiration" on its very first pages. If the deck represented an ideal to aspire toward (versus a claim of current identity), then gaps between what it said and what employees experienced were not all that problematic; they were merely opportunities for improvement. We will see in a bit that Anil and the other executives adopted this aspirational framing even more so over time and that doing so was key to employees' eventual acceptance of the deck. Nevertheless, that framing was overshadowed at first. Implicit in marketing culture is that one is marketing a description of the company's actual culture—after all, customers and prospective job candidates do not care what a company aspires to be, but what it is. In short, there was simply no getting around the fact that the culture deck was also an identity claim.

PANIC OVER VOICE

When TechCo's deck caught fire on social media and was embraced by the public, it was as a description of life inside the company, and employees took note. A year after the deck's release, an executive referred back to that time and told me, "I wonder if it hadn't been so successful with the public, would we have gotten the internal reaction we got?" He was on to something. Version 1.0 never took off externally, and employees mostly ignored it.

But the more prominence version 2.0 gained in the market, the harder it was for employees to ignore a crucial fact: They had played no role in authoring this seminal statement about life at TechCo.

Although employees appreciated the appealing external image the deck portrayed and welcomed the marketing boon it was for the firm, they were not used to accepting executive-decreed definitions of a situation. They expected voice and conversation, and just as they had earlier objected to an outside consultant defining culture for them, they did not seem to appreciate their executives doing the same now. Comments like "It's interesting how much of this is top down" and "It's weird how against the message that you can speak your mind all this is" suggested an irony not lost on the workforce: TechCo's executives had taken control of characterizing a culture that, by their characterization, supposedly valued employee voice and dialogue.

In the weeks and months following its public release, my interviews with TechCo employees began to sound eerily like those with citizens of a repressive authoritarian regime who were bitter about having their voices silenced. When I had previously asked interview subjects to describe TechCo's culture, they responded with words like "transparent," "fun," "informal." Now they responded with statements such as "Do you want my view of it, or what they tell us its like?" and "My cynical response is that it's what they tell you it is. What they say is happening when you work at TechCo. They say 'This is TechCo culture.'"

A twenty-nine-year-old with an undergraduate degree in political science even drew a direct analogy to oppressive political regimes. When I asked him how he defined TechCo's culture, he paused for a moment and then said, "That's a really good question. I don't know how I'd answer that. The culture deck is out there and people are eating it up, though marketers will eat up anything. But part of me feels like if you need 150 slides to define something, that's not a very good definition." I asked if those slides reflected his experiences of the company's culture, and he said:

Honestly, Cat, when you ask me that, I go back to my education. With dictatorships, they spend an undue amount of time branding their culture because, of course, what's really going on is not good. If you listen to North Korea, their culture is really excellent. I don't mean to draw that direct line to TechCo, but I do often feel like I'm having shit jammed down my throat.

Like many of his peers, he offered few specifics about what was "not good" inside TechCo when I probed. In fact, he said he thought TechCo's actual culture was "great," and he appeared to be an otherwise highly satisfied employee. What seemed to bother him was the feeling of "having shit jammed down my throat." He explained, "What's important to me is the experience of working here," and on that score, he preferred to speak for himself rather than have executives do it for him.

This feeling that executives were controlling the internal voice environment introduced new uncertainties. Since my earliest interviews at the company, I had been asking each employee what one question they hoped my study might explore. Prior to release of the culture deck, I had received a variety of answers to that question, the most common theme being how TechCo could maintain some of its most cherished aspects (e.g., executive's transparency, the wiki, and UGJ) as it grew. After the culture deck was released, I received variations on just one answer, over and over: Did other TechCoers really believe the marketed culture? For example, a woman in the services group answered, "Everyone says they're drinking the Kool-Aid, but I want to know if they're swallowing it, or are they just spitting it out when no one's looking?" Another woman in her group likewise hoped I might ferret out her peers' true sentiments: "I'd be interested to know, day-to-day, do they feel the 'TechCo-love' thing that people always talk about?" An engineer said he wanted me to ask other employees, "Do you feel like this place is real?" It appeared that marketing a culture that prized employee voice was paradoxically provoking concerns about suppressed dissent and pluralistic ignorance.

Trust in the firm and its leaders began to erode. The engineer just quoted said that executives' intense focus on promoting culture now made him question, "Is it really the best company to work for? . . . They keep telling us there's nothing better than this. But I wonder if it's like a cult sometimes. . . . They say 'it's so unusual you have no idea' that we have it so good. I have to trust them when they say this. I haven't worked somewhere else." Leah, the sales rep, said the deck heightened her sense that "people are scared to leave." Because she too had no prior work experience to compare with TechCo, she said, "I've asked people here about whether there's a better place to work. I want to know. . . . But the seed has been placed in my mind that there aren't [better places], that TechCo is the best place to work. And that seed gets pushed further down in my head whenever I meet someone outside the company and I say I work at TechCo and they talk about how awesome they heard it was from all the external buzz we spin."

In short, as executives flooded the airwaves with messages about Tech-Co's culture, that very culture seemed to be momentarily threatened. What employees could appreciate as savvy marketing outside the company felt uncomfortably like top-down control of their voices inside the company. "They're pushing the culture down on us," said one employee, and, in turn, he and others had begun distancing themselves from the marketed culture and expressing cynicism about it.

In his study of 1990s tech company culture, Kunda found that executive efforts to engineer culture internally provoked similar cynicism and role distancing. According to Kunda, this was one of the perverse ironies of corporate culture, for it was through such cynicism and role distancing that "real dissent is preempted."[13] By allowing employees their subtle irony during cultural events and their quiet scorn with one another behind the scenes—by tacitly acknowledging the manufactured nature of the culture, in other words—the company Kunda studied had been able to neutralize more formidable dissent. Kunda argued that the "contradictions between ideological depictions and alternative realities" were actually sinister means of control because they bred such "confusion" and "emptiness" in employees that the workforce's only recourse was to play along.[14]

Had employee criticisms been restricted to my confidential interviews or to sidelong glances and hushed conversations among friends, then TechCo would have offered further support for the model of culture Kunda described. This was not the case, however. At TechCo real dissent was not preempted, and employees did not just play along. Rather, they voiced their criticisms loudly and clearly through all the various points of openness the company had in place. It quickly became clear that any initial concerns about suppressed voice were unfounded.

Employees shared with executives the same criticism they had been sharing with me privately; namely, that the deck was not always an accurate reflection of life inside TechCo. In so doing, they also conveyed their second, even more powerful, critique of the deck: By speaking up, they were asserting their voice rights—specifically, the right to weigh in on the deck's content. A few weeks after the culture deck was released, a midlevel sales manager walked up to Anil and told him that employees felt the culture deck was not reflecting their true experiences at TechCo. On the wiki, in the Friday "Ask the Execs" Q&A sessions, and at the all-hands company meeting, employees posed direct questions to executives including, "Regarding areas where TechCo falls short of the [deck] ideal, do you feel that any progress has been made in addressing these shortcomings?" and "What would you advise us TechCoers to do when we encounter senior colleagues who might be acting out of step with [the culture deck]?"

Following the culture deck's release, the employee survey revealed that employee happiness had dropped significantly. It continued to fall in the coming months, eventually reaching its second-lowest level in company history. Employees used the anonymous comments section of these surveys to voice their frustration. One comment said, "The culture deck is not reality." Another said, "The culture deck is brilliant but more a piece of marketing content than reality" and then listed a series of gaps the employee perceived. In response to the survey question about what TechCo could do to improve the employee's score, someone answered, "To actually abide by the culture deck we share with others."

Ironically, employees even spoke with their silence. Shortly after releasing the deck, Anil wrote a follow-up wiki post that asked, "How well do we walk the walk on our [culture deck]?" On a ten-point scale and across various topics, he gave the company all 8s, 8.5s, and 9s. The usually vocal workforce responded with a deafening silence. The post got just two "likes" and only one comment, which said that on at least one of the topics Anil had listed, "we have a ways to go." Referring to this post, an employee told me, "The execs will notice it didn't get tons of likes."

OPEN RESPONSE

If all those platforms for voice were merely release valves that preempted real dialogue—if employees had just voiced their concerns and then calmed down—perhaps this story would not be so different from Kunda's after all.[15] That is not what happened, though. As openly as employees voiced their concerns, TechCo's executives listened and responded to them.

First, executives acknowledged that the culture deck was provoking internal consternation, and they opened a direct conversation with employees to understand why. Anil began having small group meetings and dinners with employees from across the company to understand how the culture deck did and did not resonate with their daily experiences. More than ever, executives dove into the comments of the employee survey, analyzing and parsing them to understand the workforce's perspective and criticisms.

Then they made efforts to address those issues. Regarding criticisms that TechCo was not transparent enough about how competitive its compensation was, the company released a recent analysis of market compensation they had collected. Regarding criticism that the unlimited vacation policy was meaningless because some jobs seemed to preclude any vacation at all, Keith announced on the wiki that every employee must take at least two weeks of vacation every year, and he put managers on warning that this would be enforced. Regarding complaints that UGJ was impractical without better training, executives pulled a widely respected employee out of his current job in HR and created a full-time position for him focused solely on building out an extensive internal training program. Regarding complaints that executives were so busy they were not truly accessible, Keith announced and then consistently held weekly "office hours."

Similar modifications, all intended to bring TechCo's internal life more in line with its marketed one, continued over the coming months. Not too long after Keith's post, the company hired a new executive to focus specifically on culture. The wiki post introducing her said that her primary job responsibility was to "audit the culture deck—identify the gaps" and "implement a plan to close the gaps." In her first weeks on the job, she held focus groups and one-on-ones throughout the organization to collect employee feedback on the deck.

As they tried to bring TechCo more in line with the deck, executives also tried to bring the deck more in line with TechCo. Anil went back to work on it, revising the slides so that they stated the deck's aspirational nature even more clearly than before. He added text that pointed out when the company still fell short of specific ideals being discussed, and he included a section that listed some of the current negatives and costs of TechCo's culture (for instance, how its openness and informality could sometimes feel chaotic or disordered). Both TechCo and the document itself were now framed as continual "works in process." Anil continued to speak of the culture deck as code, but now he clarified that it was "open source" code. It was to be "iterated" and "updated" with feedback, he said.

In time, the internal revolt subsided. Employee cries of dissension quieted. When I followed up with employees who had initially rejected the deck's internal relevance, I found they had come to see it in a new light. The culture deck was valuable precisely because it had sparked debate, they now said. Angelique explained how her thoughts on the deck had changed as she watched the discussion of it unfold inside the company. She believed that without the deck many of the issues raised by employees might never have surfaced. Recalling a recent conversation, she said:

> I was talking to [a colleague] about this. He was saying that at first it really pissed him off that Anil was doing this. I was the same way. But we both agreed that we feel better about it now. At least you have it. You have something to work toward. It gives us slides to call ourselves out on when we're not walking the walk.

Others who had expressed initial frustration with the deck seemed to have experienced a similar change of heart.

As a clearly stated ideal, the culture deck also became a powerful rhetorical weapon for the workforce. Even months later I would hear individuals invoke it to express complaints against management when they felt something fell short of the ideal. For instance, after a restructuring of the sales organization that left some sales reps frustrated and confused, I joined a few reps over lunch. I knew their views on the deck had softened since its initial release, but on that day they spent the lunch complaining about how the recent restructuring was inconsistent with some of the deck's principles. As an engineer put it to me around the same time, the deck had become a tool for "keeping the execs honest," true to the ideas about organizing they so often promoted.[16]

For their part, executives knew that employees now had this weapon in their arsenal. In meetings, I heard executives caution each other that something they were contemplating might get "pushback" from the workforce because, as one executive said, employees may see it as "going against the deck." Far from suppressing employee voices, in other words, the culture deck had become another vehicle for having them heard. Rather than a means for oppressive control, it had been a starting point for conversation.

6

A CONVERSATION ABOUT
BUREAUCRACY

S I WAS ending my ten-month stint at TechCo, I presented my
preliminary findings to the whole company. Among other things,
I discussed people's initial frustration with the culture deck. After
the presentation, employees took to the wiki to discuss my comments. Over
the prior months, they had been invited into the conversation, and they now
embraced the deck as an aspirational identity toward which they were collectively working. As one commenter on the wiki put it, "The culture [deck]
made it easier for everyone to identify areas we should be working on . . . .
The more public we are about it, the more we're committing to the ideal."

But what exactly was the ideal to which TechCo had committed
itself? This chapter will reveal the nature of the firm's true commitment–
and the resulting organizational model that emerged – by unraveling an
internal dispute over human resources (HR). To the firm's executives, the
"radical openness" they sought meant shedding the conventional trappings of bureaucracy, and nothing symbolized bureaucratic control to
them more than HR with its standard policies and formal guidelines for
how employees should behave. Yet by the end of my time in the field, a
quite conventional HR department was up and running inside TechCo.
To see how that happened and what we can learn from it, we need to
start at the beginning.

COMMITTING TO THE NONBUREAUCRATIC ORGANIZATION

"I have a visceral hatred of HR," Anil told me in our first meeting. "Eric and I agree on a lot of things, but on this we really agree," he continued. "Most HR people—people in that profession—they tend to stand for things that go against everything we value." From the perspective of TechCo's cofounders, human resources was a rotten legacy of "old school" corporate bureaucracy, a source of unnecessary rules and processes that directly threatened the sort of openness and flexibility they sought inside the organization.

Theirs is not a particularly unique perspective, of course. From the evil HR manager in *Dilbert* cartoons to meek and rule-minded Toby on television's *The Office*, caricatures of tedious human resources professionals have been standard comic fare for years. Moreover, although most companies adopt formal HR policies to conform with legal mandates or societal expectations, scholars have found that they often "decouple" their internal practices from these policies' formal dictates.[1] For many in the business world, HR is as much required "myth and ceremony" as function and utility.[2]

What was unique about Eric and Anil's approach to HR, however, was that for years they simply refused to participate in the ceremony of it all. Despite the fact that most companies adopt formal HR departments (and despite repeated pleas from its board of directors to do the same), TechCo had no HR department, no HR manager, and almost no formal HR systems and processes until it was five years old and had nearly four hundred employees. Also unique was that Eric and Anil made this fact, and their views on HR in general, very publicly known. Years before they decided to release a culture deck, TechCo had already begun to market some of its internal culture and practices, and quite often that early marketing centered around the company's rejection of conventional HR.

In speeches and interviews, Eric declared that "HR is dead" and postmodern corporations like TechCo need not, and should not, have it. In blog posts, he and Anil described how the company bucked bureaucratic convention when it came to standard HR fare like vacation policies, work hours, and expense reimbursement. Other organizations had formal guidelines, manuals, and managers to handle such matters, they noted, but TechCo did not.

In short, whereas many companies publicly bend to convention by adopting formal HR policies but then privately mold them to suit internal needs, TechCo and its executives explicitly rejected the need for conformity in the first place. Most important, Eric and Anil staked the organization's identity on that act of irreverence: Conventional corporate bureaucracies might have HR, but TechCo was unconventionally and unabashedly nonbureaucratic. Its lack of HR was evidence thereof.

Just like the culture deck did later, this act of declaring and sharing TechCo's unique personnel practices shaped the company's identity in the labor market. It attracted employees who bought into the idea that there was "a new world order," as Anil once put it, and that today's workers and today's technologies necessitated a new kind of organization. Accordingly, the workforce seemed to place great value on the company's commitment to rethink and dispatch with conventional bureaucratic trappings, including (often especially) HR.

CALLS FOR STANDARD POLICIES AND PRACTICES

Nevertheless, there came a time when TechCo employees began to question the logic of this particular act of nonconformity. Once the company reached approximately three hundred and fifty employees, the idea that it could go without HR "started breaking down," as one employee described it. According to numerous (often colorful) employee accounts, "the wheels started to come off," "it was total chaos," and "everything went willy nilly." Increasingly, those who had once embraced their executives' view of HR began to doubt it.

When thinking back to this period, which spanned the year leading up to my fieldwork, each employee appeared to have his or her own story about when exactly they realized HR was needed. For a twenty-eight-year-old engineer, it was finding crushed beer cans and a "gross, sticky" floor in the company atrium one morning. For a thirty-two-year-old woman in operations, it was the offer letter sent to a promising job candidate with the wrong name and job listed on it. For a twenty-five-year-old woman in sales, it was realizing that she did not know for sure which questions she could and could not legally ask when interviewing job candidates for her team.

In addition to personal anecdotes like these, the employees I interviewed consistently raised three issues that seemed to have made HR converts of them all. First was the lack of standardization around performance reviews and terminations. Second was the ad hoc process by which internal job changes were handled. Third was the absence of a consistent maternity leave policy.

When it came to evaluating employee performance and handling terminations, the absence of any formal guidelines left managers to rely on their own individual discretion. As a result, some managers conducted regular performance reviews with their staff; others did not. Some offered clarity around the criteria they were using for evaluation and terminations; others did not. A twenty-four-year-old woman on TechCo's entry-level sales team recounted how the lack of clarity in her group had made her continually anxious during that time. Worried that she might be getting fired and unable to stand the uncertainty, she scheduled a meeting with her boss one day, "But she said I was doing great . . . . It was still so stressful though. People would get fired. You'd have no warning, they'd just be gone." Recalling how a different manager in her group handled terminations, she said, "He'd walk by someone's desk and say, 'hey, you have a sec?' Then people would come and shut down [the employee's] system, and you'd never see them again."

Lack of structure around the company's internal labor market also caused confusion and grief for the workforce. With no formal process governing internal job changes but a preference for "hiring from within," accusations of favoritism and poaching surfaced. One woman said that she had "worked a connection" to her current manager in order to advance out of an entry-level position in customer support. "He knew my mom," she explained. Others who had wished to leave their own entry-level positions complained that cases like hers were common and that it was difficult for most to learn when a position in another department was even open. Most said that the best strategy for securing a new job was to curry favor by volunteering after hours and on weekends for the manager they hoped would hire them. This may seem like a boon for managers, but they too were frustrated by the lack of clarity around internal hiring. The head of services was known to complain that his best employees were regularly poached by other groups. In another case, a contentious situation arose between two managers when a junior software developer, who was about to be fired from engineering, secured a job in another department. The developer had not disclosed the full details of the situation to either his old or new manager, so when the engineering manager went to fire him one day but instead learned that he was transferring groups, the engineering manager became irate and wanted him fired regardless. The other manager disagreed and said it should be his call.

Finally, there was the issue of maternity leave. Several female employees had become pregnant around the same time, but because the company had no formal maternity leave policy, each had negotiated a different arrangement with her respective manager, some better than others. A few of the women returned from maternity leave to find that their jobs had been reassigned and they would need to find new positions within the organization (although one returned to a promotion). Also, because things were handled so informally, the maternity leave pay that several women had negotiated with their direct managers was not what they received once on leave because of miscommunications between their departments and the finance staff. While on leave, the women had to spend hours on the phone reconciling the issue with folks back at the company. Workers generally ascribed such experiences to disorganization, not ill intent on anyone's part. However, the experiences left some feeling mistreated, and as word of it spread, other female employees who anticipated having children in the future began to worry about how their own maternity leaves would be handled.

Looking back to this time, employees recalled that it simply stopped feeling so "TechCo'y" to not have HR. "We say we value transparency, but we weren't being transparent around the biggest decision people face in their life," a male executive acknowledged in reference to the maternity leave issue. The workforce had bought into a revolution that rejected the unnecessary trappings of conventional bureaucracy, but HR no longer felt so unnecessary to them. What previously seemed like stultifying rules and procedures now looked like a possible path to more rational organization. In surveys and meetings, employees began calling for HR.

EXECUTIVE RESISTANCE

Eric and Anil hesitated to give in to the calls. While not denying the need for new approaches to managing the growing organization, they remained committed to building a nonbureaucratic firm and believed that a human resources department undermined that. In their opinion and in their public statements, the rejection of conventional bureaucratic practices like HR was directly linked to their broader mission of building a radically open, postmodern organization. To add HR now seemed like a betrayal of that mission and the company's carefully constructed identity, not to mention a lack of conviction to walk the walk of all their prior years' talk. On more than one occasion, Eric had said, "I hate companies that don't walk the walk," and he did not want TechCo to be one of them now.

At the same time, the founders recognized that as the company was growing, it was becoming increasingly difficult to decipher which dimensions of conventional organizational life needed to be rethought in service of their broader mission and which did not. They and the company's other senior executives spent considerable time discussing and debating that question. In a conversation I had with Anil, he talked about their ambivalence over HR in particular, explaining:

> We know we want to be unconventional. It's woven into the fabric of who we are and what we do, but there's a fine line between being unconventional and not doing things that other people do because actually that's the best way to do them . . . . But our default position has always been to rethink what's conventional.

Despite that default position, the executive team finally conceded that something had to be done about HR. The firm was reaching a scale and complexity—and employee calls were becoming so adamant—that it felt untenable to hold off any longer. About six months before I started my field-work (and about six months after employee calls for HR had first started surfacing), the firm hired a professional HR manager and began building out a formal human resources function within the company.

Eric and Anil remained deeply skeptical about HR, however, and it showed. When I entered the company six months after their apparent concession to add HR, the organization's adoption of it remained partial at best. Even though executives had hired a professional HR manager, they had also appointed a long-time TechCo employee to oversee her and her team and gave him the directive to block HR practices that might threaten the company's existing culture. In my first meeting with Keith, the company's COO, he explained this logic to me: "We didn't want to bring in an HR person and just run the standard HR playbook. So, instead we took a TechCo-er and told him not to do HR. We told him to hire other people to do that, and his role is to stop them if HR is doing something that puts pressure on the culture."

Executives were also adamant that this new department not be called "Human Resources." In a wiki post titled "What to call HR," employees were asked to weigh in on this naming issue. The post read, "TechCo has been historically tentative when it comes to HR-related things because *typical* HR is old school . . . . So tell me TechCo-ers, what are we going to call this thing we don't want to call HR?" As the months unfolded, it seemed like no name ever sat quite right with executives, and despite most employees calling the group "HR" regardless, its official name changed several times during my time there, starting off as "Team Development" and eventually becoming "People Operations."[3]

Meanwhile, implementation of standard HR systems and processes moved slowly and with limited commitment from the top. Before the new HR team could do much else, they had to complete the laborious task of auditing the company's personnel files to identify and rectify any potential compliance gaps that had arisen while the company was without HR.

During this period, the company continued to rely on informal systems for tracking things as important as the size of its own workforce. "It's hard to even know the numbers of people we have coming in and going out," a manager said to me one day early in my fieldwork. "We have some spreadsheets, but it's all eyeballing still . . . . Even things like how many people in each group, it's very opaque." He and others claimed this was why TechCo had recently been taken by surprise when it ran out of physical office space (a situation that had required executives to "chase down space" throughout the building complex).

Consistent with these accounts, when I asked for an employee list so I could begin interviewing the workforce, I was told that none existed. Eventually someone gave me an Excel spreadsheet, which they said was used for current payroll and into which employee names had been hand-entered, but I quickly realized that it was out of date. It failed to include the names of some recently hired employees and included the names of some employees who no longer worked at the company. Another manager, who had worked in operations at several other companies before joining TechCo, said to me with bewilderment one day, "I've never seen a company this size that didn't have an HRIS [human resources information system]." She was unsure whether the company would invest in one even now.

Throughout this period Eric and Anil did not hide their ongoing skepticism of HR. "Every day, across the board, Eric and I feel like our soul is eroding on this stuff," Anil said in a meeting shortly after the firm created the HR department. That perspective wore thin with the staff. "Why are we so petrified of HR? We need HR as a company this size," a twenty-six-year-old sales rep asked me rhetorically over coffee one morning. A twenty-nine-year-old manager in the same department put it even more bluntly, observing, "The execs want to be a billion-dollar company but they don't want HR even though every other billion-dollar company in the world has HR . . . . I feel like this company is the guy who can't grow up, who's too old to be living with his parents."

From the workforce's perspective, the issue was quite straightforward: The company's leadership was holding on to an outdated image of the firm and so "hell bent" (in the words of two individuals) on doing things differently that they were making life inside TechCo harder than it had to be. "I mean, do the execs really think we care if you call something HR?" a twenty-eight-year-old woman on the services team asked, complaining that "People Operations" was a needlessly confusing name. After a short pause, she answered, "Actually, we do care if it makes things easier! We should just call it HR." "They just have to get over it," a colleague of hers in marketing said.

The issue for these employees was not TechCo's overall vision but HR's place in it. One individual in his midforties, who spoke glowingly about how different TechCo was from any of his prior employers, nevertheless questioned, "Why do we need to try to transform HR? Can't we just figure out how to run HR in a way that enables the stuff we really want to be transformational on?" Executives had committed to revolutionize the firm, and foot soldiers like him were not abandoning the revolution; but they were saying that HR could be decoupled from it.

LEADERSHIP AND THE QUESTION OF STANDING FIRM

It is a general challenge of any revolutionary movement to know which elements of the old regime can and should be discarded and which should be retained. In the executives' minds, that was the issue they were facing. It was not an unreasonable perspective. Although HR has been adopted by nearly all businesses, it is also disparaged by many of those same organizations for its inefficiencies and rigidities. It may well be that some (or even many) conventional HR practices are outmoded in today's environment, and it is reasonable to think that they may need to be reconceived for an organization to fully transcend the conventional bureaucratic form (and reasonable to think that it may take some time to figure out exactly how).

Moreover, good leadership often entails dogged commitment to one's ideals in the face of others' wavering. TechCo executives were understandably concerned that reversing an earlier commitment simply because things had become challenging might be a lapse of resolve on their part rather than an example of wise stewardship. In my first meeting with them, Eric and Anil said that as the organization grew they expected to face pressure to "get pulled away" from their founding vision of being nonbureaucratic, pressure to "migrate back to the conventional wisdom" on issues like HR. Their role, as they saw it, was to make sure TechCo resisted such temptations.

In his seminal book *Leadership in Administration: A Sociological Interpretation*, Philip Selznick agreed with Eric and Anil's definition of leadership. In fact, Selznick wrote that when the core values of an organization are at stake, leaders should hold so firmly to their ideals that they actually limit their own—and the organization's—freedom to reverse course by making irreversible commitments.[4] We have seen how that very dynamic proved to be a benefit of marketing TechCo's internal practices and culture. Whenever TechCo publicly articulated a version of its ideal self, it became more accountable to it. Key audiences such as employees and customers would now hold the organization to its stated commitments, and the organization had clearly defined guideposts for future action. Not having HR was one of those clear guideposts, so it is not surprising that executives tried to stay the course.

Finally, an extensive line of research on Silicon Valley technology companies offers further support for executives' hesitancy to embrace conventional HR after their initial rejection of it. In the 1990s and early 2000s, the Stanford Project on Emerging Companies (SPEC) found that when high-tech companies forge clear labor market identities around their specific personnel practices as TechCo had, changing those practices can be treacherous.[5] Companies that alter their original employment model (e.g., by adopting formal HR policies and procedures when informal practices were previously the norm) experience higher subsequent turnover, worse financial performance, and higher rates of organizational death than organizations that maintain their original approach. The reason, scholars argue, is that a firm's employment model influences who comes to work there and what expectations they carry. Over time, social relationships, routines, and tacit knowledge develop around the company's practices, and changing any given one can trigger a "cascade" of unanticipated consequences and disruption throughout the organization.[6]

According to this perspective, one major challenge is that employees take their company's personnel practices to be a reflection of management's "core beliefs and values."[7] If management then alters those practices, it can feel like a betrayal. James Baron, who worked on the SPEC project, observed, "Firms that alter an established labor market identity . . . risk being viewed by current and prospective employees as mercenary or duplicitous, rather than authentic in their commitment to a set of principles governing the employment relationship."[8] Adding HR after committing to building a nonbureaucratic firm would seem to surface just this issue.

But was that really the commitment TechCo had made? After all, when it came to HR, TechCo's workforce was calling for conventional bureaucratic practices, suggesting they may never have taken management's nonbureaucratic stance to reflect the firm's "core beliefs and values." Indeed, as we have seen throughout the book, employees seemed to expect and value the firm's commitment to voice above all, and what could be more of a testament to that than employees speaking up and calling for the introduction of bureaucratic practices and policies in defiance of their leaders' perspective?

Nevertheless, TechCo's workforce was not exactly right when they criticized their leaders for trying too hard to be different or for holding onto an outdated image of the firm. The real issue was that executives were so concerned with being nonbureaucratic that they simply failed for a time to appreciate what was truly revolutionary about the organization they had created—failed to see what was unfolding right before their eyes in the dispute over HR. Namely, they had not built a nonbureaucratic firm; they had built a conversational one. And it was that fact, ironically, that helped them navigate this period.

THE CONVERSATIONAL FIRM ADOPTS HR

Even though the company's leadership opposed HR and even though they believed that it betrayed a key commitment they had made to being nonbureaucratic, the conversational firm they had actually built contained a ready-made mechanism for challenging their thinking on the matter: employees had voice. On the wiki, in company meetings, and through the quarterly survey, people continued to share their opinions on the need for HR. Hearing such persistent and consistent feedback, executives became more persuaded of the need for standardization around things like performance evaluations, job changes, and maternity leave, and by the end of my time in the field, Eric and Anil had granted the new human resources department increased autonomy and supported the adoption and implementation a variety of HR processes and systems. They still wished they could have found a more "creative, visionary" approach to HR, as Anil put it, but they had come to value the department's rather conventional place in the company. "Eric and I were dubious, but we were wrong," Anil said.

As I watched the HR saga unfold over the year, the nature of TechCo's conversational model became clearer. The model was not predicated on an absence of all bureaucratic practices, but rather on the idea that employees could speak up and weigh in on what practices were most appropriate at any given moment. In my interviews, I was repeatedly struck by how employees never seemed to share their executives' fear that HR might somehow compromise the internal culture they all valued so much. The sales manager who had said the company was like a "guy who can't grow up" had followed up that statement by explaining that TechCo would simply "never get away" with introducing excessively rigid rules and processes because of the internal debate that would inevitably erupt. HR would only ever be done in a "TechCo'y way," he said, so there was no risk to adding it in his opinion. Likewise, a woman in the services group said that even though she believed many of the negative stereotypes of HR, "TechCo is good at dispensing with the stupid things." She trusted that executives would bring employees into the conversation and adopt HR without compromising its values or harming the staff. There was no reason to fear TechCo becoming some sort of oppressive bureaucracy just by adding HR, in other words, because employees knew they had voice and trusted the firm to evolve with their interests in mind.

This was also why, when the company outgrew its rejection of HR but executives did not immediately budge—when "the wheels started to come off," when "it was total chaos," when "everything went willy-nilly"—the staff did not make a mass exodus for the door. Rather, they voiced their opinions, trusting that eventually they would be heard and the company would respond. In their conversational firm, they did not have total control over decisions like this (and as we saw in earlier chapters, they may not even have wanted that in all cases), but they knew their voices informed the firm-level decisions that were made. In some instances, like HR, employees got exactly what they called for. In other cases, they did not. For example, executives never did release a formal org chart; but they did roll out a software application that addressed the workforce's desire for an employee directory and which offered some visual representation of formal reporting relationships (see chapter 2). In short, the firm's commitment to ongoing dialogue ensured that executives were continually hearing from employee voices on the ground, and it gave the workforce a level of trust that afforded their leaders the space and time to respond.

Still, we must ask the question: Isn't the introduction of bureaucratic practices at TechCo simply the iron cage reasserting itself? Isn't this all just proof of the ultimate inescapability of bureaucracy? To appreciate why it is not, it is first important to recognize that adopting bureaucratic practices is not the same as adopting a conventional bureaucratic model of the firm. The implementation of HR at TechCo (as well as successful experiments with "representative" or "enabling" bureaucracy in factories, where employees play a role in designing the rules and processes that govern their work) demonstrates that bureaucratic practices need not be top-down mechanisms of control that dehumanize the workforce.[9] They can come from the bottom-up demands of employees trying to make their organization a more humane place to work. Second, when bureaucratic practices like HR were adopted by TechCo, they remained as subject to employee critique and firmwide dialogue as any other practice or topic in the company, and they were often modified accordingly. There is no mechanism for that in the conventional bureaucratic model of the firm.

After the introduction of HR, TechCo modified its 401(k) plan (making it more generous) in response to employee feedback on the wiki and in the quarterly survey. After the introduction of standard performance evaluations, employees offered periodic thoughts and ideas on the wiki about how these evaluations could offer even more useful feedback or be structured differently. The firm's nonbureaucratic practices evolved similarly—for instance, when TechCo developed training programs to support UGJ after the workforce complained about a lack of clarity around the policy. The point is this: The constant in TechCo's organizational model was not bureaucracy, nor was it the complete rejection of bureaucracy; it was conversation. The firm's practices would change and evolve with the circumstances because its true commitment to employee voice did not.

This did not mean that things always went smoothly. Conversation and the unique capacity for change it enables can make for a messier and more chaotic environment than anything we are accustomed to seeing in bureaucratic firms. Situations like HR were constantly arising. "It's not just HR. We run into this all the time actually," a manager told me one morning at a local coffee shop. He recounted how the company had publicly rejected certain conventional approaches to public relations, outbound sales, and organizational structure in the past, only to realize they needed them later on. As a fast-growing firm in a rapidly changing market, there was often a "dissonance," in his words, between the practices the firm embraced in one moment and the reality they confronted in the next, and it often took time to work through that. However, the dissonance was not fatal, he said. "It's something we can live with."

It was something they could live with because what mattered to the workforce was not the firm's commitment to any given set of practices but to engaging in an open discussion about them. There was always some dissonance at play: dissonance between what the firm publicly committed to and the reality it lived (like with the culture deck), and dissonance over what those commitments should even be at any given time (as with HR). But employees were patient with the gaps. In a wiki discussion about the culture deck, one employee wrote that because TechCo was clearly listening and incorporating employee feedback, the organization and its executives should "release any shame about the gap between the vision and the reality." Being authentic to TechCo's ideal did not mean having a perfect match between some stated vision and internal reality. It meant being willing to talk about the gaps openly and to confront them in ongoing dialogue. And that is how a conversational firm can evolve while remaining firmly committed to its ideal.

* * *

Employees met the institutionalization of HR with great enthusiasm. A twenty-four-year-old woman in services, who had previously had difficulty with her manager and recently sought counsel from the head of HR, told me, "HR has been one of the greatest additions to TechCo that ever could have happened." A thirty-four-year-old engineering manager said that for all the past talk about the potential "evils" of HR, "You know what? Now we have HR, and I'm so glad we do." As a manager, he was particularly grateful to have a formal process for conducting performance reviews. The junior members on his team embraced the new performance review process as well. For them, it offered the transparency and clarity they felt had been lacking in the past.

As processes and systems were rolled out, employees praised executives for having engaged in an open conversation about their concerns and for adopting HR in a way that did not compromise the organization's values. The engineering manager just quoted said that like other issues TechCo had tackled in the past, "the company has done HR incredibly effectively. They've clearly tried to avoid bringing in big company rules just for the sake of bringing them in. They genuinely seem to want to only bring in the good." Another employee said simply, "We got to where we had to."

7

CONVERSATIONAL SPACES

NTHROPOLOGISTS HAVE LONG observed that a group's physical space and architecture often reflect its cosmology—how it understands the world, what it values, and what it believes. In this regard, TechCo is little different from the remote tribes of anthropological study. In fact, this modern tribe embraces the symbolic aspects of space quite explicitly, for its chief, Eric, believes "the office is an idea" and that the ideas informing TechCo's office design should be those that inform its overall organizational design.[1]

Just like its approaches to communication, control, and culture, TechCo's physical workspace is intended, as Eric and Anil often say, "to match the way modern humans live and work." During my time at TechCo, I came to see the company's physical space as a concrete metaphor for its approach to so many other areas of its organizational life. The firm rejects conventional bureaucratic solution and shoots for something more open in its place; what it creates in the end is a conversational environment. The company's vast, open workrooms and lack of dividers are meant to support open, unob-structed communication. Managers and executives do not sit in private offices but rather alongside everyone to signify and encourage transparency and information sharing. Common areas like the kitchen are designed to foster informal exchange and dialogue. And four times a year everyone in the organization changes seats so they can make new connections and strike up new conversations.

When I first arrived at TechCo, the company had just hired an architecture firm to help build out additional space for its rapidly growing staff, and the architects were set to hold a series of meetings across the organization to collect employee and manager feedback on the existing space. I decided to tag along, curious to hear what the workforce would say about the environment built to accommodate their conversational ways.

What they said was: "I can't hear myself think." "Sometimes I just want to escape." "There are so many people all sharing the space—it's a total shit hole." "By 3 P.M. it smells like a goat farm." It was not what I had expected to hear.

Yet for all of their complaints, I noticed that not one person told the architects they would prefer to sit in an office. Outside of the meetings, it also struck me that the workforce seemed quite happy in their wide-open rooms. In my spare moments, I began asking people how they would feel if the company switched to a more conventional office setup. To that question they said: "That'd be terrible." "I'd be on the barricades to protest." "We'd probably riot." "There would be a rebellion." Or, as Emma, the millennial worker who kicked off our tour of TechCo in chapter 1, said simply, "That'd really depress me. Something key would be lost."

Understanding this puzzle—why the workforce might complain vehemently about the problems of working in this open environment but, in the next breath, say they would lose something key and revolt if faced with an alternative—offers one final window into what may well be new and different about workers like Emma, or at least what is new and different about the overall environment TechCo has built for them. We will see in TechCo's physical space what we have seen elsewhere in the firm. Namely, there are costs to pursuing such open communication, and with their empowered voices, employees complain about those costs often. Nevertheless, they choose to live with them because they value a set of countervailing benefits more and because they trust in the firm's open, ongoing conversations to confront the tensions head on.

NOISE BUT ALSO BUZZ

Over the last thirty-five years, a growing body of academic research has found that employee satisfaction is generally lower in open layout offices than in conventional (or "cellular") offices because of problems with interruptions, lack of privacy, poor air quality, and even germs.[2] According to surveys in this literature, the most common employee complaint about open offices is noise.[3] Open spaces can be noisy places, especially when they are intended to encourage free-flowing conversation, and noise was by far the most common complaint about TechCo's workspace too. With a multiplicity of voices in the background, it was often hard to hear the other side of your own conversation, let alone have a moment's quiet reflection. During the architect meetings, employees offered their own vivid descriptions, with several complaining that between their colleagues' phone calls and face-to-face interactions in the workroom, it could sound like "a call center in India" or "a telethon." Across the organization, people had downloaded white noise applications onto their smartphones. When they needed to concentrate or simply escape the din, they pumped white noise through their headphones to drown out the cacophony of voices in the background.

In other moments, though, they spoke as if those voices were a symphony of sorts. The same employees who complained about noise also talked about the energizing "buzz" of the open workrooms. The sound of human conversation appeared to signify a connected, collective spirit that they valued. Grace, a twenty-five-year-old woman in marketing, said she felt charged, "When you come in and everyone is eating breakfast at their desks and talking—'What'd you do last night?' 'How was your weekend?' When it's humming like that, that social atmosphere gets you really pumped for the day." Laura, a product manager at TechCo three years' Grace's senior, said she was not averse to pumping white noise through her headphones when the need arose, but in other moments the buzz from everyone working side by side seemed almost transcendent to her:

There's that collective sound of people doing their work, you know? Sometimes I put my headphones on without any sound and it creates this amazing white noise—the sound of everyone in the background. It inspires me because there are all these people working hard, and they depend on me to do my job well too.

Like Grace and Laura, many employees noted that the steady stream of human voices gave TechCo's workrooms a vibrant, "alive" feeling, which they contrasted with the "dead," stultifying feeling of more conventional firms. Matt, a long-time member of TechCo's marketing group, had recently visited several local companies for meetings; when he returned, he told me he could not imagine working at places like them. "One had these real Dilbert-style, high, high cubicles," he described. It was quiet there, he acknowledged, but consequently "dead." "It felt like there was no activity. No conversation. It was depressing. It was like nothing was happening, no one talking." By contrast, Matt said, "When you walk into our offices, you feel like 'Holy shit! Stuff's happening here! People are doing things!' . . . Just the energy, it's palpable here."

In short, TechCo's workforce was not deaf to the racket they coproduced in their wide-open spaces. They complained about it and looked for ways to manage it. They wore headphones when needed, and one after another they asked the architects to build "quiet rooms" into the new space (a request the company ultimately obliged), places where they could retreat to work and think when the symphony turned to cacophony. Yet they never asked for offices. The noise in their rooms was like the virtual noise on the wiki and on social media in general—a tension to be navigated. It could be a burden for sure, but it also signified a more vibrant, connected experience, and they were uninterested in the alternative.

DISTRACTIONS BUT ALSO LEARNING; INTERRUPTIONS BUT ALSO TEAMWORK

It was not just the decibel level that was challenging about TechCo's open offices. With no barriers or dividers, employees were easily distracted by what they saw and heard right around them, and easily interrupted by their colleagues. Mia, a twenty-nine-year-old who had been at the company for just under a year, told me that she had recently moved her seat to a back corner of her workroom. She explained that she had had trouble focusing in her two previous seats because they were more centrally located: "I could hear everything everyone was saying. I could see people walking by. They would stop by to chat."

A twenty-eight-year-old engineer complained that the distractions and interruptions were "hugely negative" for his productivity. He analogized interruptions stemming from the company's open offices to interruptions stemming from HipChat's open virtual rooms where he and his peers spent their days as well. "HipChat's open to the rooms you're in, and it blinks when something is added. So, like every ten to thirty seconds you see it blink and check over," he said. Similarly, he was constantly glancing up from his desk "to see who's walking by."

At the same time, the ability to see and hear what others were doing and the ability to interrupt and be interrupted were cherished attributes of the space. Shortly before I began my fieldwork, the company had installed dividers for a team of workers in customer support. The team had been complaining about noise and distractions in their workroom for a while, so it had seemed like a reasonable solution to place cubicle barriers between their individual workstations. Yet as soon as the barriers went up, the workers took them down. I heard this story several times before asking the team's manager one day why the staff had done this. He shrugged, "It's a cultural thing. . . . The workers hate the dividers." As I continued to explore people's feelings about the space, I came to understand that workers were bothered by the noise and distractions of the open workrooms, but they simply privileged the feeling of connectedness and the opportunity to converse and learn from one another more.

In particular, the lack of dividers enabled employees to access and share information in ways they valued and that came naturally to them. They talked about "learning by osmosis" because they could hear and see so much. Customer support reps learned how to troubleshoot new problems by leaning over and watching neighbors handle calls (as well as by following the ongoing stream of HipChat "interruptions"). Sales reps said they learned new sales strategies by overhearing "sound bites" from their colleagues' calls and then following up with questions. Programmers described stopping work to listen in on one another's conversations when they concerned topics about which they were unfamiliar and wanted to learn more. Laura, the product manager, described how she liked to "scan" and "browse" the room to see what other people were working on and then go over to them if she felt she could learn something new or offer a hand. When I heard these descriptions and saw people doing this, I was reminded of their analogous online activity (and most everyone's these days)—the steady feed of information and updates on social media accounts, the rapid browsing and scanning, the double clicking to dig deeper and learn more.

The more time I spent in the workrooms, the more I realized that Tech-Co's workforce valued a style of collaborative learning that conventional offices simply would not have accommodated. There was a distinct preference for team-based learning and troubleshooting versus solitary toiling. Just as I had seen support reps like Emma use HipChat to solicit help on customer calls, I saw numerous examples of crowdsourced problem solving in the physical space. When someone nearby encountered a problem or was working on something particularly challenging, others stopped what they were doing and jumped in to tackle it together.

A few months after our first exchange, I ran into Mia again, the woman who had struggled with all the distractions and moved her seat. I asked how she liked her new spot in the back of the room. She smiled and confessed that even though she found it easier to concentrate, she missed the stimulation and learning she had experienced in her old seat. She now made an effort to walk around the room to see what other people were working on and to inquire about their projects, and she said she was looking forward to trying out a different location soon. Like the overall noise, the distractions and interruptions were a part of life in TechCo's offices, and they held a dual meaning for workers like Mia, posing challenges to be managed but also benefits to be gained. Such a thick and open communication environment was overwhelming at times, but it was also rife with opportunities for connection and learning.

CONFUSION BUT ALSO CONNECTION
AND A CAPACITY FOR CHANGE

The company's practice of seat rotation created additional opportunities for connection and learning but also a certain amount of confusion. Mia was not the only one to change seats it turned out; four times a year everyone in the entire company moved to a new spot. The idea was that people could meet new colleagues and encounter new perspectives. However, employees sometimes found the constant dislocation to be disorienting, and they complained that it made navigating the offices difficult.

During the period of my study, there was no centralized directory showing where someone sat, so trying to find a person's desk after one of the rotations felt like setting off on an uncharted expedition. One day, as I wandered up and down the aisles of one of TechCo's larger rooms looking for someone I was scheduled to meet with, I passed by Kelly, whom I had recently met, typing at her desk. She asked what was up, and I confessed, "I'm supposed to meet with Kevin, but I'm realizing I don't know where he sits." Kelly said, "Yeah, the amount of time it takes to find where someone sits, it's ridiculous . . . . We just changed again. Check the back row maybe?"

Despite the occasional frustrations, the workforce never called for abandoning the practice of seat rotations. They reported that the constant flux energized them and that the practice worked as intended, allowing them to forge connections and encounter perspectives they otherwise would not. They identified both individual and organizational benefits to that. Grace, for instance, said she learned from meeting new neighbors and hearing what they were working on because it exposed her to a range of skill sets and let her see what work went into other jobs at the company. That broader perspective, she said, made her better at her current job and was useful professional development for the future. The new connections fostered by seat rotation also made the organization more effective, she explained. "All the great experiments we've had that have solved big problems [for the company] came from people from different areas coming together . . . [from someone saying] 'oh, you've got that problem, well I have something from over here that might help.'"

Academic literature supports Grace's perspective. Physical proximity, especially among similarly aged individuals, has been shown to aid in the formation of network ties (i.e., connections between people through which information and resources can flow).[4] Furthermore, it is "weak ties"—ties between people with non-overlapping networks and knowledge bases— that carry the most novel, generative information.[5] (Sitting next to people you know well and whose networks overlap with your own can be comfortable and certainly less disorienting than having new neighbors every few months, but it also limits the amount of knowledge transfer that will happen.) Conceptually speaking, what quarterly seat rotation enables is the repeated generation of new weak ties and the individual and organizational learning that comes from that. Employees like Grace valued the practice, in short, because it encouraged a set of connections and conversations that transcended the firm's formal structure and helped create new capacities in them and in their organization.

Perhaps the greatest capacity promoted by seat rotation, however, pertained to change. Institutionalized practices are generally associated with stability and a resistance to change, but the quarterly rotation of seats was a way to institutionalize change itself and acclimate the staff to it.[6] Matt compared the oft-changing seats at TechCo to his last job where he sat in the same office for several years. "I still feel it's my space here, but I feel more agile. I'm not putting down the same roots like I did in an office." Others who had worked in more conventional offices said similar things. A woman from operations linked the staff's frequent seat changes to an overall collective spirit and tolerance for growth, noting, "Very few folks seem to feel much of a sense of entitlement to their space, and they're pretty flexible when it comes time to find a slot for someone new . . . . In my old office, there was a real sense of turf in the cube areas, and people were very grouchy when we needed to rework space to accommodate growth."

Summarizing the sentiments of many, Matt put it simply, "The constant seat shuffle keeps everybody OK with change." And that was important because TechCo was all about change. It was an organization built to accommodate the transformations in worker habits and expectations brought about by social media and represented by the millennial generation. In turn, the organization itself had to evolve and adapt repeatedly as its experiments with organizational change surfaced new and unexpected challenges and tensions that had to be navigated.

SURVEILLANCE BUT ALSO FLEXIBILITY AND ACCESS

One tension that I expected TechCo would have to navigate as a result of its open environment concerned surveillance. Its workspace was not just communicatively open but also visibly open, and prior studies have found surveillance of workers to be an issue in such environments.[7] When I first heard that TechCo allowed its workers to set their own hours, take free food from the company kitchen, and drink beer in the office, I wondered if such ostensible freedoms were possible simply because employees knew that any abuses of them would be visible. We saw in chapter 4 that the firm did not have to formally restrict employee voices on social media because the visibility of what was said on those platforms acted as a disciplining force, and it seemed reasonable to assume that a similar dynamic might operate in its physical space.

My initial observations seemed to confirm this. As I spent time in the workspace, I noticed that employees availed themselves of the freedoms TechCo bestowed, but within bounds. It was not unusual for people to come in late, leave early, or even work from home on some days, and the workforce said they greatly valued this flexibility; and yet it was still the case that on most days most people at TechCo worked normal business hours. What is more, when confronted with behavior that deviated outside certain bounds, employees often invoked the specter of visibility. A programmer who had just spoken to me about the freedom he enjoyed in TechCo's open offices told me that he was worried about a friend of his who had recently joined the company: "Everyone can see him strolling in late, and he's only been here a few weeks. I pulled him aside and told him to wait a while . . . . People notice that stuff, especially if you're new."

Explicitly acknowledging the potential for surveillance in the space, managers confirmed the programmer's assessment. Several said that it was impossible for them not to notice their employees' behavior in the workrooms. However, they also seemed to appreciate the risks of reneging on promised freedoms and creating a sense of oppressive monitoring, and they said they tried not to act on their observations as a result. Matt, who managed a small team of other marketers, explained, "There's no face time. If they don't want to come in that's fine," but he added, "Don't get me wrong, it's hard for me, and you have to be really careful as a manager to watch yourself." A woman who reported to him sat several seats down from his workstation, and for the last two weeks he could see that her seat was often empty. "I think she should come in more and be there for her own team," he said. "But I won't tell her that because that's the wrong message to send . . . . It would feel like [she's] being watched." Other managers spoke of disciplining themselves similarly.

At times, their efforts seemed to be paying off. When I asked employees whether they felt monitored in the open workrooms, they spoke of flexibility instead. For example, I asked Grace, the junior woman in TechCo's marketing group, whether she felt it was a burden that her manager could see everything she was doing. She intuited the point of my question and responded, "I don't feel surveillance if that's what you're asking. Because I can go work wherever I want in the office or work from home, it would be pretty crazy to assume that if I wasn't at my desk that I'm not working . . . . I'm not at my desk a lot of the time." Likewise, in response to a similar question, Laura acknowledged that people's activities were visible to those around them, but she said surveillance was not relevant because there were no consequences to doing things that might be frowned upon in another setting:

No one cares what you do here, so long as you get your work done. Sometimes I look over and someone's watching the latest viral video but then ten minutes later they're back working. That's just how it is, they let people do their thing here . . . . If I were in some buttoned-up financial firm and you saw someone on Facebook and they were reprimanded for it, then it'd feel like there was all this surveillance.

Nevertheless, even as employees downplayed the relevance of surveillance to their daily work lives, and even as managers spoke of consciously resisting the temptation to police their workers, I witnessed specific instances of what could only be defined as surveillance. When a customer support rep jokingly swore on a phone call, a manager sitting nearby overheard and immediately reprimanded her. In the room where many sales reps sat, managers listened to the staff's sales calls, and as the reps spoke to prospects on the phone, the managers often sent them instant messages with suggestions for what to say next or critiques of what they had just said.

I made a point of probing these specific instances, and when I did, employees acknowledged that it could be stressful to be so constantly visible to their supervisors, "always under the microscope" as one put it. However, they still maintained that they preferred the open seating plan to any alternative. Sure, there was occasional scrutiny, they said when I pressed, but more often than not they felt their managers' watchful presence and interventions offered valuable feedback and learning opportunities. With their supervisors sitting alongside them, they felt they could ask questions, receive on-the-spot feedback, and learn by watching. Laura, who had said she liked to "scan" and "browse" the room to see what she might learn, told me, "Sometimes I'll lean over and see that my manager is working on a report I've never seen before, and I'll ask him what it is and how he created it." If he sat in an office, she said, "I would feel like I wouldn't have as much access to him."

Employees across the organization seemed to feel the same. Because of the perceived learning benefits, the young workforce placed more value on the conversations they could have with their managers than the risk of surveillance by them. As one sales rep explained, "I'm not going to say it doesn't bug me when I'm in the middle of a call and I've got to look over [to HipChat] and see what she's [my manager] telling me I should be doing different. But nine times out of ten she's got something useful that helps me out . . . . Net-net, it's worth it."

This rep's perspective is understandable once we recognize that flexibility, access, and oversight are inextricably linked in a space like TechCo's. The workforce did, indeed, experience more flexibility and access to managers than they would in a closed office setup, but they received those benefits precisely because they were willing to sit in the open and accept a bit more surveillance in exchange. Contemporary surveillance scholarship makes this point more broadly, observing that historical notions of surveillance (as something imposed on individuals top-down and without their consent) are outmoded today. More often these days, we as a society voluntarily embrace tools and technologies—whether social media and networking sites like Facebook and Twitter or our mobile devices and applications—that enable a certain amount of surveillance because we want the convenience, connections, and freedom they give us in exchange.[8] Without ascribing false consciousness to them, then, it may simply be that TechCo's employees were unconcerned with surveillance because, like many of us, they have already made the tradeoff between flexibility and access, on the one hand, and surveillance, on the other; and because, at least for now, it is a tradeoff with which they can live.

ABSENT MANAGERS BUT ONE-ON-ONE CONVERSATIONS

Whatever the potential for surveillance in these open rooms, it was clearly less relevant to the workforce than the access of which they more often spoke. And yet that treasured access to managers did not always look like what I expected it would. Yes, I saw people conversing with their managers in the open workrooms as they had described to me (and, yes, I sometimes saw some evidence of managerial surveillance), but just as often I was left wondering where all the managers were. When I sat out on the floor to shadow workers, I watched as people repeatedly swung by managers' desks only to find them empty. Workers who sat near a manager's desk were subjected to frequent questioning about the manager's whereabouts. Laura, who said she liked to look over at what her supervisor was working on, also complained to me that he was rarely at his desk and, as a result, "five or six times a week, I get people stopping by and asking me if I know where he is. I'm not his keeper!"

Managers themselves fully acknowledged their frequent absence from the workrooms. Whenever I offered to swing by someone's desk later to catch up, the standard refrain I heard from managers was some version of "I'm never at my desk. We'll have to schedule a time." Some were at their desks so rarely that they gave them up entirely when space was scarce. A manager who gave her workstation over to a newly hired junior employee explained, "We were low on desks and I don't really need one since I'm almost never there. I can be a nomad for a while." In such instances, the conventional corporate association between status and space seemed to have been turned entirely on its head: Managers at TechCo were marked not by their fancier offices or better equipment but by their disconnection from the physical space entirely.

As observations like this accumulated in my field notes, I wondered whether one reason the workforce felt such flexibility was because managers were rarely present to surveil them. I also struggled to comprehend how the workforce could maintain such strong feelings of access to people who were so rarely around. Soon I at least learned where all the managers were. It turned out that every manager at TechCo held a weekly one-on-one meeting with each member of his or her team, and because these meetings were held in the various conference rooms scattered throughout the building complex, managers were often away from the workrooms.

When I learned of this practice, it answered my question about managers' whereabouts, but it opened up others. In past studies or even my own work experience, I had never encountered anything like the frequency and number of one-on-one meetings that I saw at TechCo. Some managers had more than fifty of these meetings each week, and for several months I struggled to make sense of what seemed like a bizarre, unnecessary practice. On the one hand, I assumed that employees might consider the practice a burden, a source of unwanted and excessive managerial attention. On the other hand, I reasoned that if the workforce truly valued having managers so accessible in the workrooms, then managers' consistent absence must be problematic. Eventually, though, I came to see that the workforce was unfazed by these issues because they saw the one-on-one meetings as offering a different, even more personalized form of access that they valued.

When I asked a manager in the operations group why the company held so many one-on-ones, he said matter of factly, "Everyone does it. It's a new generation." Someone senior in the customer support group explained, "It's almost a right for them [the workers]. They want it and expect it." Surveys of millennials as well as public and scholarly commentary on them suggest they value and are used to personalized attention and frequent, detailed feedback.[9] One-on-one meetings gave them that and, even more important, offered yet another platform to speak up and be heard. In the meetings I observed directly, employees arrived with their own written agendas that covered personal topics (such as skills they wanted to improve upon in their current position as well as long-term career objectives, both within and beyond TechCo) and organizational topics (such as questions and thoughts about whatever was being debated on the wiki that week or an idea for how to improve a specific work practice in their group). For their part, managers offered feedback on the worker's recent performance and helped troubleshoot any problems they were having. By way of example, Mia and her manager used a one-on-one meeting to discuss Mia's struggle with the noise and distractions in the workroom, and it was there that they jointly hatched the idea of her moving to a new seat and having a white noise machine at her desk.

Far from imposing excessive managerial control, the meetings seemed to offer a sort of personal connection and dialogue with supervisors that the staff appreciated. "I'm a huge one-on-one geek! I think they're great," Laura, the product manager, told me when I asked about her experience with one-on-ones. She explained that it was only because of her one-on-one meetings with a prior manager that she had obtained her current position in the company:

> The one-on-ones let [my manager] really get to know me . . . . She really heard me when I said I was interested in certain things. So when a project came up that was a good fit, she thought of me and brought it to me . . . and it led me to this [new job]. She'd never have known I'd be interested in that project if I'd not had all those one-on-ones and the opportunity to make myself understood and known to her like that.

Ironically, to be heard and understood in this way apparently required a particular physical environment for these meetings that, at first glance, seems to challenge the company's goal of radical openness. When I asked Laura and others why their one-on-ones were held in private conference rooms and not at their desks given the company's preference for transparency (thinking that managers would be away from the workrooms less often that way too), they were puzzled by my question. In a tone that implied I was failing to grasp the obvious, one responded, "It's not like we don't value privacy." One of the findings of research on open offices is that for all the supposed communicative benefits, people sometimes communicate and share less in open spaces than in private ones, and TechCo's workforce seemed to have intuited this.[10] But the privacy they sought was not for protection from their managers' watchful eyes; it was for the ability to converse freely and directly with them. With their lack of barriers and constant interruptions, the workrooms offered neither the privacy nor the possibility of their manager's undivided attention that workers sought in these particular conversations.

Given how many one-on-ones were held each day and given the company's limited number of private rooms, finding a space for all these meetings posed a persistent challenge. In their comments to the architects, employees and managers alike repeatedly asked for more private spaces to accommodate them. This request came up so frequently, in fact, that I eventually realized they were asking for nearly as many private meeting rooms as other companies had manager offices. But it was never once suggested that managers might just sit in offices. Several months after my fieldwork ended, the new office build out was completed, and just as it included "quiet rooms" for people to escape the noise and distractions, it included rows of small, private rooms for the popular one-on-one meetings. It was another step in TechCo's ongoing process of facilitating the unique habits and expectations of its millennial workforce and supporting the many conversations they valued.

As I watched all of this unfold, I came to understand why employees would talk about access in the open rooms despite their managers being so often away from their desks. The company's "no office policy," as it was called, had symbolic meaning for the workforce, and what it symbolized was the very same thing employees received in the one-on-one meetings: voice and conversation that cut across hierarchical lines. Grace acknowledged that her manager was not always at his desk but said she would still feel a great loss if he moved into an office. "Even if a lot didn't change practically, it'd still mean something if [managers] had offices . . . like there was less access overall," she explained to me. Because of the no office policy, she said, "I feel like I can walk up to Eric [the CEO] and ask him a question or start a conversation . . . . I value that accessibility. It's unparalleled here." A twenty-six-year-old in engineering said, "There are still all these managers and directors," but because of the no office policy, "they don't feel all high and mighty." Like others, he felt comfortable walking up to any of them to ask a question or share an idea. From these perspectives, access was less about hands-on learning (although both Grace and the engineer said they valued those opportunities when they arose) and more about communication being unbound by the firm's hierarchy.

Academic studies of open office layouts have found that they are often symbolically associated with nonhierarchical organizations, but here they were taken more specifically to mean access within and communication across the hierarchy.[11] As we have seen throughout the book, no one denied the existence of hierarchy at TechCo, but the no office policy was taken as a symbol that conversation could be decoupled from it. When I asked Matt—the marketer who had compared TechCo's alive, buzzing offices to the stultifying, dead ones of other firms—what the company's no office policy meant to him, he answered, "It means we don't want any unnecessary hierarchy. We definitely want some; you need people to take responsibility for things and make decisions. But we don't want any more than you absolutely need, and offices feel like unnecessary hierarchy." The lack of physical barriers between company leaders and the workforce signified a lack of conversational barriers between them, and for this particular workforce, the symbolism of unrestricted connection and communication was as salient a form of access as a manager's physical presence.

CONTROLLING CHAOS

TechCo employees accepted certain costs of their workspace because they valued the countervailing benefits more. But what happens when there is a cost the workforce does not want to tolerate? More generally, what happens when a conversational firm confronts a problem that conversation alone cannot fully resolve? One issue in TechCo's workspace presented a test case for these questions.

The issue is that nearly all space at TechCo is shared space—whether in the open workrooms where people sit side by side, in the kitchen where they prepare and eat their food, or in the various common sitting areas where they go to relax. Moreover, the firm has dispensed with much of the conventional bureaucratic separation between corporate and personal property by encouraging employees to treat the property and free amenities as if they are their own and to feel comfortable expressing themselves in the space. There are benefits to all this, but one major cost: The organization is not immune to the problems of the commons that economists have long identified, and the shared spaces can become littered and chaotic places at times. In its physical space, as elsewhere, the firm cannot escape the question of control.

The main benefit of TechCo's open, shared spaces should be clear by now: connection and conversation that fuels the vibrancy and "buzz" so many cherish. Beyond that, the freedom and flexibility employees enjoy create an informal, playful atmosphere unlike anything resembling a conventional corporate environment. The workforce cherishes that too. Once, while I stood waiting for my next meeting to begin, ten or so employees gathered nearby and began doing push-ups on the ground, having self-organized on the wiki earlier in the day. Another time, I noticed a band's worth of musical equipment in the software developers' workroom, including a full drum set, microphones, and amplifiers. Later that week, I listened as a handful of programmers held band practice right there. My field notes from other typical days include references to a bowl of goldfish atop someone's desk, a poster of Justin Timberlake at another, and along one wall life-sized cardboard cutouts of several mariachi players.

Nevertheless, the quirky, relaxed feel that the workforce likes so much can become a disordered, messy place that they loathe. In short, there is a fine line between people feeling comfortable enough to express themselves and simply feeling too comfortable. When employees complained that the workspace was a "shit hole" or "filthy" or "smelled like a goat farm," this was what they meant, and I understood the complaints. People brought their dogs to work, and on two different occasions I heard reports of dog excrement in the halls. Before meetings, I cleared empty take-out containers off of conference room tables, remnants of the room's prior occupants. While I was at the company, a new kitchen counter was installed. Despite bottle openers having been mounted on the nearby fridge as well as right above the counter itself, I noticed that within just a few weeks of its installation, the counter had multiple chips along its edge due to people using the edge to open beer bottles. I heard the facilities team instruct an outside design firm that, when it came to purchasing furniture or equipment, the guiding principles should be "WBS" ("we break shit") and "SFS" ("solve for spillage"). There was also talk of putting steel corners on all the walls because of how they got "hacked" and "bumped" as employees made the space their own, rolling white boards, desks, and even kegs from one room to another.

For many on the workforce, TechCo was their first job, and lack of familiarity with basic corporate norms undoubtedly played a role in all this. By multiple accounts, the workroom that housed the company's youngest team (the entry-level sales group) was said to be the "worst" and the "stinkiest." A woman in her late twenties who sat in that room said that the younger workers regularly left food and garbage lying around. "I feel like the den mother," she complained. The period of my study was one of rapid growth for TechCo, and the company was often playing catch up in building sufficient space to house the workforce, so sheer density added to the general sense of human-created chaos. But youth and density aside, employees complained that not everyone on staff felt a "vested interest" in the space (as several put it) and that this more than anything accounted for the mess and disorder of it all.

As elsewhere, the company's executives had historically taken a hands-off approach when it came to exerting control over the space. They noticed the mess and filth and sometimes commented about it on the wiki, reminding people to respect the space. But they had wanted an informal workplace, and I sensed some of them even derived a bit of pride in having created an environment in which employees felt so free and comfortable as to have this problem. Employees, in contrast, were increasingly vocal about their frustrations, and over the years, the issue had become a topic of conversation on the wiki.

One day during my fieldwork, one of the company's software developers walked into the company kitchen to find the counter covered with trash and half-eaten food. Disgusted, he snapped photos with his smartphone and posted them on the wiki for all to see, taking it upon himself to create a bad judgment post of sorts that he hoped might influence the staff's behavior. He titled the post, "Why I'm embarrassed to be a TechCo-er," and answered with the subtitle, "Because I work with slobs, meanies and jerks." Next to a picture of an empty yogurt container, he included the caption, "That's not an empty yogurt container, it's an art installation." Accompanying a photo of the trash-strewn countertop, the caption read, "Hey I found my water. It's right next to the used cup, random bits of food and other crap I'm going to leave for the next person. Cause you know, I like to share. I'm TechCo'y!"

The discussion that unfolded in the comments section to his post demonstrated the extent of employee frustration with the issue, as well as the desire for a more effective mechanism of control. This was not the first post about office mess, and people seemed to have had enough. One commenter wrote, "These kind of companywide call outs help put a Band-Aid on the problem for the time being, but things just recede back to how they were after a few weeks." He and others wanted a "more actionable plan" rather than just another conversation.

The first suggestion came from a marketing executive, a senior manager whom I had heard joke about the mess at times but who had also written wiki posts of his own pleading for people to show more respect for their shared space. Indicating that perhaps it was time to adopt a more direct form of control (and simultaneously revealing the temptation for surveillance that is inherent in these spaces), the executive suggested installing a webcam and "checking video footage and firing people." An executive from engineering responded, "HELL F*CKING YES!" It was not entirely clear to me whether they were serious or just offering a reminder that TechCo could adopt alternative means of control if people did not start picking up after themselves. Either way, it got a discussion going about what some of those alternatives might be.

Some people proposed collectivist solutions. For example, a twenty-eight-year-old customer consultant suggested, "I think we should all take turns cleaning the kitchen." Others countered that individuals should have to pick up for themselves, not create work for everyone else. After some back and forth, the customer consultant seemed persuaded and revised his proposal. "How about a combination of the two ideas: The webcam would expose offenders and publicly shame them, and then force them to clean the entire kitchen as punishment?" The marketing executive endorsed the suggestion. Someone from sales wrote in, "Nailed it." Someone from services called it "an awesome idea."

Others did not think the idea of direct surveillance and public shaming was such an awesome idea, however. Sure, some minimal surveillance was tolerable in exchange for flexibility and access, but a camera recording your every move? Dissenting voices arose and preached caution. A woman in marketing asked, "What's the actual goal here? To identify us some red-handed perpetrators? Or to keep the place clean?" A woman in the services group wrote, "For what it's worth, I don't really subscribe to the public shaming option. I'd like to think embarrassing a specific individual and naming them isn't the necessary course of action for people to respect the office and their coworkers." As described in chapter 4, the point of bad judgment posts was not to shame individual offenders but to get a collective conversation started. A conversation was already under way here so calling out offenders any further seemed unnecessary.

But that was the issue all along. Those who entertained the webcam idea were saying that maybe this time conversation was not enough. Whether the organization knew it or not, they were facing a test of the limits of the conversational firm. Would they opt for direct surveillance because they had finally encountered a problem for which the benefits did not outweigh the costs and that conversation did not seem capable of resolving?

The results of this test were revealed over the next several days as debate and dialogue continued on the wiki. There was never a definitive decision to drop the webcam idea, but it garnered less and less attention over time, until eventually no one referenced it anymore. Confronted with the possibility of direct surveillance and control, the organization just kept talking, implicitly renewing its commitment to conversation despite knowing that it was not a perfect solution to the problem at hand. At a certain point, there seemed to be a collective acceptance of the inevitability of at least some mess and the corresponding need to tolerate it while still working against it. A woman from marketing wrote, "It's a never-ending battle. The universe tends towards freaking entropy and disorder and chaos, we all know that. So we humans just need to get in the habit of beating back the damn chaos."

Complaints about the mess never fully abated during my time at the company, nor did the mess itself. However, each time the conversation resurfaced, the organization grappled with, but ultimately resisted, the temptation to adopt more oppressive controls and surveillance. Throughout the book, we have seen that a bit of chaos and disorder was the cost of openness in other areas of TechCo as well. Over and over, the organization faced the dilemma of how much chaos it could live with versus when it was necessary to adopt more formal controls to tame it; and over and over, the organization confronted that question through ongoing dialogue that temporarily resolved but never fully closed the issue. Sometimes formal controls were adopted; sometimes they were not. Either way, things would inevitably change again. New conversations would be launched, and old ones would be reopened and revisited. The conversational firm worked not by resolving every problem perfectly but by being able to surface and collectively reflect upon the never-ending tradeoffs and tensions of organizational life.

* * *

When I first asked Matt, the marketer, what he thought about the company's open office layout, he seemed surprised by my interest in the topic. He said, "Nobody really talks about it or notices it. It's just something that is, and is good . . . . It would be really weird—like alien-landing weird if [the company] started sitting in offices."

This did not mean the environment built to accommodate TechCo's workforce did not have its own challenges, of course. Despite Matt's assessment that nobody really talked about it, employees complained about the challenges of working in the open offices often. However, they complained because they had been given the right to do so, and because they trusted that management would take their complaints seriously and engage in a dialogue about them. Management, for its part, wanted that dialogue too. It offered a way to confront the costs and benefits of difficult decisions transparently and to arrive at solutions the workforce would accept. Thus, just as employees chose to live with the noise, distractions, and occasional chaos of their conversational spaces, executives chose to live with the noise, distractions, and occasional chaos of facing so many, often critical employee voices on these and other topics. For both parties, the costs were real, but the benefits great—and neither wanted an alternative. Conversation was the one path that everyone at TechCo trusted to help the organization evolve and improve.

8

THE CONVERSATIONAL FIRM: IMPLICATIONS FOR THEORY

O N THE SURFACE, today's high-tech firms seem quite different from conventional bureaucratic firms. Google touts an "open" culture in which "Googlers ask questions directly to Larry, Sergey and other execs about any number of company issues" and where employees share ideas and opinions with one another in company cafes and lounge areas.[1] Facebook declares, "We don't have rules, we have values," and one of those values is "to be open" and "make sure everyone at Facebook has access to as much information about the company as possible."[2] Netflix has distributed a public statement about its organizational form in which it notes, "most companies curtail freedom and become bureaucratic as they grow," whereas Netflix's model is "to increase employee freedom as we grow, rather than limit it."[3] The online shoe retailer Zappos has gone so far as to abandon formal manager roles and titles entirely. Meanwhile, hundreds of smaller high-tech firms are emulating these tech giants and experimenting with their own unconventional approaches to organizing and managing their workforce.

Not surprisingly, considerable hype and hyperbole have surrounded these developments—from the revolutionary claims of some corporate executives, to news coverage of these firms' quirky and unexpected ways, to Hollywood caricatures of them in movies like *The Internship* and television shows like *Silicon Valley*.[4] This book's agenda has been to get beyond all the hype and hyperbole however, by investigating what is really going on inside one high-tech firm's attempt to discard conventional wisdom and become "radically open." I set out to study TechCo because I wanted to understand the impact of the social media revolution on organizations and, fundamentally, whether it is possible to transcend the conventional bureaucratic form.

Listening only to the hype, we might expect to find no remnants of conventional bureaucratic organizing inside a company like TechCo. Alternatively, absorbing only the academic literature on past attempts to transcend bureaucracy, we might have expected to find that whatever is going on is either destined to fail (history has repeatedly shown just how hard it is to pry open the iron cage of bureaucracy) or all just rhetoric (perhaps masking even more pernicious forms of control than bureaucracy itself). But what we have actually found through this book's ethnographic tour of TechCo is born less radical than the proclamations of some pundits and more hopeful than the predictions of past scholarship.

As we watched TechCo shoot for "radical openness" in multiple dimensions of its organizational life, we saw it challenge conventional bureaucratic approaches to organizing but also confront the limitations of openness as an alternative philosophy. Along the way, we saw that TechCo has ultimately succeeded in building something quite new. More than its openness, however, what is truly radical about the organization is its conversational nature—the ongoing dialogue the firm maintains with its workforce. In this chapter, I draw out the theoretical implications of this finding by examining how the conversational firm TechCo has built challenges traditional scholarly understandings of the firm and how it might be transformed.

RETHINKING BUREAUCRACY, RETHINKING HIERARCHY

Since the publication of Weber's work in the 1920s, a staple of bureaucratic theory has been that leaders of corporate firms will command strict control of their communication environment. Weber believed that bureaucratic administrators derived their authority from two sources: their expert knowledge and their position in the organization's hierarchical structure.[5] Open communication would seem to undermine both of these bases of authority and call the entire firm's legitimacy into question. If leaders really have superior expertise, then allowing others to weigh in on important matters will merely interfere with the firm's capacity for rational, efficient action, not enhance it. And, if leaders derive authority from their position, then any challenge to them is a challenge to the whole hierarchical structure itself. Accordingly, Weber observed that the modern bureaucratic firm tended to "hide its knowledge and action from criticism as well as it can," and that meant carefully restricting the conversations that happened within the firm's own ranks and with the outside world.[6] Over the years, empirical evidence has generally supported this position. A consistent finding from past corporate ethnographies is how hierarchical firms either stifle employee voice and dialogue entirely, or promote merely ceremonial forms that constitute no real challenge to executives' authority.[7]

And yet if the bureaucratic form depends on control over its conversational environment, consider the challenge today's world poses. These days firms operate in an environment in which it is increasingly difficult to control the conversations happening within and around them. Customers are demanding more voice and dialogue in the market, employees are carrying similar expectations into the workplace, and all sorts of new tools and platforms exist to meet these expectations.

In this conversational age, TechCo has shown that it is now possible (and possibly necessary) to create a more conversational firm. Such an organization offers a far more open communication environment than has been seen before, and it challenges us to rethink the relationship between corporate communication and control. TechCo's experience has shown that a firm's hierarchy of communication can be subverted quite profoundly without directly subverting or delegitimizing its hierarchy of authority. Its experience also suggests that certain types of hierarchical control may even be necessary to support the sort of open communication that is valued by many of today's workers.

But why are we only now seeing that such open communication is possible? For starters, prior attempts to rethink the bureaucratic firm lacked the conversational tools and expectations afforded by today's environment. But that is not all. Prior attempts to rethink the bureaucratic firm also made a very specific and, as it turns out, needlessly narrow assumption about how such a transformation must come about. One way or another, transcending the conventional bureaucratic firm has almost always been taken to mean transcending its hierarchical structure of authority.[8] TechCo's experience suggests that a different path is available; to appreciate the novelty and significance of that, it is worth reviewing some of these earlier attempts.

Consider first the grassroots collectives that emerged during the countercultural movement of the 1960s and 1970s—organizations such as free schools and clinics and various worker and producer cooperatives. Founders of these organizations were explicitly and ideologically opposed to the conventional corporate firm, and they sought an alternative by rejecting hierarchical authority and embracing the principles and practices of democratic decision making. Scholarly analyses of these experiments suggest that democratic governance was possible in some, but it did not come easily, was not always stable, and could only survive under certain limited conditions that do not pertain to most corporate projects.[9] In particular, consensus decision making and shared authority seemed to work best where skills were shared and scale was small. As the need for specialization and scale increased, hierarchical approaches to managing tended to slip back in, and many of the countercultural experiments floundered and failed over time.

In the 1980s, new approaches to bureaucratic management emerged inside some large-scale industrial enterprises. Unlike the 1960s and 1970s collectives, these experiments were not intended to eradicate bureaucracy entirely but to transform its nature and improve its functioning, specifically by enhancing worker empowerment and loosening manager's hierarchical grip on local decision making. Inspired by the Japanese model of management and the Toyota Production System in particular (and fearful of being outpaced by global competition), businesses began to give factory floor employees more direct control over their job tasks and to let them design the workflow and rules they would follow on the line. A canonical example from these experiments was the andon cord, a cord that workers could literally pull to stop the production line if they identified a quality or safety problem. Called "enabling bureaucracy" or "representative bureaucracy" by scholars, some observers viewed these developments optimistically, seeing them as a path away from more "coercive" or "compliance-oriented" forms of bureaucratic management.[10] Others saw them as just another way to get workers to consent to their own exploitation.[11]

Finally, in the late 1980s and 1990s the rise of the knowledge economy spurred a new wave of talk and experimentation with alternative approaches to organizing, especially in the high-tech world. Leveraging the network communication technologies of the day, a number of firms began reorganizing and distributing work, emphasizing horizontal collaboration and teamwork over hierarchical command and control. At the time, some observers believed these "network organizations" marked the beginning of a postbureaucratic era in which distributed modes of authority would replace rigid hierarchical ones.[12] Others noted that the supposedly looser, less hierarchical structures of these firms simply allowed more insidious forms of cultural and moral control to take hold, and that bureaucratic practices tended to slip back in anyway, just as they had with the earlier wave of countercultural collectives.[13]

Despite its mixed results, the tradition of rethinking the firm by rethinking authority continues. Today, many of the high-tech firms experimenting with alternative organizational models are doing so by rejecting the conventional structure of hierarchical authority. Medium, a blog-publishing platform company located in San Francisco and founded by one of Twitter's original cofounders, made waves in the tech world when it announced it had absolutely no managers, nor a traditional organizational structure. The firm relies instead on a form of nonhierarchical, constitutional governance called "holacracy," which uses self-organizing teams and frequent meetings to clarify responsibilities and reach democratic decisions.[14] Zappos recently moved to a holacracy form of governance as well, and the video game developer Valve and other firms have been experimenting with their own approaches to building so-called bossless organizations.[15] These experiments are still unfolding, but like the three earlier attempts to take on hierarchical authority, there are reports of challenges arising in the process.

Common among all these approaches is not just that they try to subvert and reimagine hierarchical authority but that they have done so by directly equating changes in the firm's communication environment to changes in its decision-making structure. The countercultural collectives saw dialogue as a path to democracy and conversation as a path to consensus decisions. Because worker participation initiatives focused on local empowerment, they rarely distinguished voice and decision making at all: Pulling the andon chord was both a way to speak up and a way to stop the line simultaneously. The new economy firms of the 1990s assumed that distributed communication meant that distributed authority would follow. Holacracy posits open, democratic dialogue in small groups as a way to "revolutionize how a company is structured, how decisions are made, and how power is distributed."[16]

What a conversational firm like TechCo does that is different—and what today's new tools and platforms for voice and conversation allow—is to attack the bureaucratic firm's structure of communication while leaving the structure of authority largely intact. As we have seen, TechCo executives use their authority to share information far more openly than corporate executives have in the past, and they extend internal and external voice rights to the workforce in ways that were previously unimaginable. What is more, when executives try to subvert the firm's hierarchical structure of authority and delegate decision rights as they have voice rights, it is the organization's open conversations—and the employee voices expressed in them—that surface the challenges of doing that and often argue against it.

The result of all this is that some bars of the iron cage remain firmly in place inside the conversational firm, but the bars encaging communication have been pried open more than ever before. That is not insignificant. It means that we can rethink the conventional bureaucratic firm by rethinking communication. By leveraging the spirit and technologies of social media, firms today have new tools and ideas at their disposal, and they can come at the iron cage from a different angle. Weber argued that modern communication made bureaucracy, in the form he imagined it, the most effective modern form of organization.[17] However, communication has changed drastically since his time, and new forms are now possible. A conversational firm like TechCo is an achievable model today and one suited to the conversational age in which we all live.

A NEW BASIS FOR LEGITIMACY

As noted, the conversational firm that TechCo built is neither entirely post-bureaucratic nor entirely open. The firm as a whole retains a fairly conventional hierarchical structure of authority. Consequently, some may come to the end of this ethnographic tour and still question why TechCo's workforce accepts that hierarchy as legitimate and wonder whether this is all not just some new form of false consciousness. Chapter 2 indicated that the structured upbringing of millennials might make them an extreme case with regard to a preference for hierarchical direction, but that is at most a small piece of the puzzle. A more complete answer to these important questions can be discovered by considering one of the key functions and dilemmas of hierarchy itself and how the conversational firm uniquely addresses it.

On the one hand, scholars who have examined why firms exist in the first place (as opposed to, say, having all work contracted for in the market) often refer to Weber's notion that legitimate authority stems from managerial expertise. These scholars observe that corporate managers hold valuable knowledge and information that employees do not, and that this knowledge and information is quite difficult to transmit.[18] From this perspective, hierarchy is a functional and legitimate way to coordinate: Managers can simply direct employee behavior without employees having to absorb all of the manager's wisdom.

On the other hand, the last several decades have seen a growing recognition of the limits of managerial wisdom and a growing appreciation for the ways in which information and knowledge are distributed throughout the organizational ranks.[19] For example, models like "enabling bureaucracy" and "networked firms" were predicated on the idea that workers' local knowledge often surpassed that of their supervisors and that decision making should be delegated accordingly. This observation suggests that the other basis of authority Weber identified—a manager's hierarchical position—may not be fully legitimate on its own.

Taken together, these two perspectives leave us with a puzzle. Those at the top of a hierarchy often do possess knowledge and a perspective that those below them do not. At the same time, other important knowledge is often dispersed and local, which makes hierarchical authority problematic. The conversational firm takes both realities into account and, in doing so, finds a new basis for legitimacy.

Through the conversational firm's open dialogue—and across all of its open spaces and platforms—managers and workers continually confront one another's knowledge, developing a mutual appreciation for each other's wisdom. As employees weigh in with their own information, ideas, and opinions, executives gain valuable local perspective but also crucial insight into which decisions they can delegate effectively. In turn, as executives share their information and knowledge, they foster a better-informed workforce, which means the scope of delegation may be expanded over time. Most important, the terms of delegation are worked out together. Employees share their opinions on which decisions they feel equipped to make and which they do not, and they develop trust in the decisions that executives choose to retain because they know their voices have informed the decision-making context.

With his two conceptions of authority, Weber seemed to understand that simply occupying a hierarchical position of control was not a basis for complete legitimacy, but he saw no other path at the time. With our new tools for voice and conversation today, there seems to be another way. The conversational firm works—it has legitimacy for employees and is not just false consciousness—because, even as the organization retains a conventional, hierarchical decision-making structure, the decisions themselves are shaped and shifted by the conversational environment and the employee voices within it.[20] Whether employees are given control over the ultimate decision or not, the firm's decision-making process is more legitimate in their eyes because their own voices have played a part in shaping it.

Consider what TechCo was able to achieve with this model. Through its ongoing dialogue, the firm was able to experiment with the use good judgment policy and letting employees sound off on social media, with marketing culture and a physically open workspace, with having no HR department and no org chart. At each decision point, its commitment to open discussion enabled it to leverage the collective wisdom of the entire organization, surfacing and confronting the tradeoffs of both openness and conventional bureaucracy directly, finding its way to a reasonable solution for the given moment and moving forward into the next. What resulted is not entirely ahierarchical, not entirely postbureaucratic, and not as radically open as some might want. But with far more open communication than previously seen, a deeply committed workforce, and a unique capacity for navigating change, it is a radical transformation of the corporate firm nevertheless.

9

THE FUTURE OF THE CONVERSATIONAL FIRM

E
XPERIMENTS LIKE TECHCO suggest that today's new tools for voice and conversation have the potential to permanently change how firms are organized. So we must then ask: Is the conversational firm the firm of the future? As corporate leaders recognize the opportunity to have more committed workers and more adaptive organizations, will this model diffuse across the corporate landscape in years to come?

Employees, after all, are apt to embrace the model just as they have rapidly embraced new forms of voice and conversation in their personal lives. However, unlike the way in which Facebook, Twitter, or texting have transformed personal communication, the future of the conversational firm does not depend solely on individuals' adoption of new technologies. Many of the necessary communicative tools already exist. The key issue seems to be whether and how these tools will be embraced by the corporate hierarchy. The future of the conversational firm, I argue, all depends on the willingness of corporate leaders to support truly open, honest dialogue. This is no small order.

LESSONS FROM TECHCO'S
CONVERSATIONAL FIRM

This book's ethnographic tour of TechCo has revealed some of the work involved in building a conversational firm. It is a project both laden with opportunities and fraught with tradeoffs. For corporate executives hoping to organize their firms more effectively for the social media age, TechCo's experience illuminates many of these opportunities and tradeoffs. This section thus reviews the tour we have taken through TechCo and what we learned from it.

We began by observing Emma at work, a digital native who grew up on social media and whose habits and expectations for voice and conversation represent the very cultural change that inspired TechCo's project in the first place. In chapter 2, we examined the firm's attempt to meet those expectations by creating a more open communication environment for workers like Emma. Rejecting the strict hierarchical control of information and communication often associated with bureaucracy, TechCo executives used a corporate wiki plus a variety of other open spaces and platforms to share information broadly and to promote employee voice. However, open communication did not always come easily, and we saw that TechCo's executives had to remain alert to the many forces that naturally suppress voice and dialogue in a corporate setting (e.g., impression management and fear of manager reprisal). They supplemented public spaces for dialogue with anonymous ones at times, and most of all, they worked hard to foster trust that employee voice was genuinely welcome. In turn, the workforce embraced the voice rights delegated to them, and the result was a type of company-wide conversation and employee engagement foreign to many corporate environments.

In chapter 3, we watched as executives tried to move away from other conventional bureaucratic approaches to control—specifically, centralized decision making and formal rules and guidelines to direct employee behavior. However, blasting open the firm's hierarchy of authority proved even more complicated than blasting open its hierarchy of communication.

In settings like the Experiments Meeting, TechCo executives tried to delegate decision rights, but employees pushed back. The millennial workforce wanted to weigh in and be heard on high-level strategic issues, but they nevertheless respected and valued the firm's hierarchy of authority and expected executives to take ultimate responsibility for firm decisions. Also, when executives tried to do away with formal rules for things like work hours, vacation, and certain job tasks—adopting instead the more informal principle of use good judgment (UGJ)—a fair bit of confusion and chaos ensued. The firm's physical and communicative openness made it difficult to achieve cultural consensus on what "good judgment" even was. Only in engineering—the one corner of the organization where voice and conversation were not as free and open, and where the group's leaders imposed their own definition of good judgment for all to use—did open control in the form of UGJ work seamlessly. From all this, we began to see that building a conversational firm does not necessarily mean relinquishing all hierarchical control over a firm's decision-making environment; in fact, it may necessitate retaining some control.

In chapter 4, we looked at the complicated relationship between open communication and control from another angle. Whereas bureaucratic firms have historically put strict limits on who can speak on their behalf, TechCo gave its workforce external voice rights, letting them say whatever they wanted on social media so long as they (again) used good judgment. From Brian's story, we learned that a conversational firm can, indeed, delegate external voice today far more broadly than firms have in the past, but this is possible precisely because the openness of social media makes any deviance immediately visible to executives and because the firm still retains a key form of hierarchical control—namely, the threat of firing those who speak out of turn. Here again we encountered the paradox that certain types of hierarchical control may actually be necessary for the sort of open communication upon which conversational firms are built.

In chapter 5, we followed TechCo as it embraced a new approach to corporate culture increasingly popular in the high-tech world. Rather than use culture as a mechanism to bolster bureaucratic control by socializing individuals into their appropriate corporate roles, TechCo executives saw culture as something to be marketed for recruitment purposes. By attracting like-minded individuals, they hoped to diminish the need for bureaucratic control entirely. However, when executives declared the company's culture to the world, they momentarily took control of corporate communication to promote a culture that purportedly supported open communication. This did not go over well with a workforce that had come to expect voice and conversation, and only after executives shifted to using the culture deck as a basis for dialogue with the staff was morale restored. From their experience, we learned that marketing an open culture may help a firm recruit like-minded employees and minimize bureaucratic control in certain respects, but a firm that has committed itself to conversation will need to use such cultural decrees as a starting point for internal voice and dialogue as much as an external identity claim in the labor market.

In chapter 6, the true nature of TechCo's conversational model was revealed. Although TechCo executives associated their corporate revolution with the rejection of conventional bureaucratic practices such as HR, the workforce did not. The commitment employees held their executives to concerned voice and conversation, and they demonstrated this quite clearly when they began demanding that HR be adopted. Whereas executives believed HR was merely a dysfunctional "myth and ceremony" of bureaucratic organizing, employees increasingly concluded that an HR department and formal personnel policies would afford them greater openness and transparency than the absence of them was allowing.[1] From their calls for HR, we saw that bureaucratic practices are not always just myth and ceremony; sometimes they are the most open option available. Most important, we saw that a conversational firm is predicated on the ability to talk such matters out.

In chapter 7, we concluded our tour of TechCo with a tour of its wide-open workspaces. In its physical environment, the firm rejected bureaucracy's isolating office structure as well as its strict separation of personal and corporate property. With the noise and mess and the buzz and vibrancy that resulted, the workplace's physical openness became a metaphor and summary of what we had seen throughout the book. Specifically, a conversational environment presents a number of challenges, but it also offers a corresponding set of benefits and the ability for executives and workers to confront the costs head-on in open dialogue.

In chapter 8, I drew out the theoretical implications of this new organizational model. I argued that with today's tools and platforms, it is now possible to rethink the firm by rethinking communication. Organizations can support far more employee voice and conversation than ever before, and this constitutes a radical transformation of the firm and our understanding of it.

BUILDING MORE CONVERSATIONAL FIRMS

For corporate leaders wishing to rethink communication and build a conversational firm of their own, the key lesson is that open, honest dialogue does not come easily. Building a conversational firm may not mean forsaking every element of hierarchical authority, but it is not as simple as adopting a corporate wiki or chat system either. For starters, the tools themselves will not generate more open conversation. Some scholars even argue the tools do the opposite. In her books *Alone Together* and *Reclaiming Conversation*, technology theorist Sherry Turkle argues that our general human capacity for authentic dialogue is declining, not expanding, in the social media age.[2] She observes that people perform particularly shallow versions of themselves on the open platforms of social media, using tweets and Facebook posts to project how they want to appear rather than who they really are and what they really think. In hierarchical firms, where employees are conversing with the managers and executives who evaluate them and control their professional fate, the pressure to present an appealing image to those in authority is great, and this could easily suppress dissenting voices and close off honest exchange.

The fact of the matter is new technologies never carry an inherent transformative capacity.[3] They afford only the changes we are willing to make. As we saw at TechCo, the same tools that can support open dialogue can just as easily be used for impression management, bullying, surveillance, and the like. Organizational leaders need to be genuinely committed to using today's new platforms and technologies to promote open conversation. If employees try to express their honest opinions, but management then punishes dissenters, the tendency to be inauthentic will quickly dominate. The conversational environment will shut down as employees silence themselves, saying only what they believe management wants to hear.

The sort of open dialogue that makes a conversational firm work also requires a diversity of perspectives. If only certain employees feel comfortable speaking up, and others remain silent, the power of the conversational model will be limited. Moreover, when companies use social media to market their culture and attract like-minded employees, there is a risk of creating an echo chamber in which the existence of dissenting voices is limited from the outset and management only encounters views identical to their own. Marketing culture may be useful for building a workforce committed to the organization's project and philosophy, but corporate leaders must walk a fine line so as not to build an organization incapable of challenging their own conventional wisdom when necessary. These concerns are worth heeding. As open as TechCo's conversational environment was, we still saw that not everyone was equally comfortable participating in it, and the firm's corporate philosophy and marketed culture attracted a homogeneous workforce in terms of age and outlook. To harness the full potential of open dialogue, firms like it need to work continually to support and attract a multiplicity of voices and perspectives.

Corporate leaders trying to build conversational firms from scratch as TechCo has done will encounter all sorts of difficult tensions and tradeoffs like this. Those trying to transform conventional firms into more conversational ones may face an even more complex set of issues. In both cases, executives must be ready to confront all of the challenges head-on. Most of all, executives must recognize that the whole point of conversation is to surface the tensions and probe the tradeoffs of any new endeavors they attempt. This requires a thick skin and a tolerance for a lot more noise than most managers are used to. Some comments will sting, not every idea expressed will be a thoughtful one, and not every conversation will move things forward. Successful leaders, though, will accept the noise and discomfort as the price to be paid. Only when a workforce trusts its leaders not to suppress the sometimes uncomfortable discussions that arise along the way will employees be patient with the chaos and uncertainty that accompany change. Only when executives have proven that they are really listening can the conversational model work and allow that capacity for change so unique to it.

For corporate leaders willing to suffer the slings and arrows of building a conversational firm, this ability to confront and manage the complexities of change may be their greatest reward. By promoting voice and conversation with its workforce and not wavering from that commitment, TechCo's executives were able to challenge convention repeatedly, experiment with approaches that seemed better suited to today's environment, and then continually iterate and improve as they learned from the open, ongoing dialogue that followed. Fostering such a capacity would seem invaluable for any firm. After all, time marches on, and social media will not be the last major technological and cultural development that firms have to face. Harnessing social media to build a conversational firm today may, in fact, be just the way to navigate whatever tomorrow brings.

Consider, for example, how a conversational firm can confront new technological developments. A company's executives or staff cannot know the precise impact of a given technology, nor can they predict exactly the contingencies that may arise from its adoption. This is obvious even today. Numerous enterprise social media tools are available to corporations, and more seem to come onto the market each year. Products such as wikis, Slack, Yammer, HipChat, TinyPulse, and many others enable all sorts of new ways for people inside organizations to share information and ideas. However, each is distinct, and each presents its own specific affordances and constraints, which are difficult to foresee at the outset.[4] TechCo demonstrated some of the benefits and challenges of a corporate wiki, but the specifics of its experience will not translate exactly to these other platforms or even to wikis in different organizational contexts. Opinions and perceptions about any given tool are likely to vary across individuals and firms—what is perceived to be a means for voice and freedom in one context may be seen as a nuisance or a mechanism of control in another.

One generalizable lesson from TechCo's experience, however, is the way in which a firm can support an ongoing dialogue about new technologies. Inside TechCo, there were frequent meta-conversations about how conversations on the wiki were changing as the company grew. There were discussions about the "noise" as more and more voices sounded off on the wiki, discussions about trolling and appropriate norms for engagement, discussions about authenticity and impression management on the platform. There were also discussions about what sort of new tools might be of use, which, in turn, led to experimentation with home-grown solutions and alternative products available in the market. In short, one way for corporate leaders to navigate any technological change is to support an open, ongoing dialogue about it and to try to leverage the organization's collective wisdom to understand the technology's affordances, limitations, and unexpected consequences. A conversational firm is built to support just these sorts of meta-discussions.[5]

Something similar can be said for navigating cultural changes in the labor force. The business press has had a field day in recent years writing about the millennial workforce, chronicling what they are supposedly like, how they are different from generations past, and what companies must do to accommodate their unique ways.[6] Generations that follow will undoubtedly intrigue and mystify us anew, sparking uncertainty and speculation about their unique ways and what they mean for organizations. What we can take from TechCo's experience is that, no matter the public rhetoric, corporate leaders should never assume they know exactly what any group of employees wants or what will make for an optimally productive workplace for them. Instead, executives should engage those employees in conversation to continually probe and decipher that.

TechCo's gen X leaders built a firm they believed millennials wanted but then learned along the way that some of their assumptions (in particular around the workforce's views of authority and control) were not entirely accurate. Also, what the workforce did want from their organizational environment—what they saw as enabling or constraining practices and features—changed over time. For instance, it was only as the staff aged that employees began to see value in certain HR policies such as parental leave.

In each case, though, the firm was able to learn and adjust because it encouraged its employees to speak up. As with technological change, the key seems not to organize for the change we imagine or hope is unfolding but to understand the reality we face in any given moment so that we can navigate it effectively.[7] The open dialogue that unfolds inside a conversational firm is a powerful way to surface a multidimensional understanding of today's reality, to reflect on ways to confront it, and to realize when even more changes are afoot.

By supporting such dialogue, corporate leaders may find their way to more thoughtful, self-reflective organizations overall. One of Turkle's key concerns with social media is how our performances on these platforms can hinder our ability to engage in the sort of solitary self-reflection through which we come to know ourselves and gain true wisdom. Turkle may well be right when it comes to our personal uses of these technologies, but when we bring the spirit and tools of social media inside firms to create more conversational environments, perhaps it can have an opposite effect on our organizational lives. When TechCo marketed its culture on social media, employees spoke up and raised concerns about the external presentation. Together, executives and workers began to discuss the gaps between the organization's public, aspirational self and its internal, actual self and how they might move closer to the ideal. What resulted at the organizational level was just the sort of mindful self-reflection and wisdom that Turkle says is being sacrificed in our individual lives. Because organizations are collective entities, they can only come to know themselves through collective reflection, and that, it seems, is the real power of a conversational firm.

For years, the seminal challenge facing corporate executives has been that of control. We have seen from TechCo's experience that that challenge remains. But today corporate leaders can begin to think of organizing as a problem of collective self-reflection too. Building more conversational firms is not going to be easy, but it seems achievable now, and the payoff for those who do it is likely to be great. What firm does not want a more deeply engaged and committed workforce? What firm does not want to improve its capacity for change—to be able to challenge the market's, and even its own, conventional wisdom in order to adapt to the present moment and face tomorrow? Today's environment presents many new challenges and complicated tradeoffs but also significant opportunities. So will tomorrow's. For those willing to embrace it, a conversational firm seems a powerful tool for navigating it all.

METHODOLOGICAL APPENDIX

N OW IT IS my turn to be open. In this appendix, I aim to be "uncomfortably transparent" (to borrow a phrase from Anil) about my research process and the decisions I made along the way.

WHY TECHCO?

I had heard a lot about TechCo before I thought about studying them. The firm was a darling of the technology trade press, which I still followed as a holdover from my days working in the industry. Also, a college classmate of mine started working at TechCo in 2008, and ever since he joined I had been equally captivated and perplexed by his stories of life inside the company.

I was surprised by how little of what Greg said resonated with my experiences of tech darlings in the first Internet era. Gone were the cubicles and offices, org charts, and standard work hours. Instead, Greg spoke of unlimited vacation, free beer, hours spent debating issues on a wiki, and a management team that shared the sort of information most executives preferred to guard. In the late 1990s and early 2000s, I had seen Web 1.0 firms break with convention by offering playful amenities like foosball tables and unlimited Pop-Tarts, but TechCo's unconventionality seemed to run deeper. It seemed to guide the firm's entire approach to organizing.

TechCo put no restrictions on employees' social media use, and Greg posted about events inside the company on his personal Twitter and Facebook accounts. His posts led me to those of other TechCo employees, and then to the company's own Twitter feed and blog. Over the years, as I read about yoga classes in conference rooms, pop stars performing at company events, and company-wide Hack Nights extending late into the evening, I waivered between thinking TechCo might be the firm of the future and thinking it all sounded rather ridiculous. Either way, I found myself checking for Greg's online posts, wanting to learn more.

Soon I came to realize that what I had thought of as one unconventional firm was actually representative of a broader phenomenon. Not only the high-tech trade press but also major papers like the *New York Times* and *Wall Street Journal* began reporting on a slew of Web 2.0 companies that sounded a lot like TechCo. As several other college and business school classmates entered these firms, I heard more and more stories like Greg's. I became intrigued by the self-conscious nature of this apparent organizational revolution. TechCo and its Web 2.0 peers were publicly rejecting the conventions of bureaucratic organizing, and in their pronouncements about change, they appeared to be drawing on the tools and spirit of social media. Openness and sharing were the watchwords of this revolutionary sect.

As an ethnographer, I have always been guided more by my interest in particular phenomena than by some overarching theoretical agenda, and the phenomena that attract me tend to lie at the intersection of economic and sociocultural trends. In the past, I had been driven into the field by a curiosity to understand such things as the rise of private equity as a powerful force in American capitalism, the commercialization of motherhood and the booming stress reduction industry, and the lucrative but often morally suspect personal injury market. The rise of social media was the latest cultural trend to capture my attention, and here were firms seemingly inspired by these new media to reimagine the corporate form.

Could this work, I wondered. Was any of it even real? Maybe it was all talk—a savvy presentation of corporate self that masked the same bureaucratic and hierarchical practices firms have had for years. Then again, maybe it would carry lessons for how corporations really could change. One December morning I woke up and decided I had to study TechCo.

NEGOTIATING ACCESS AND ANONYMITY

I asked Greg what he thought about my studying the firm, and when he responded positively, I asked for an introduction to the executive team. Just after New Year's 2013 I headed to TechCo's offices for the first time. In one of the glass-walled conference rooms I would come to know well, I met with Keith, the company's COO.

I made my pitch, explaining that I was interested in understanding high-tech culture in the Web 2.0 and social media enabled world we now inhabit. I explained that I was particularly intrigued by TechCo's message of organizational change and curious to understand how its attempts to buck convention worked on the ground. I was not a consultant, I clarified, but a researcher who wanted to learn from TechCo's experience. My goal was to understand the organization's culture from the perspective of its members, and my ethnographic fieldwork would entail "living" inside the company for a period of time to observe its daily activities and to conduct interviews.

I promised to share my findings at the end and hoped my observations might be of some value, perhaps enabling the company to see itself in new or deeper ways. I gave Keith the names of two ethnographic monographs that represented the sort of research I conduct: Katherine Chen's *Enabling Creative Chaos,* which in my opinion was a flattering portrayal of an organization and its leaders, and Gideon Kunda's *Engineering Culture,* which in my opinion was not. Finally, I offered to share some of my own past papers. (Later, another executive took me up on this offer, although I do not know how widely, if at all, my prior work was read and circulated.)

Keith was responsive to my pitch. Given the company's rapid growth, he said there would be value in "just having someone come in and tell us what the company's culture even is now." We discussed how any study of

TechCo would have to entail studying the wiki and its other communication platforms because so much of company life unfolded there. Keith also noted that much of TechCo's cultural past was recorded on the wiki so it might offer useful historical perspective as well. As for TechCo's message of change, Keith said he, too, was interested in how some of its more unconventional practices were working on the ground. "TechCo was founded on the idea that the old way of marketing and selling—the old technologies—don't work," he said. "I think the same principles apply to how you deal with employees. The old ways don't work." But how well the new ones were working, and what employees thought of them, he suggested, might still be an open question.

When I met other TechCo executives over the coming weeks, they expressed similar sentiments. Eric and Anil, as committed to rethinking everything as they were, saw value in the line of inquiry. In our first meeting, they told me that they grappled constantly with what—and how much—to rethink, and they said they often worried about the risks of bucking convention. It was important to ask "What if we're wrong? What if you need all this [conventional] stuff?" Eric said, adding, "It'll be interesting to see if you come away thinking we're nuts."

Their reactions intrigued me. I seemed to have stumbled upon a management team self-reflective enough to ask the same questions an outsider like me wanted to ask: What was the place's culture really like? How were their attempts to reinvent the firm going over on the ground? Was this all nuts? When my fieldwork got under way, I learned that the workforce was grappling with the very same questions. In short, I got lucky. I had found an organization as interested in my questions as I was. I hoped Hortense Powdermaker's observation was right that "when a topic is interesting to both anthropologist and informants, the data on it are usually full."[1]

In that first meeting with Keith and in my subsequent discussions with other executives, I broached the issue of confidentiality. I explained that I wanted to maintain employee confidentiality so the staff could feel comfortable speaking openly and without risk of reprisal. When quoting from confidential discussions with employees in my research, I would change names and details so that individuals could not be identified by their peers or supervisors.

I worried about how this would go over. I knew that TechCo promoted itself as radically open and transparent, but I did not yet know the extent or nature of that radicalness. What if it meant nothing at all was private? As it turned out, my promise of confidentiality was a selling point to the management team. For all the multiple points of communication they had with the workforce, they were not naïve to the fact that information and opinions were filtered and warped as they traveled to the top. They hoped my safeguarding of people's confidentiality might encourage even more openness from the workforce.

During these early discussions, executives and I also discussed the issue of anonymizing TechCo itself in my research. At least one member of the executive team suggested that naming the company might be consistent with their commitment to openness. Some others felt that protecting the company's identity would be wise, mainly to ensure that everyone would be open with me. Anonymizing a company to manage reputational risk to the organization is common in organizational ethnographies. I stated clearly that I could make no commitment regarding the nature of my findings or arguments. Given that I had never met anyone on the senior management team before Greg facilitated my meeting with Keith, I expected there might be skepticism of a stranger asking for such deep access into the firm.

From my perspective, I felt anonymity was going to be crucial for the integrity and validity of this particular study. After all, TechCo was an organization that publicly declared its "radical openness" and touted its unconventional ways by regularly sharing flattering details about its internal organization online. Yet my central question was what life was really like at TechCo. I wanted to know how radical their openness really was, and whether it was experienced as good or bad by those subject to it. If I could not penetrate the firm's backstage—if executives or employees let concern about the company's reputation influence their interactions with me—the study would be a failure, and I would collect little more than I could gather from the company's blog posts and Twitter feed.

Accordingly, I entered into a nondisclosure agreement (NDA) with the company at the start of the project. Under the NDA, TechCo gave me full control over whatever findings and arguments I might make in publications or presentations resulting from my research, and I committed to make reasonable efforts to disguise TechCo's identity in those publications and presentations. As discussed later in this appendix, the question of how much to disguise the company, and whether or not to anonymize it at all, arose once again when I had a complete draft of the book. During the period I collected data, however, everyone's understanding was that I would not name the firm in any research resulting from my fieldwork.

ENTRY AND DATA COLLECTION

As soon as we signed the NDA, the company gave me complete access to its wiki and chat system for my analysis, as well my own TechCo email and calendar account for communication. The latter provided my first lesson in openness at TechCo: like everyone there, I could now see the personal calendar of every other employee, including the executives.

Upon the recommendation of several people, I took to the wiki to introduce myself and the project to the workforce. I emphasized the academic nature of the project and explained that as an ethnographer I studied companies "the way anthropologists have traditionally studied remote tribes—by living with them and asking lots of questions." I promised not to disclose what individuals told me in confidence to others at the company, and I explained that I would disguise both the company's and individuals' names in my work. I wrote that I would follow up with a company-wide email including more details and a consent form for those interested in being interviewed or shadowed while they worked. In the comments to the wiki thread, one employee asked if he and others would be able to see the final results of my study, and I said yes. As I had in past organizational ethnographies, I felt it would be important to present my findings to the entire company, not just the executives, once my fieldwork was complete, and this was something Keith had wanted too when we first spoke.

During my first few weeks at the company, I focused on getting the lay of the land. TechCo was growing so rapidly that it was running new hire training every month, and I decided to participate in this rite of passage. As Gideon Kunda's study of a high-tech firm and multiple studies of socialization in the professions attest, how an organization trains its people provides a useful window into its culture. This proved true at TechCo. My later analyses were aided by having been able to see how the company introduced new employees to things like use good judgment, the open office layout, and the role of the wiki. I got an inkling of things to come when I noticed that several presenters flashed an org chart on the classroom screen by way of introducing themselves and their role at the company, only then to apologize and note that TechCo did not technically have an org chart. As I participated in the weeklong training class, I also got to know a few of the new hires. At lunch, I heard what colleges they had gone to and, if they had worked before, where and what it had been like. I asked how they had found their way to TechCo and what they expected and hoped it would be like. When I followed up with several of these classmates later in the study, it was useful to compare those early expectations with their evolving understanding of the organization.

The wiki was another valuable starting point, and as soon as the company granted me access, I dove in, employing the techniques of digital ethnography.[2] Just as Keith had said, the wiki offered a rich chronicle of the company's entire history. I could see seminal debates and decisions from the past exactly as they had unfolded on the platform, not as they were filtered through people's retrospective accounts. Throughout the study, I spent hours reading and analyzing old wiki posts to understand the past and the players and to contextualize what I was seeing today.

The wiki was also a window into the immediate scene. Doctoral students often ask me how an ethnographer knows where to look and what to ask when first entering a setting. I tell them to train their ethnographic eye toward two things that more often than not overlap.[3] First, look where your subjects are looking. That is, study what your subjects find most compelling and puzzling about their own world—what excites them, what baffles and worries them, what sparks conflict among them. When I logged onto the wiki each morning, those issues appeared right before my eyes in the top trending posts, and as I began my fieldwork in earnest, I focused my observations accordingly. Ethnographers Colin Jerolmack and Shamus Khan have noted that interviews are most powerful when they probe people's definition of the situation as it is being worked out in real time. Because of the wiki, I knew what key issues or events were unfolding on any given day or week, and I used my interviews to probe staffs' in situ perspectives on them.[4] The second thing I tell my students to look for are instances in which people say or do something unexpected relative to our current theories. So many of TechCo's wiki discussions defied my theoretical expectations about things like employee voice, hierarchy, and culture that the platform guided my research in that way as well. Over the course of the study, I tracked and analyzed more than four hundred and fifty wiki discussions, past and present.

Shortly after entering the field, I also began to conduct formal interviews and to shadow employees. I distributed my IRB consent form in a company-wide email and explained that if people were interested in being interviewed or scheduling a time for me to watch them work, they could reply "I agree to participate" to that email. After the email, a steady stream of "I agree to participate" responses came in, and this continued for several weeks. However, to address selective nonresponse bias and obtain as representative a sample as possible, I also obtained a list of all employees at the company around this time and sorted it by function and (where it was possible to tell) rank. As I began to construct my interview sample, I randomly selected names from each function and level. If these individuals had already consented, I contacted them to set up a time. If they had not, I reached out to ask if they might.

As my fieldwork progressed, I came across certain people whose perspectives I thought would be uniquely valuable, and I sought them out specifically. For example, I oversampled executives to make sure I captured that perspective in addition to the staff's.[5] I also tried to note any time an interviewee spoke of a disagreement with another individual at the company. I thought counterperspectives and contested meanings might surface if I explored this, so I made a point of reaching out to the other individual to chat informally or to see if they might be willing to be interviewed (careful, of course, never to reference the original employee and to maintain both employees' confidentiality).

In total, I conducted just under one hundred interviews and reinterviews with seventy-six employees during the initial study, each lasting one hour or longer. In addition, I interviewed a handful of former employees to understand their perspectives. In the year after the study, I stayed in touch with and interviewed (in some cases, multiple times) nine individuals at the company to track developments and to follow up on certain issues I wanted to learn more about.

During the course of my interviews in the field, I often asked if I might shadow the individual in some aspect of his or her work. Employees generously let me listen in on sales calls and customer support calls, accompany them to individual or group training sessions, sit in on one-on-one meetings with their managers or direct reports, and just generally follow them around as they went about their daily work. In addition to these formal shadowing appointments, I also regularly hung out with staff in the company kitchen and common areas, grabbed coffee and lunch with them at the popular local haunts, and in the process had hundreds of informal conversations about work and life at TechCo.

Early in the study, I realized TechCo had lots of meetings, and the company gave me broad and deep access in this regard. Meetings quickly became a staple of my observational diet. I attended those meetings that were open to all employees, such as the quarterly company meetings during which executives took questions from the workforce and reported on the state of the business over the past quarter. I attended the multiple recurring meetings held to encourage information sharing across the organization such as those in which the product team demoed new product features to the rest of the company and those in which the marketing, sales, and services groups reported their performance over the past month. I also joined the hundreds of TechCoers who regularly sat in on "TechTalks," lunchtime presentations delivered by employees or visitors on topics ranging from positive attitude to what TechCo could learn from Apple.

I received access to numerous smaller, departmental-level meetings, attending a daylong planning meeting of a product training team as well as regularly held sales management team meetings and monthly marketing team meetings. Special purpose meetings proved particularly interesting because they often brought together people from multiple departments to address an important issue. For example, I observed a cross-functional group trying to redesign the front-end customer experience, and I followed preparation for the company's annual user conference by joining the group that met weekly in the months leading up to the event to coordinate its planning and execution.

Some of my most fruitful observations came from cross-hierarchical meetings. These included recurring events such as the Experiments Meeting described in chapter 3 where junior staff members presented new business ideas to executives, as well as monthly reporting meetings in which sales and marketing staff presented their results to executives and the group collectively troubleshot issues in the business. (Before one of these, I sat in on a fascinating "meeting about the meeting," in which the group of executives and employees grappled together with how the staff could become more comfortable sharing negative information with the management team while knowing that the management team was also evaluating them.)

As described in chapter 7, I followed around the team of architects as they met with various employees about the company's office space. I sat in on meetings of the newly formed women's group, and in one of my more memorable fieldwork experiences, I participated in a training session in which we all took personality tests and then shared the results with one another. (I was grateful when my personality type suggested I was conscientious, albeit a bit dull. After taking the test, I had begun to panic over how it would look if the researcher in the room was revealed to have a personality type known for snap judgments or lack of attention to detail.) After hours I stayed for Hack Nights and attended out-of-office events like the Mystery Dinner profiled in chapter 2 and employee recognition award dinners held at nearby restaurants. In short, my approach was to observe people interacting in as many different settings as I could and to follow events over time by returning to the same gatherings again and again. When I was not observing interactions in person, I was often observing them on the wiki and in the HipChat chat rooms.

While I was immersed inside TechCo, I also followed press coverage of the company and tracked its external communications, observing management presentations to industry analysts and attending the company's annual user conference during the year of my study and the year following. I tracked news and social media coverage of speeches the executives gave around the country, and I read the company's blog and social media posts every day.

The period of intensive fieldwork lasted ten months from February through November. For six of these months, I typically spent four days a week at the company. I slowed down to several days a week after that, eventually making more targeted visits to meet with people and follow specific events I was tracking over time. In the field, I took notes in a spiral-bound reporter's notebook, getting down as much direct dialogue and interaction as I could. (If I was in a meeting in which others were typing notes on their laptops, I took notes directly onto my computer). At night, I typed up the day's notes, accumulating 1,678 pages over the course of the study. I used weekends to write analytical memos on what I had seen in the field the prior week, generating 350 pages of in-process analysis and reflections over the course of the study. Taken together, the primary data for this study are my observations of actual and digital life at TechCo, the formal interviews I conducted with organizational members, and the hundreds of informal conversations I had during the course of my fieldwork.

REFLECTIONS ON RAPPORT AND COMFORT IN THE FIELD

STUDYING UP, DOWN, AND ALL AROUND

Some organizational ethnographers take as fact the notion that it is easier to build rapport with individuals lower in the hierarchy than those at the top. My colleague John Van Maanen has advised, "Members of the lower caste will make better informants (reveal more). Not only do they have less to lose objectively but they are under less strain to appear faultless to either their internal or external audiences."[6] I do not doubt the experience of other ethnographers on this point, but I have not found this to be a general rule of ethnography in my experience. Across all of my projects, I have found both executives and employees to be both open to and skeptical of the research process (and me).

Contrary to what others may have encountered, the employees I have met have always seemed acutely aware of just how much they have to lose (their jobs, for one). As a result, promising them confidentiality from supervisors and peers has proven crucial for gaining their trust. At the same time, executives have often been quite willing to engage when the topic is of interest to them, even in settings like the closely guarded private equity industry. In short, I have had to work equally hard, although in different ways, to earn each group's trust. My experience at TechCo was no different in this regard.

When researchers talk of difficulty accessing executives, one argument they make is that the corporate ethnographer must pick a side and study either employees or management, the logic being that rapport with one group precludes rapport with the other. I do not agree. Gaining access up and down a hierarchy is certainly challenging. Trust is not easily earned, and there have been days in all of my field studies when I have felt like a double agent trying to identify and connect with people who did not see eye-to-eye with one another—people whose interests were not aligned given the positions in the hierarchy they occupied. And yet the burden rests on us as ethnographers to find a way past these obstacles. Given that so much of the drama of organizational life (and social life in general) stems from contestations over meaning by people who are positioned differently but must nevertheless coordinate, we miss the point entirely if we include only one party to the contest. As ethnographers, we have known for a long time now that our craft is not about discovering a single native point of view but about discovering the multiple points of view in a setting. If we fail to capture the beliefs and values of one level of a hierarchy, we fail to capture the working of that hierarchy.

Over the years, some corporate ethnographers have openly identified with the workers at their field sites. This can be a perfectly legitimate strategy depending on one's research question, but it closes off other questions. So does open identification with executives. If we want access to all levels of a hierarchy, what we need is the "psychological mobility" to move between those levels, not a singular identification with just one.[7] Accordingly, I have tried to follow Powdermaker's advice when navigating hierarchies at TechCo and elsewhere. She counseled that ethnographers must maintain compassion for, and a genuine curiosity to understand, all of their research subjects, not just those with whom they most identify. She chastised fieldworkers who think they have to "take a side," just as she chastised herself for having done that in her study of Hollywood, writing, "An exclusive identification with the underdog (or with the top ranks) may prevent the necessary social, intellectual and psychological mobility necessary for fieldwork in a complex power structure."[8] This is not to say we need to like every one of our research subjects, but it is to say that if we want to understand them, we need to respect their human dignity and maintain a genuine curiosity for their lived experience.

While in the field, I tried to remain equally curious about the perspectives of TechCo's workforce and its executives. My attempt to extend ethnographic empathy to all subjects is evident in the text when I move between levels, presenting a situation from the perspective of the employees first and then from the perspective of the company's leadership next (or vice versa). Some academic readers of this book have responded with surprise and even some dismay that I presented an empathetic understanding of the executives' perspective at times and was not as critical of TechCo's management team as they expected me to be. My response is this: Over the years, fieldworkers have extended ethnographic empathy to criminals and gang leaders, sidewalk vendors and chefs. When we do the same for corporate executives, I believe many of the assumed barriers to access fall away and our portraits of corporate life become more full. In my interactions with both workers and executives, I tried to convey my genuine desire to understand and learn from them, and I hope this is reflected in the portrait I have drawn.

As an aside, I should note that there are always more groups we could, and often should, include in our studies and to whom we should extend our ethnographic empathy. As the anthropologist Joseph Mitchell once noted, "The unit of interacting relationships . . . is larger than the tribe,"[9] and every organization has numerous relationships beyond that of its management and full-time staff. A coincidence at TechCo drilled this lesson home for me.

One day while chatting with two women from TechCo's marketing group in a lounge area, I looked up and saw my high school prom date standing next to a ladder. It turned out that he worked on the crew building out TechCo's new office space. I had not seen him since high school, but we now started running into one another nearly every day. Because of the unusual coincidence—and undoubtedly because of the slight awkwardness of it all—I never failed to notice when he or his fellow electricians walked by. Then again, I figured everyone noticed them; amidst a sea of skinny jeans, ballet flats, and Chuck Taylors, his crew's identical yellow T-shirts, baggy jeans, and work boots marked them as "other."

As time went by, however, I sensed they might be invisible to some at the company, or at least a taken for granted part of the background. Like other invisible workers, they were in the scene but not entirely of it, going unnoticed as they laid cable in the backs of unfinished conference rooms while workers held meetings at makeshift tables, dodging people in the halls as they wheeled dollies stacked with digital screens on route for installation.[10] Yet their experience of TechCo was as legitimate as anyone's, and when I bumped into them a few times on cigarette breaks outside the office, I got to hear a bit about it. It turns out my prom date and his colleagues would have made pretty good ethnographers themselves, for they had their own incisive observations of life at TechCo.

In the end, I had to draw some boundaries around the project, and I did not formally pursue, nor do I include in this book, the perspectives of these contract workers, or those of TechCo's investors or customers (groups I have included in past organizational studies). I did observe customer interactions at the office and on phone calls, and I tracked TechCo's exchanges with them on social media. However, the questions I was most interested in for this study pertained to the manager–employee relationship, so I trained my eye there, even while knowing this left other paths unexplored.

COMFORT IN THE FIELD

Certain aspects of my own biography may have aided my access and integration at TechCo. Being on the faculty at MIT when asking for access to a tech firm helps. It is also possible that I was particularly comfortable engaging with TechCo management, and they with me, because of my past experience interacting with high-tech executives when I worked in technology investment banking and when I later reported to executives at a software firm. I had been in my early twenties when I worked in tech and had those experiences, so there was also much I identified with in TechCo's young staff.

Leveraging one's biography to build rapport with subjects, however, can cut both ways. When I told employees I had worked in software, they invariably asked which firm, and I seemed only to lose credibility and date myself when they learned it was a Web 1.0 dinosaur by their accounting. As for Eric and Anil, 1990s tech firms epitomized the "old school" thinking they were rebelling against. Eric liked to say that he "underrated" experience, and I noticed that employees who had worked in more conventional firms almost never referenced these past experiences in meetings or conversations. A hiring manager explained it to me one day, saying, "We rarely hire people from other places, and when we do, their experience is discounted. I have to coach people not to talk about their experience. They have to frame it as an idea that came to them rather than something their old company used to do." I stopped mentioning my experience in high tech after that.

In truth, I never felt fully comfortable at TechCo regardless of whether my past work experience helped or hurt. Ethnography is not a comfortable practice in general, and I felt more out of place at TechCo than I had in prior field sites. Part of it was probably my age. Thirty-five at the time, I was one of the older women at the company. I was excited to see so many young workers and intrigued to learn the millennial perspective if there was one. (When starting out, I did not take the popular press coverage of millennials as fact but rather as an empirical question to explore.) When I saw they often had a different take on issues than I would have assumed, it was both refreshing and intellectually intriguing. Sometimes it was humbling. One day at a company sponsored dinner, I chatted with a twenty-five-year-old sales rep. He was well spoken and confident, and it was easy to forget that I had a decade on him. He asked what I had found most surprising about TechCo so far. After stumbling around for an answer, I finally blurted out something about it having such a young workforce. He laughed and said, "Yeah, I guess so! And it's not like you're even that old a lady." I bought my first tube of antiwrinkle cream on the way home that evening.[11]

It was not just my age though. It was my temperament too. I am an introvert who craves structure and routine, and I was operating inside a company that privileged communication over control and had a unique tolerance for disorder and chaos. In addition, the whole place operated at warp speed relative to my natural cadence. After my first two weeks in the field, not a week went by that someone didn't stop to ask me what my findings were. I knew I couldn't answer with the truth—that, honestly, I'd probably have no idea until a year or so after I left the field and had time to analyze my data and really think about it. I felt called upon to have a clever 140-character takeaway, but all I had were some inchoate thoughts.

Most of the time, it felt like I had landed in a world for which I was severely maladapted. Even as I was studying it, the extent of sharing and openness often took me by surprise. One employee tweeted about a conversation we had right after we finished talking, and I felt violated until I reminded myself that I had extended him confidentiality, not the other way around. The most embarrassing part of it all was that I was studying a firm steeped in social media while being fairly uncomfortable on those media myself. The irony is that I am fascinated by social media as technological and cultural phenomena yet rather ill-suited for them personally. Sharing personal information unnerves me, and I can never settle on what about myself I want to present on any given profile. In fact, even though I spend hours a day on Twitter, Facebook, Instagram, LinkedIn, and the like, I do not at this writing have my own accounts. (I log on through my husband's or mother's accounts, the utter absurdity of which I fully appreciate.)

None of this went unnoticed by my digital natives. People looked me up online and asked why I was not on one or another platform. Several commented that my "personal brand" could stand to be upgraded, and one young woman generously offered to help me set up a personal website that could promote my academic work better. (By the time this book comes out, maybe I will have followed some of their counsel.)

Finally, as is always the case in fieldwork, I had to work hard to check my own biases throughout. I am, by nature, a cynic and a skeptic. When I saw people doing push-ups in the lobby or when I overheard someone suggest that people should carry a card with the results of their personality test on it "so people know what type you are," I had to stop myself from a knee-jerk, "Are you shitting me?" and instead explore what those actions and experiences meant to them. Also, I tend to take little at face value, and a fascination with the gaps between what people say and do is probably why I became an ethnographer in the first place. If anyone was going to cursorily dismiss TechCo as all talk and no walk, it was me.

If I had a saving grace from all this, it was simply how interesting I found the setting. Throughout the study, I could not shake my intense curiosity about the organization and its people. The short, simple question Clifford Geertz said all ethnographers should ask—"What's going on here?"— seemed to play on repeat in my head. Asking it again and again helped drive me past those knee-jerk reactions and brought me to what I hope is a deeper understanding of the organization. It also gave me a deeper understanding of what Geertz meant when he wrote, "Understanding a people's culture exposes their normalness, without reducing their particularity. The more I manage to follow what the Moroccans are up to, the more logical, and the more singular, they seem."[12] Yes, what I saw often looked weird to me at first—that's why I had been interested in the first place—but the "natives" are never fools. To understand their behavior from their point of view—to see how it is sensible and rational to them, not wrong or absurd— is to achieve real ethnographic understanding.

Personally, I think it is impossible to shut off our natural emotions and dispositions during fieldwork. But I think it is quite possible and often quite fruitful to use them as cues to dig deeper.[13] Some of the deepest insights

I gained from TechCo came from events or incidents that I initially wanted to dismiss as absurd but that my curiosity forced me to explore further. I like to think that TechCo made a bit more of an optimist out of me in the process.

MANAGING ONE'S (WHOLE) SELF IN THE FIELD

There is another reason I was uncomfortable: fieldwork is excruciating. From what I hear, that's true for everyone to some extent. It entails hard work and long hours, and it can take a physical, not just an emotional and intellectual, toll. For me, fieldwork is a particularly physical labor because I have a genetic illness that affects multiple organs and systems and that significantly saps my energy and strength even on the best of days.

Like others with my condition, to manage the symptoms I have had to use a wheelchair at times, and I sometimes walk with a cane. However, I have never done fieldwork in my wheelchair, and I only used a cane at TechCo toward the very end of the study when I felt I had collected sufficient data and felt more comfortable in my position there. Even then I used it rarely. I can get by without these assistive tools on most days, although not without some consequence to my health when long days strain my muscles and autonomic nervous system. And there are many of those days during fieldwork.

I say that I do this because I worry that people would react differently to me if my illness were more visible, that it would prevent them from developing the comfort necessary to share their thoughts and experiences with me. I know there is some truth in that; it does not take an ethnographer to see the reactions a wheelchair provokes in many. Yet this excuse is unfair to the people I've studied and unfair to others with visible disabilities whom I believe are entirely capable of doing excellent fieldwork. In reality, I am so self-conscious when my illness is visible that I worry I would pay less attention to my subjects and their world, than to me and mine. And good ethnography that would not make. As it is, I let myself get so distracted managing my presentation of self and masking physical symptoms that I often wonder what I miss in the scene I am supposed to be studying.

Indeed, there is an argument to be made (I've made it myself) that full-time fieldwork is simply too physically demanding given my situation. TechCo generously let me into their backstage for this project, but thank God they never saw mine: I vomited in their bathrooms, spent a night in a nearby emergency room hooked up to an IV before returning to the field the next morning, and on one particularly grand day walked to the nearby parking garage to lie down in my car before having to return for an interview, only to realize my car was not there because I had taken a cab that morning. Unable to concoct a better plan and feeling like I might pass out if I did not lie down soon, I sat on the dusty garage floor, leaned my back against the cement wall, and hoped no one would come to retrieve their car while I took a break.

I don't share these details to suggest I have nobly sacrificed for the craft. I share them so you will believe it when I say that I constantly compromise my work for this illness and that this is a limitation of my work that should be taken seriously. During my time at TechCo, I canceled interviews when I felt ill, left the company early on some days even when I knew something interesting was happening later on that I should observe, and took days off from collecting data to give myself time to rest and recuperate. I detest anodyne sentiments that suggest life-threatening illnesses somehow make one wiser or encourage one to make the most of every experience; mitochondrial disease has made me a worse ethnographer than I would otherwise be, and I am no wiser for it.

It has made me a worse person too. Because of the toll fieldwork takes on me, this work is an act of extreme selfishness on my part. I cannot do it on my own, and I do not do it gracefully; I impose costs on everyone around me. During my time at TechCo, I depended on my husband's strength and resilience to keep our day-to-day life going while fieldwork consumed my every ounce of stamina. I leaned on loyal friends and colleagues who tolerated my spectacularly self-absorbed bouts of pessimism when I repeatedly asserted that I couldn't do it any longer, but then woke up the next day and did it anyway. And as I have during all my life, I relied on a brother who appears in hospital emergency rooms at just the right time with a cup of coffee and a funny story, a father who has never thought any pursuit was too ambitious for me but knows what a battle it is so serves as wartime consigliere whenever called upon, and a mother who has always known exactly what to say when no one else in the world does.

Ethnography is an inherently selfish act. We ask people to open their worlds to us, and when they so generously do, we record, dissect, and analyze them to advance our own knowledge and careers. With the social costs I impose on those I love, I have taken this narcissist's game, this soul-sucking enterprise, to a whole new dimension. It is one of the many moral ambiguities I accept when I choose to do this work.

EXIT

It is always hard to put a firm date on when fieldwork ends. I collected data throughout most of 2013 and stayed in touch with the company for more than a year after that, following up on certain lines of inquiry and meeting with people to stay current on unfolding events. But around nine months into my fieldwork, I started to slow the pace of data collection because I was teaching. Around that time, the management team also began asking what my findings were. It seemed like a reasonable time to take stock.

I had not yet done the sort of systematic analysis I would do later, but I had been reflecting on my data throughout in analytical memos. I was particularly interested in two empirical puzzles. The first was that in a company in which executives seemed genuinely interested in limiting formal, hierarchical control over the workforce, employees were in some cases calling for more structure and hierarchy. The second was that the simple act of publicizing the company's culture had seemed for a time to complicate, or perhaps even erode, the very culture being described. I decided to organize my presentation to executives around these puzzles and share some findings and analyses that pertained to them. I created a presentation of about fifty slides in which I discussed a number of the topics that would later end up in this book (e.g., org charts, HR, use good judgment, and the culture deck).

One afternoon I delivered the presentation to a small group that included Eric, Anil, Keith, and several other top executives.

The management team's initial interest in this study had been to receive an unvarnished account of life on the ground at TechCo, and I took them at face value on that score. Also, I knew I would be writing about my findings down the road, so there was no point hiding anything from them now when they would only confront it later. Plus, I wanted to know what they thought. Learning from your subjects' reactions and insights is not the same as mindlessly adopting the native point of view, and I trusted my ability to distinguish the two.

I prefaced my remarks by saying that I wanted the meeting to be useful to them so was going to focus more on the challenges I observed the organization facing than on the successes I had observed. That was probably a mistake in retrospect. I should have spent time talking about both. Focusing exclusively on the challenges misrepresented my overall impression of the organization. Also, when the executives asked what ideas I had for addressing the challenges I had identified, I had nothing to offer and felt like a fraud, even though I knew it was not my role. I reminded them I was not a consultant and made an awkward joke that I was more like a psychoanalyst who helps people identify their problems but offers no suggestions for how to confront them. The analogy resonated more than I would have liked.

Even had I nailed the presentation and provided useful recommendations, I don't think it would have made the meeting that day any easier. If there is a way around the awkwardness and discomfort of presenting one's findings to the subjects of your study, I have not learned it. As I always am in these situations, I was nervous and nauseous leading up to and during the meeting. When we reveal our final analysis, the ethnographer–subject relationship is laid bare. And as Janet Malcolm wrote about journalism—in a statement that applies equally well to ethnography—the subject comes to see that the individual who was "so keen to understand him fully, so remarkably attuned to his vision of things, never had the slightest intention of collaborating with him on his story but always intended to write a story of his own."[14]

When you reveal that story in person as I was doing here and have done in past projects, you sign yourself up for sitting by your subjects' side as this realization takes hold. No matter how uncomfortable I find this process to be, though, I see no reason for people to give us the access they do without us giving them something in return; and what we have to offer is the knowledge we gained from studying them and the human decency to tell it to them straight. They may not agree with us, and we may not always be right in our final analysis; but it is all we have to offer, and it is what we owe them if they ask for it.

At TechCo my task was made somewhat easier because I was not the only channel these executives had into their organization. Most of what I shared that day they had already heard directly from employees in open discussions on the wiki and weekly Q&A sessions or anonymously through the quarterly survey. I was offering my own analytical take on issues, and the executives seemed genuinely interested in that, but the findings themselves were not entirely surprising to them. In fact, the management team was, as I might have expected, an open-minded audience that day. They asked questions to probe certain topics more deeply and at times paused for sidebars with one another to consider various ideas for addressing one or another issue.

Several weeks later I delivered a lunchtime TechTalk in the largest meeting hall at the company. This talk was open to the whole organization and recorded for those who could not attend in person. In advance of the talk, I worked with a woman from TechCo's people operations team to settle on an appropriate format for it. We opted for a "fireside chat" during which she would ask me a series of prepared questions about my research and findings, and then we would open it up for questions from the audience. The prepared questions allowed me to discuss my initial interest in studying TechCo, my research methods, what I had found to be uniquely impressive about the organization, and what I felt organizational scholars like myself could learn from it. But I also used the planned Q&A to discuss at length the two empirical puzzles I had discussed with executives. I spoke directly about the challenges I saw stemming from policies like UGJ and the desire to minimize managerial control, and

I discussed what I felt were some inherent challenges to marketing the company's culture.

When I took questions from the audience, employee questions ranged from how I had constructed my sample, to whether departmental sub-cultures were a problem at TechCo, to my thoughts on work–life balance. After the talk, a handful of employees came up to me and thanked me for capturing their perspectives. In the sort of comment ethnographers live for, an engineer whom I had never met approached me and said, "I've worked at TechCo for five years and just wanted to say thank you for representing my experience." An executive who had not been able to attend my presentation to the management team but who had seen my slides and attended the TechTalk pulled me aside and said I had "nailed it" in my analysis. Have no doubt, I was aware of the obvious selection bias in these interactions. People who did not like the talk were unlikely to come up and tell me right then and there. But reactions like this are what make ethnography worth it, so I cherished the wins I could get, knowing that my study was far from perfect.

Because I still had access to the wiki, I was able to follow the posttalk discussion online, which was less subject to this sort of selection bias. This proved immensely valuable for my research. By the time of my TechTalk, I had already observed a shift in employees' reaction to the culture deck, but I did not yet have a good handle on what exactly was happening. I knew that individuals who had been quite negative initially were speaking of it more positively now. I had some hypotheses for why, but I had not had enough time to sit with my data and examine the question closely. During my TechTalk, I voiced some strong skepticism about the practice of marketing culture, and in the wake of my talk a discussion unfolded on the wiki in which employees—many of whom initially had been critical of the deck—defended the practice. As I watched the discussion unfold, it became clear to me that the workforce had come to see the deck as an aspirational statement and publicizing it as a way to commit the firm to a shared ideal. This insight helped me understand the data I had collected and directed my ethnographic gaze to parts of the data I may otherwise have overlooked. In the process, my understanding of what it meant to market culture changed and deepened. That never would have happened had I not had the opportunity to share my initial impressions with the company and hear their reaction.

DATA ANALYSIS AND WRITING

By early 2014, I was out of the field and had begun more systematic data analysis. First, I read my full set of field notes and memos several times through. I have never been able to jump right into line-by-line coding and find it necessary to understand the dataset as a whole initially. On my second pass, I began looking for empirical puzzles in the data, things that were unexpected from the perspective of existing theory or just my own intuition and common sense. Such puzzles had guided my data collection along the way and that helped at this stage. Next, I began reading and coding data specifically in pursuit of understanding those puzzles. (When I eventually sat down to write, those puzzles wound up organizing the book's chapter structure.)

There is no one label I would apply to my analytical strategy nor a particular school of thought I think my approach represents, but I have been influenced by both Geertz's writing on thick description and Burawoy's extended case method, and I find these to be complementary approaches, although I know some would disagree with that. Like Geertz, I believe making sense of ethnographic data "is like trying to read a manuscript—foreign, faded, full of ellipses, incoherencies, suspicious emendations and tendentious commentaries . . . written not in conventional graphs of sound but in transient examples of shaped behavior."[15] My overriding objective when first confronting my data is simply to understand "what the devil is going on in the setting," as Geertz once put it.[16] The way I do this is to reconstruct the logic of the situation for those in it, in other words, to interpret what the natives' actions and words meant to them at the time, what the devil they thought they were up to in the moment. Such thick description is absolutely necessary in my opinion, but also not sufficient.

As Burawoy notes, "We are interested not only in learning *about* a specific social situation . . . but also in learning *from* that social situation."[17] Once I feel I understand a situation deeply, I then start to ask what it is a case of more generally and how it conforms to or defies our existing understanding of the social world. To be sure, there are other ways to approach data analysis in ethnography, but I have never found a way around this iterative process, wherein puzzles guide my interpretive gaze and my interpretations revise my understanding of those puzzles.

It is not until the ethnographer sits down to write that he or she fully confronts the promises made in the field. I faced this reality as soon as I started to write. On the one hand, I needed to honor my commitment to disguise employee identities. I had promised that their confidential statements to me would not be identifiable to their peers or supervisors, and if I failed at that, I might be putting their jobs and relationships at risk. On the other hand, I needed to maintain the integrity of the data and not distort the facts of the situation. As anyone who has tried to anonymize qualitative data knows, meeting both of these objectives is not always straightforward. My approach was to keep the tension continually in mind and, given the stakes involved, to err on the side of protecting people's identities if ever there was a question. In most cases, it was as simple as giving employees a pseudonym. In rare instances, when I felt particular details were not crucial to the specific point being made but might risk revealing a person's identity, I left them out or changed them (e.g., changing someone's college major or adding or subtracting one year to a person's age). In the most sensitive cases (e.g., where there were very few men or women in a particular group or where the nature of someone's work made him or her easily identifiable), I did more, such as combining details from similarly situated individuals so no one person would be singled out. More often, though, I just left out an illustrative quote that I might have preferred to use because I feared it would identify the speaker. I worried that some changes might make employees unrecognizable to themselves, but my commitment had been to protect their identity from others, and I tried to honor that without sacrificing the integrity of the story as best I could.

As I began to write, I also confronted a question regarding the wiki. The company had given me complete access to the wiki so I could understand and analyze its online culture and communication. Moreover, people posted on the wiki knowing that what they said would be visible to the entire company, so these data were substantively different from data individuals shared in confidence during my interviews. Yet I quickly realized I would need to proceed carefully, or I might still compromise confidentiality. If I quoted someone from the wiki and then linked that statement to something the individual had shared in confidence to me, others could conceivably identify the person by searching the wiki archives for the original quote. I consulted recent texts on methods in digital ethnography and concluded that I simply could not link data in this way and still maintain my commitments to confidentiality.[18] (Other options suggested in the literature, such as changing quotes from the wiki so they could not be as easily searched, seemed to sacrifice the integrity of the data and not offer sufficient protection.) My approach precluded some interesting analyses I might have presented, but I think it was the right call.

Finally, I had to confront my promise to anonymize TechCo itself. Disguising a company that was "radically open" and "shared everything" about itself publicly was not seamless. Throughout the study, in fact, I had worried about how I might disguise various things but also maintain the integrity of the data and create a portrayal that was recognizable to TechCo itself. When it came time to write the book, I solicited advice from several contacts at the company and did my best to take what felt like reasonable measures. I gave the organization a pseudonym and was careful not to quote from publicly available materials that would directly link back to it. I could have done more to disguise it at that time, but I did not want the organization's first look at their representation on the page to be an alienating experience. Instead, before finalizing the manuscript and submitting it to any publisher, I sent a draft to the company for their reaction, along with a number of ideas for how I planned to disguise TechCo's identity even more fully once they had read the draft I was sharing with them.

When I did not hear back immediately, I hatched numerous paranoid theories about their likely reaction to what I had written, and I predicted the end of my academic career. I felt I had written a fair account, but I also knew there were things in it most companies would prefer not to have exposed publicly and interpretations with which executives might disagree. Under the NDA we had signed, they had no ability to influence my arguments or analyses. Nevertheless, I worried that if they hated the manuscript, it would mean either I had failed in my attempt to represent the organization fairly or they were not as open as I thought and the book's argument was bunk. Either way, I concluded that the project was doomed, as was I. For those who had to put up with me during this time, I apologize.

As it turned out, the slight delay was due to the management team sharing the manuscript internally with a number of people to solicit their opinions (something I might have expected given the argument of my own damn book). When I received the company's definitive response, they stuck to their word and to our agreement by not asking me to change any of my arguments or interpretations. All they asked was that I redact one-half of one sentence in which I had inadvertently mischaracterized a piece of information shared at a company meeting. I recognized my mistake immediately and cut the phrase.

Instead of adopting my suggestions for how to disguise the company further, they said they were comfortable with TechCo being loosely disguised as I had done in the draft they read. In fact, the executive team said they were comfortable with my using the company's name at that point. After careful deliberation, I chose not to pursue that path, but I told the company that I would support whatever decision they made regarding identifying themselves as the book's subject.

I recognize the tradeoffs of this decision, but I believe it was the right one. First, in light of the NDA, I had told TechCo employees—both verbally and in writing throughout my fieldwork—that I would not be naming the company in my research. The individuals who allowed me to observe, shadow, and interview them did so with that understanding. Ethically, I find it problematic to modify the terms of subjects' participation ex post. Even if all employees were to consent to my naming the company now, I could never be sure they would have agreed to participate in the first place under these terms, nor would I know whether they were truly comfortable with the change or merely bending to internal pressure. From a practical standpoint, future research subjects would have reason to doubt my upfront commitments if I had a track record of retrading them.

Second, stepping outside of the NDA (which, as noted, gave me full control over my research findings and arguments) ran the risk that something might change at the company and someone there might try to influence the content of the manuscript before its publication. My interactions suggested that executives and staff believed I had presented a fair and honest account of the organization, but I also knew there were certain things I described and certain interpretations I offered that would not be put in a marketing or PR document. Not every conclusion I drew from my vantage point as an outside ethnographer was exactly as insiders would describe their world. For all its remarkable transparency, TechCo (like all firms) quite understandably cares about its image in the market, and its executives and staff think carefully about exactly what and how they will present themselves to the public. The NDA was written to make sure these concerns could never interfere with my work or its publication, and I wanted to maintain that protection through publication so readers could be completely confident that I had not let the firm influence my work at any step of the process.

For these reasons, I declined to pursue the suggestion of discarding the NDA and naming them. It would not surprise me if the company publicly reveals itself to be the book's subject on Twitter or their corporate blog some day. I would welcome them disclosing this information if that is what they decide. I simply believe the decision is theirs, not mine, to make.

To be sure, there are pros and cons to anonymizing in ethnography (lower book sales is one con, a few people have told me). And I am familiar with recent academic critiques of the practice in urban ethnography—namely, that anonymizing subjects makes it harder to verify the scholar's work.[19] However, I also know that corporate ethnographies are often anonymized for good reason. If we stop offering to anonymize companies, I strongly believe much corporate ethnography will grind to a halt, or at least change drastically in form and lose much of its value. Firms may be more hesitant to give strangers deep access into their organizations, and the data they allow scholars to access may be warped by concern for their reputations in the market. Yes, popular business books profile companies all the time and use their real names, but I believe we seek, and I hope we receive, something different when we pick up a scholarly ethnography.

Even for TechCo, which may have been willing to identify itself from the outset had I pushed the issue, and which proved quite willing to be identified at the end, there were compelling reasons to offer anonymity for the sake of the project's validity and integrity. As the book attests, the data I collected over the length of my study led me to develop a healthy respect for the organization, its vision, and the challenges it navigated in pursuit of it. I concluded the study with an appreciation for the complexities of change but also with a sense of optimism regarding what TechCo's experience might mean for the future of corporate organization. Because neither TechCo nor I believed the company's reputation would be affected by the data I was collecting at the time (given the NDA), I feel more confident in my conclusions than I would otherwise. Also, I always knew that I would share my findings with the company in the end (and I think all ethnographers should share their work with the subjects of it), so my compulsion to "get the story right" was strong regardless of whether TechCo was named or not.[20] I never had any doubt that the company and its employees would speak up if they felt I was representing them inaccurately or unfairly. Whether TechCo chooses to disclose its identity or not, I hope to have many future conversations with them about this book and about their ongoing experiments to build a more conversational firm.

ACKNOWLEDGMENTS

T HIS BOOK WOULD not have been possible without the openness of Techco. They let in a stranger and shared their world with me. I will be forever grateful for that and for all they taught me. I learned from every conversation I had there.

I had never really spoken with Peter Bearman before I received an email from him one Sunday afternoon. He had come across a draft chapter from my book and said, when I was done, I should send the manuscript to him because he wanted to help get it published. I have yet to delete that email. Peter's support of this project has meant the world to me, and I am honored to be a part of his and Shamus Khan's new series at Columbia University Press (CUP). Brayden King was a reviewer on this book at CUP, and I could not have asked for a better one. His enthusiasm for the manuscript and incisive suggestions for its revision were invaluable. Eric Schwartz was my editor at CUP, and every conversation we had only deepened my already great respect for his editorial talent and vision. Eric is an author's editor, and he is going to have a hard time shaking this author.

I would not have survived the process of researching and writing this book were it not for three individuals at MIT. Kate Kellogg knows the trials and tribulations of ethnographic fieldwork firsthand and how to talk me off of the many ledges I walk myself out onto while doing this sort of work.

She took my calls at all times of the day and read a draft of the manuscript. Ray Reagans was the first person with whom I shared the manuscript, and he made a critical observation about organizational culture that has shaped my entire thinking on the subject and that I continue to contemplate. Ray may be a quantitative researcher in practice, but his ethnographic eye and instinct rival the best, and his wisdom guided me throughout the project. Ezra Zuckerman taught me how to be a sociologist, and I will never stop learning from him. He has been my intellectual mentor and true friend ever since I started graduate school. During this project, he read my analytic memos and the complete manuscript, engaged with my ideas, challenged my thinking, and tolerated my panic attacks. As many parts of this book attest, his own work on the nature of the firm and hierarchical control had a profound influence on me.

There are three individuals outside of academia without whom this book simply would not have come together. Rick Burnes was unfailingly generous with his insights into today's tech world. He responded to every inane question I asked, taught me much, and was instrumental in bringing the project to fruition. Dedi Felman has my deepest gratitude. She pushed me, my thinking, and my writing in ways I never could have done on my own, and her intellectual companionship on this journey was invaluable. I would need her help to craft the perfect words to thank her as much as she deserves. Finally, TJ Murphy offered wise advice when it was most needed.

I am fortunate to work in a community of exceptional organizational scholars who create a rich environment in which to pursue the sort of questions this book explores. At the risk of leaving off the many other MIT colleagues who offered support and inspiration during this project, Kelly Basner, Emilio Castilla, Roberto Fernandez, Bob Gibbons, Erin Kelly, Tom Kochan, Tom Malone, Fiona Murray, Wanda Orlikowski, Paul Osterman, Susan Silbey, Scott Stern, and John Van Maanen are just a few of the people whom I wish to thank.

Outside of MIT, I have a number of amazing friends who happen also to be brilliant scholars, and they supported me both intellectually and emotionally while I researched and wrote this book. Sarah Halpern-Meekin is the best friend a girl could have. She knows me and my work better than

I do, and life would not be the same without her. Damon Phillips means more to me than he knows. Our conversations over the years have continually renewed my sometimes flagging confidence in being an academic, and his work and life offer a model of integrity I try to emulate in my own. I am also deeply grateful for the intellectual engagement and friendship that Rodrigo Canales, Jason Greenberg, Mako Hill, Sara Shostak, and Jocelyn Viterna offered me during this project.

Drs. Caroline Birks and Amel Karaa from Massachusetts General Hospital make it possible for me to do this work. They both know how much I hate letting mitochondrial disease slow me down, and they did everything they could to help keep me going during this project. MitoAction also deserves thanks for all the organization does to support mito patients like me.

I have been focused on my professional life since I was in the third grade and declared that I wanted to be a tax lawyer. Yet the single most important thing to me has always been my family. My mother Joanne Turco cared for me during the writing of this book as she has throughout my whole life. My father Albert Turco believed in me and my ambition and offered sage counsel at every step of the way as he has throughout my whole life. And my brother Al, a writer himself, showed once again that he will never stop being the generous big brother who taught me how to throw a spiral and shared all his notebooks with me.

Philip Borden read every word of this book multiple times and never let me give up. He is the love of my life, and it is to him I dedicate the book. If Philip will humor me this one last time, I will give Rumsfeld the hammer. The best dog in the multiverse, Rummy sat by my side as I wrote every page.

NOTES

PREFACE

1. In a 2001 article "Digital Natives, Digital Immigrants," Mark Prensky defined "digital natives" as the cohort of students then entering educational institutions who had grown up on digital communication technologies and who consequently (by his estimation) communicated, thought, and processed information in radically different ways than past generations of students. The term "digital native" took off in popular media and the research community. Both the Pew Research Center and the Berkman Center for Internet and Society, for example, have research initiatives devoted to understanding digital natives, their habits and values, and how they differ from past generations.
2. Pew Research Center (2010, 2014) and Fosse (2014). According to survey research, millennials appear to constitute a new cultural group, marked by distinctive habits and beliefs relative to past generations, especially concerning technology use.
3. Pew Research Center (2010, 2014) and PWC (2011).

INTRODUCTION

1. For a thoughtful discussion of the history of organizational scholarship on this topic, see Leonardi and Barley (2010).
2. In the 1950s and 1960s, contingency theorists argued that different technological systems demand different organizational forms. Classic works in that tradition include Woodward (1965) and Perrow (1967). Barley (1986) moved beyond the technological determinism of contingency theory to observe that new technological systems do not always demand new organizational practices but can instead serve as objects with which social actors envision

and claim new organizational roles and routines for themselves. Social constructivists argue that technology influences organizations not through its material properties but through the various meanings actors attach to the technology. Some classic works in this tradition include Fulk et al. (1987), Orlikowski (1992), Fulk (1993), and Orlikowski and Yates (1994).

3. For various treatments of this issue, see Powell (1990, 2001), Heckscher and Donnellon (1994), Fulk and Desanctis (1995), Volderba (1998), Adler (2001), DiMaggio (2001), Stark (2001), Girard and Stark (2002), and Greenwood and Lawrence (2005). At the time and in the years following, some argued that this postbureaucratic discourse was more rhetoric than reality and that conventional bureaucratic elements (and sometimes even more onerous forms of control) emerged in supposedly postbureaucratic projects. Adler (2012) as well as Courpasson and Reed's 2004 special issue in *Organization* offer this perspective, for example.

4. Benkler (2006) and Shirky (2008). As with the earlier wave, there is debate about whether such projects are truly postbureaucratic. Some argue that bureaucratic elements slip back in and that even these projects are subject to Michels's (1915) "iron law of oligarchy" (e.g., Shaw and Hill 2014).

5. Malone (2004) and Davis (2014).

6. See O'Reilly (2005), van Dijick (2013), and Fuchs (2014). Also, even though Rainie and Wellman (2012) call their recent book on social media *Networked: The New Social Operating System,* their discussion is quite different from the 1990s talk of distributed networks. The new "social operating system" they describe is one of constant expression, sharing, and conversation.

7. Facebook S-1, Letter to Shareholders, https://www.sec.gov/Archives/edgar/data/1326801 /000119312512034517/d287954ds1.htm (Note: all weblinks cited throughout these endnotes were accessed and valid as of December 2015.)

8. https://www.google.com/about/company/facts/culture/

9. The popular press has made a cottage industry of profiling their quirky and unexpected ways. See Hardy (2014) and Heller (2013) as examples.

10. Extreme examples are firms trying to create open decision-making environments by eliminating managers entirely. See Silverman (2013) and Shaer (2013) for press coverage of this trend. Related to this trend, the blog publishing platform company Medium and shoe retailer Zappos have both recently adopted "holacracy," a form of nonhierarchical constitutional governance that uses self-organizing teams and frequent meetings to promote open dialogue, clarify responsibilities, and air tensions. See Wohlsen (2014); also http://www .holacracy.org/how-it-works/. In chapter 9, I discuss these trends in more detail and explain how they differ conceptually from TechCo's conversational model.

11. Mahler (2014).

12. Huh et al. (2007) and DiMicco et al. (2008).

13. Power (2014a, 2014b).

14. Barney (2000), Bauman and Lyon (2012), and Gilliom and Monaham (2013).

15. Kunda (1992); also Courpasson and Reed (2004).

16. Shirky (2008).
17. Morozov (2011).
18. Morozov (2009) and Gilliom and Monaham (2013).
19. Gladwell (2010).
20. Turkle (2011).
21. Weber (1978, 989, 988).
22. In his 1938 book *The Functions of the Executive,* Chester Barnard built on Weber's work by characterizing the bureaucratic firm as a carefully constructed system of communication and authority, although he added to Weber an appreciation for the informal and moral bases of cooperation. Taking inspiration from both Barnard and Weber, the Carnegie School theorized how bureaucratic structures and practices created the conditions for rational organizational action despite the firm's necessary reliance on cognitively limited, boundedly rational individuals (e.g., Simon 1947; March and Simon 1958).
23. Whyte (1956), Mills (1951), and Wilson (1955).
24. Merton (1940).
25. Gouldner (1954), Selznick (1949), and Blau (1955).
26. See Braverman (1974), Burawoy (1979), and Edwards (1979).
27. Meyer and Rowan (1977, 340).
28. DiMaggio and Powell (1983).
29. The Carnegie School was an influential line of organizational theory that built on Weber and conceived of the organization as a parallel pattern of communication and authority (see Barnard 1938; Simon 1947). Scott (1992) critiques Weber for making implicit assumptions about the interrelationships between the various elements of bureaucracy. Like Gouldner (1954), Scott also critiques Weber for conflating authority and knowledge. In chapter 9, I discuss how this conflation is likely what leads Weber to assume that hierarchical firms necessarily tend toward secrecy and the suppression of conversation.
30. See Nohria and Berkeley (1994).
31. Rothschild and Russell (1986) review various "alternatives to bureaucracy" and note that all took aim at the conventional firm's hierarchical decision-making structure. In chapter 9, I discuss these alternatives in greater detail and explain how they differ from TechCo's conversational model.
32. Weber (1978, 980). Weber is referring to the influence of press, party bosses, and the public sentiment of the "propertyless masses" on state bureaucracies, but the same logic extends to corporate bureaucracy and its staff and public. Building on Weber, Herbert Simon (1947) made a similar point in his book *Administrative Behavior.* Simon noted that a firm's formal communication had to follow its formal lines of authority because letting people throughout the hierarchy offer up their ideas, advice, and opinions would risk "destroying the organization structure" (216). Although he appreciated that considerable informal communication was happening outside the formal lines of the organizational chart, Simon believed there was no way for a firm to harness this information formally. For example, he suggested that the only way an executive could get the pulse on "public opinion" within the organization was through informal gossip. He did not contemplate the sort of formal

communication mechanisms that have become possible with today's technologies and that TechCo embraced.

33. Merton (1940, 561).

1. THE SOCIAL REVOLUTION

1. Others have noted this trend too. One early statement directed at practitioners was the *Cluetrain Manifesto: The End of Business as Usual* (Levine et al. 2009). Originally published in 2000 but reissued in updated form in 2009, the book offers ninety-five theses about how the Internet and associated technologies have changed how businesses must engage with customers in the market. TechCo's founders cite the book as an early inspiration for their project, its primary thesis being, "Natural conversation is the true language of commerce" (ix). In particular, the *Manifesto* argues, "Through the Internet, people in your markets are discovering and inventing new ways to converse. They're talking about your business. They're telling one another the truth, in very human voices" (xxi), and to survive firms must join those conversations. Recent scholarly work has also noted these changes in market dialogue. In their 2012 book, *Networked: The New Social Operating System*, Rainie and Wellman note how social media has inspired new expectations for voice and expression; for example, how customers now regularly go online to share their experiences and opinions on the products they use and the businesses with which they interact.

2. In this regard, the founders of TechCo also draw inspiration from the *Cluetrain Manifesto* (Levine et al. 2009), which notes, "The same technology that has opened up a new kind of conversation in the marketplace has done the same within the corporation or has the potential to do so" (90). Like TechCo's founders, the *Manifesto* directly links today's technologies and their associated changes in conversation to ideas about "openness," and specifically to "non-hierarchical" and "anti-bureaucratic" modes of organizing both in the market and inside firms (87, 2).

3. Hargitai (2010) and Boyd (2014) contest the "digital native" characterization of millennials, arguing that many are actually digitally naïve when it comes to understanding their technological devices and gadgets and, especially, the privacy they may forfeit with them. However, TechCo explicitly screens for facility with digital and social media tools in its hiring, and the term "digital native" seems quite apt for its young workforce. Also, regardless of their actual digital savvy, both millennials and older generations believe that what distinguishes today's younger cohort from past ones is their more intensive use of and relationship to technology (Pew Research Center 2010). Neither Emma nor TechCo are alone in linking her generational identity to her experience with technology.

4. There is increasing recognition of both the potential and pitfalls of millennials' hyperconnected, "always-on" communication style (which, of course, has become the communication style of so many of us nonmillennials too). Pew Research Center's Internet and American Life Project surveyed more than 1,000 technology experts, asking whether they expected millennials would benefit or suffer over the long term on account of their

"interconnected lives," and the sample was split almost evenly (Anderson and Rainie 2012). Scholars and pundits alike have also documented the social, emotional, and cognitive costs of such constant communication (see, for example, Carr 2011; Turkle 2011).

2. OPEN COMMUNICATION

1. See, for example, Bernstein (2012).

2. Various perspectives on this issue over time can be founded in Taylor (1911), Mayo (1933), Adler and Borys (1996), Sewell (1998), and Bernstein (2012).

3. See Fung, Graham, and Weil (2008).

4. WikiLeaks (2011, section 1.3); cited also in Fuchs (2014, 216).

5. Fuchs (2012) and Scholz (2012).

6. Many millennials entered the labor market during the "great recession" early in the twenty-first century, and they were often lucky to find unpaid internships with the promise of learning in lieu of pay.

7. The literature offers some support for Kylie's perspective. Several organizational behavior (OB) scholars have argued that early life socialization instills in people "implicit voice theories" that govern how likely they are to speak up or to stay silent (Detert and Edmundson 2011, 461; Kish-Gephart et al. 2009). What is more, scholars who have looked at cross-national variation in employee voice have found that opportunities for voice may be more important to people raised in cultures that have less tolerance for power differences (Tyler, Lind, and Huo 2000; Brockner et al. 2001; Macoun 2005). To the extent that millennials were raised to expect greater access to figures of authority, it may have relevance for their expectations of voice.

8. See Desmond (2007) for how organizations can leverage affinities between workers' general habitus and specific organizational/occupational practices.

9. See Freeland and Zuckerman (2014) for a discussion of voice rights within hierarchical firms.

10. Morrison (2011, 2014) provides comprehensive overviews of the literature on informal, upward internal voice, defined as instances when employees voluntarily offer suggestions, opinions, or information to someone above them in the hierarchy. A strong assumption in this literature is that opportunities for, and instances of, such voice are quite limited in most firms; for example, see Morrison and Milliken (2000), Detert and Trevino (2010), and Detert and Edmundson (2011).

11. Mowbray, Wilkinson, and Tse (2015) compare and contrast how voice is defined and studied by scholars in the OB versus human resources (HR) fields. For discussions of how voice is treated within the industrial relations (IR)/HR fields, see Spencer (1986), Dundon et al. (2004), Wood and Wall (2007), and Klaas, Olson-Buchanon, and Ward (2012). For a detailed discussion of unions and their role in employee voice, see Verma and Kochan (2004).

12. See Benkler (2006), Shirky (2011), Boyd (2010), and Lindgren and Lundstrum (2011).

13. Habermas (1989).

14. Calhoun (1992) discusses this aspect of public spheres.

15. Jackall (1988, 19).

16. Jackall (1988, 17).

17. Jackall (1988, 118).

18. In one form or another, restrictions on employee voice and dissent are a common finding of past corporate ethnographies. Studies of corporate life conducted in the 1990s and early 2000s did not seem to encounter the situation we see today at TechCo in which individual workers voice their dissent directly to top management in a company-wide forum. In *Engineering Culture,* Kunda (1992) described a high-tech firm in which voice and dissent were suppressed by the firm's strong cultural order. John Weeks's (2004) study of a British bank, *Unpopular Culture,* found that employee complaints were ever-present in that setting but entirely ritualistic; employees never intended the complaints to reach top executives or to amount to anything. In *Managing in the Corporate Interest,* Victoria Smith (1990) found that middle managers disliked top executives' orders to restructure their departments but did not vocalize their resistance so much as find ways to skirt or co-opt the executive edicts for their own agendas. Finally, in his book on conflict management in corporations, *The Executive Way,* Calvin Morrill (1995) found that direct expression of conflict and disagreement was limited to certain contexts even among people at the same level in the corporate hierarchy. When it came to employees disagreeing with a superior, strategic compliance with authority and conflict avoidance were generally the norm.

19. See Leonardi and Barley (2010) for a discussion of technological affordances and a review of the social construction of technology literature.

20. For a thoughtful critique of the public spheres literature, see Adut (2012). For critiques of social media as a public sphere, see Dean (2005), Gladwell (2010), and Morozov (2011). For a review of the emerging literature on enterprise social media, see Treem and Leonardi (2012).

21. In the OB voice literature, some scholars have pointed out the challenges that arise when too many voices weigh in on a given subject, noting that it impedes decision making and makes it difficult to reach consensus (Morrison and Milliken 2000; Ashford, Sutcliffe, and Christianson 2009). As you will see more clearly later in the book, TechCo's wiki is not used as a mechanism for consensus decision making, but the general point remains that the more voices that sound off, the more "noise" people have to contend with.

22. See Fuchs (2014).

23. Recent studies of social media use within corporations have noted that social media's visibility affects what information people share on it, when they share it, and how they present themselves. For example, Treem and Leonardi (2012) include an extensive discussion of the visibility afforded by social media and its implications. For specific empirical examples of these dynamics, see Giordano (2007), Huh et al. (2007), Danis and Singer (2008), Holtzblatt, Damianos, and Weiss (2010), and Leonardi and Treem (2012).

24. Adut (2012, 244) and Goffman (1963).

25. On how attention and social recognition can motivate contributions on social media platforms at work, see Muller, Ehrlich, and Farrell (2006), DiMicco et al. (2009), Farzan, DiMicco, and Brownholtz (2009), and Yardi, Golder, and Brzozowski (2009). For how

impression management and desire for personal advancement influence employee voice as defined in the OB literature, see Burris (2012) and Morrison (2014).

26. Adut (2012).

27. See Treem and Leonardi's (2012) review.

28. For wiki use being correlated with manager use, see Wattal, Racherla, and Mandviwalla (2009). More generally, work in OB notes that employees are more likely to speak up when they feel it is safe to do so and that such a feeling of safety is strongly related to how employees perceive their supervisor's overall openness; see, for example, Edmundson (1999), Morrison and Milliken (2000), Milliken, Morrison, and Hewlin (2003), Detert and Burris (2007), Ashford et al. (2009), and Detert and Trevino (2010).

29. This relates to the earlier point about workers' tendency to silence themselves if they feel less safe in their position within the organization.

30. For a general discussion of distorted public valuation as well as the role of visibility in the production of market bubbles, see Turco and Zuckerman (2014).

31. See Baker, Gibbons, and Murphy (1999) for a thoughtful discussion of why (decision) rights can never be fully delegated.

32. Morrison (2014, 175); see also Ashford et al. (2009) and Detert and Trevino (2010).

33. Later in the book, when I talk about TechCo's culture, I discuss another analogy to work on distorted public valuation, wherein a sort of pluralistic ignorance inhered and employees privately questioned each other's public performances of commitment and loyalty to the company. See also Turco and Zuckerman (2014).

34. Nohria and Berkeley (1994).

3. OPEN CONTROL

1. Foss (2003).

2. See, for example, Vallas (2003). Gouldner's 1954 study of a gypsum mine is also instructive. Employees became discontent after a mine, which was previously managed informally via implicit contracts, came under more formal bureaucratic control with a new manager.

3. Gibbons and Henderson (2012, 2013). These papers provide an overview of the literature on relational contracts and discuss why such contracts are so hard to implement within organizations.

4. Freeland and Zuckerman (2014); see also Zuckerman (2010).

5. In chapter 9 I discuss this issue in greater detail, describing how prior attempts to build postbureaucratic firms have generally tried to subvert the firm's hierarchical structure of authority and, in the process, have directly linked changes in the firm's communication environment to changes in its decision-making structure. For example, studies of workplace democracy and worker participation often discuss "employee involvement" and "empowerment" in ways that imply both voice and decision rights but rarely delineate them. Rothschild (2000) offers a review of some of this literature that suggests how issues of open communication and open decision making have been treated in it.

6. This view is consistent with popular portrayals and some surveys of millennial workers that suggest millennials do not like rigid corporate structures (e.g., PWC 2011). Also, an overall distaste for institutional rules might be consistent with that finding, and survey research has suggested that millennials are more detached from conventional institutions than past generations (e.g., they have lower political party and religious affiliation); see Pew Research Center (2014) and Fosse (2014).

7. Desmond (2007) discusses how organizations can tap into and build on workers' general habitus, which derives from their earlier socialization and upbringing.

8. Hays (1996), Laureau (2003), Twenge (2006), and Friedman (2013).

9. Hierarchical levels create clear career paths and upward mobility, both of which these employees were seeking.

10. Gibbons and Henderson (2013) discuss metaphors as being the basis for how employees understand relational contracts. Baron and Kreps (1999) discuss how organizational models may resonate with specific workers if they draw on blueprints or metaphors familiar to them from other settings. Studies coming out of the Stanford Project on Emerging Companies discuss the various ways in which metaphors or blueprints are significant both to workers and to overall firm performance (e.g., Baron, Hannon, and Burton 2001).

11. See Powell (1990), Fulk and Desanctis (1995), DiMaggio (2001), and Stark (2001).

12. For general treatments of the procedural justice framework, as well as how it has been applied to the study of firms to understand such things as employee reactions to layoffs, see Folger (1977), Thibault and Walker (1978), Lind and Tyler (1988), Bies and Shapiro (1988), Tyler and Lind (1992), Brockner, Tyler, and Cooper-Schneider (1992), Bies and Tyler (1993), Lind et al. (1993, 2000), and Folger and Cropanzano (1998). Another interesting precedent for this insight comes from the literature on social movements. Osterman (2006) analyzed a social movement organization that was oligarchical in structure (i.e., had concentrated power at the top) but that avoided the typical costs of oligarchy (such as loss of member commitment and displacement of organizational goals) by creating a culture in which members were encouraged to speak up and assert themselves against management. In other words, the organization promoted employee voice while maintaining hierarchical control. Under that model, Osterman found that members' commitment remained strong and the organization's focus remained steady.

13. See Spector and McCarthy (2012) and Gibbons and Henderson (2013).

14. The Toyota Production System, in which employees are given discretion to pull the "andon cord" and stop the line when they deem it necessary, is another famous example of a relational contract, as well as being a famous example of a relational contract that many non-Toyota plants struggled to replicate; see Gibbons and Henderson (2013); also Adler (1993).

15. See Gibbons and Henderson (2012, 2013).

16. See Baker et al. (1999, 56); also, Williamson (1996).

17. Baron (2004) discusses the challenges of making universal claims that end up being unequally applied.

18. See, for example, Joel Best's 2011 book, *Everyone's a Winner: Life in the Congratulatory Culture.*

19. See Gibbons and Henderson (2012, 2013).

20. Freeland and Zuckerman (2014, 41–42) discuss the importance of the "definition of the situation" for coordination in firms, and their insights informed much of the analysis in this chapter. See also Perrow (1986) and March and Simon (1958).

21. What I found in TechCo's engineering group is consistent with Freeland and Zuckerman's (2014) argument. They argue that to adopt informal methods of control for employee decision making, firms must "control the public sphere much as authoritarian regimes do" (42). Drawing on Perrow (1986) and others, they note that a "common definition" of the situation is necessary for informal coordination, and then they make the further observation that "a situation cannot be defined if anyone can speak publicly to define it" (Freeland and Zuckerman 2014, 42). Thus, Freeland and Zuckerman distinguish voice rights from decision rights and argue that it is the consolidation of voice rights that enables managers to delegate certain decision rights. In their opinion, however, the delegation of decision rights is what firms must do to minimize the alienating effects of hierarchy and obtain consummate employee performance. TechCo, by contrast, suggests that there are employees for whom, and circumstances under which, worker commitment and identification can be fostered by delegating voice rights while keeping decision rights fairly consolidated at the top.

22. For a discussion of the work that goes into supporting relational contracts, see Gibbons and Henderson (2013). See also Milgrom and Roberts (1990, 1995).

4. OPENNESS CONTROL

1. Sources for this chapter include Associated Press (2013), Cutler (2013), Hill (2013), Holt (2013), Koetsier (2013), Musil (2013), Zandt (2013), and Ronson (2015). See also, https://www.reddit.com/r/TumblrInAction/comments/1alg55/woman_at_pycon_tweets_a_picture_of_two_guys/; https://twitter.com/adriarichards/status/313417655879102464/photo/1?ref_src=twsrc%5Etfw.

2. http://en.wikipedia.org/wiki/Dongle

3. http://www.scholarslab.org/research-and-development/forking-fetching-pushing-pulling/

4. She later blogged about the incident and offered an additional motivation for her tweet: http://butyoureagirl.com/2013/03/18/forking-and-dongle-jokes-dont-belong-at-tech-conferences/.

5. Associated Press (2013).

6. The developer's comment is here: https://news.ycombinator.com/item?id=5398681.

7. The blog post by Andy Yang, CEO of PlayHaven, can be found here: http://blog.playhaven.com/?p=1387. See also Associated Press (2013).

8. Cutler (2013).

9. Anonymous's message was posted here: http://pastebin.com/ubmznGhn.

10. Koetsier (2013).

11. The blog post by Jim Franklin, CEO of SendGrid, can be found here: http://sendgrid .com/blog/a-difficult-situation/.

12. See Freeland and Zuckerman (2014) for a discussion of external voice rights.

13. The technology trade press has extensively reported on this trend and documented what such policies commonly include (e.g., Lauby 2009; Meister 2013). A cottage industry of consultants has also emerged to advise companies on how to craft their policies, and professional associations for HR managers offer conference sessions on the topic as well as templates on their websites (e.g., http://www.shrm.org/templatestools/samples/policies /pages/socialmediapolicy.aspx; http://socialmediagovernance.com/social-employee-advocacy -software-buying-guide/; and http://socialmediagovernance.com/social-employee-advocacy -software-buying-guide/). Finally, the National Labor Relations Board has recently begun to weigh in on which restrictions on employee speech can be lawfully included in these policies and what speech is protected by law. Generally speaking, protected speech is that which is intended to speak for a group of employees in a concerted effort to improve working conditions. See http://www.nlrb.gov/news-outreach/news-story/acting-general -counsel-releases-report-employer-social-media-policies. Greenhouse (2013) reports on the protections of employee speech on social media.

14. http://www.ibm.com/blogs/zz/en/guidelines.html

15. http://forums.bestbuy.com/t5/Welcome-News/Best-Buy-Social-Media-Policy/td -p/20492

16. Excerpts of Apple's social media policy can be found here: http://modmyi.com/forums /mac-news/790947-apple-retail-blogging-online-social-media-guidelines-leaked. html; excerpts of Oracle's can be found here: http://gillin.com/blog/2010/07/oracles -social-media-policy/.

17. http://www.scribd.com/doc/17249115/SAP-Social-Media-Participation-Guidelines-2009

18. http://www.ibm.com/blogs/zz/en/guidelines.html

19. Dishman (2010).

20. Beal quoted in Schweitzer (2010).

21. Facebook came under scrutiny for releasing individual's information to third parties like this, and at the time of this writing, they had announced that people would be given more control over what information was released; see Goel (2014). Nevertheless, even if TechCo had not appeared next to Brian's comment, all Scott would have had to do was google Brian. Scott would have been led directly to Brian's LinkedIn page, which said he worked at TechCo, to an article Brian wrote on TechCo's corporate blog, and to his Facebook and Twitter accounts, which at the time specified his employer as TechCo (information he subsequently removed from those accounts).

22. There was precedent for this executive's position. In September 2012, the National Labor Relations Board ruled that BMW had not violated federal labor law when it fired a salesman for posting insensitive photos of a car accident online. The photos were unrelated to work and did not constitute "concerted activity" intended to improve workplace conditions, so they were not considered protected speech under federal labor law; see https:// www.nlrb.gov/news-outreach/fact-sheets/nlrb-and-social-media.

23. The initial incident occurred immediately prior to my first discussions with TechCo staff and management about the possibility of conducting this study. In each of those conversations, the people with whom I met spoke of the incident, which was clearly still top of mind for them. I took notes of their comments at the time, and once my fieldwork formally commenced I explored the incident further in interviews and analysis of the wiki.
24. Freeland and Zuckerman (2014) point out a similar analogy.
25. Baker et al. (1999, 56).
26. Zuckerman (2010, 299–300).
27. Zuckerman (2010, 300).

5. OPEN CULTURE

1. Kunda (1992).
2. Kunda (1992, 8).
3. Baron (2004).
4. The idea of a firm's employment model is discussed in Baron, Hannan, and Burton (2001) and in Baron, Burton, and Hannan (1996). The Netflix culture document can be found on slideshare.net: http://www.slideshare.net/reed2001/culture-1798664/netflix.
5. Companies embracing this approach seem to define culture loosely as the overall workplace environment, and a "good" culture is one that makes the workplace feel as little like work as possible. In Silicon Valley, generous perks, attractive (even fanciful) office spaces, and promises of autonomy and informality may have started out as a way to differentiate one organization from competitors in the labor market, but these offerings are now so commonplace that descriptions of any given firm's "unique" culture often sound just like the next one's. The increasing number of perks offered by leading companies like Google and Facebook can be seen as an escalation in the war for top talent too. The list of perks in TechCo's culture deck did not differentiate it from many other tech companies, but the full articulation of its organizational model was rather unique.
6. Rivera (2012) found hiring for cultural fit to be prevalent in elite professional service firms. Turco (2010) found that cultural fit could influence posthire outcomes such as integration and advancement.
7. Baron (2004).
8. Sandberg quoted in Shontell (2013) and Ferenstein (2013).
9. Turkle (2011).
10. On one side of this scholarly debate are theories that define culture as a coherent, semiautonomous system that constrains and enables action (e.g., Alexander and Smith 2002). On the other side are theories that define culture as a toolkit or repertoire (and sometimes a contradictory one at that) for action (e.g., Lamont 2000; Swidler 1986).
11. Patterson (2014).
12. See Geertz (1973).
13. Kunda (1992, 158).

14. Kunda (1992, 222).

15. Weeks (2004) offers another case like Kunda's in which employee complaints functioned merely as a release valve, amounting to no real change in the end.

16. Turco (2012) offers another example of how employees can co-opt a firm's external declarations of self for their own purposes.

6. A CONVERSATION ABOUT BUREAUCRACY

1. For discussions of decoupling in the context of personnel policies see Kelly and Dobbin (1998), Edelman (1992), and Kellogg (2009).

2. Meyer and Rowan (1977, 340).

3. Google also refers to its human resources department as "People Operations" and talks of how it promotes the firm's unconventional culture: http://www.google.com/about/careers/teams/people-operations/.

4. Selznick wrote, "The acceptance of irreversible commitments is the process by which the character of the organization is set" (1957, 40). See Zuckerman (2010) and Freeland and Zuckerman (2014) for a trenchant discussion of the relationship between irreversible commitments and organizational identity.

5. See Baron, Hannan, and Burton (2001), Baron (2004), Baron and Hannan (2005), and Hannan, Baron, Hsu, and Kocak (2006). The literature on relational contracts also identifies the costs of reversing such commitments (e.g., Gibbons and Henderson 2012).

6. Baron (2004, 7).

7. Baron (2004, 15).

8. Baron (2004, 24).

9. Adler and Borys (1996) develop the distinction between coercive and representative bureaucracies that Gouldner (1954) first identified. Adler (1993) profiles the NUMMI plant, which operated by representative bureaucracy. In chapter 9, I discuss why models of representative bureaucracy are nevertheless distinct from the conversational model embraced by TechCo.

7. CONVERSATIONAL SPACES

1. It is increasingly common, especially among today's ambitious high-tech firms, for companies to infuse their buildings and interior designs with their values and beliefs (or, at the very least, the values and beliefs the company's founders and executives hope to instill). For example, it was reported in the *New York Times* (Hardy 2014) that the exposed wires and hanging plywood within Facebook's complex were intended to convey an "under construction" feel appropriate for a company that values hacking and rapid change above all; meanwhile, data-driven Google was reported to measure its employees' experiences throughout

its office complex and then use that data to inform everything about the physical environment from the size and shape of the ergonomic chairs employees sit in to the selection of office plants they gaze upon while typing.

2. See, for instance, Oldham and Brass (1979), Hedge (1982), Sundstrom and Sundstrom (1986), Brennan, Chugh, and Kline (2002), Banbury and Berry (2005), De Croon et al. (2005), Pejtersen et al. (2006, 2011), and Davis, Leach, and Clegg (2011).

3. Noise comes up repeatedly in academic studies of open office layouts. For some illustrative treatments of the issue, see Hedge (1982), Sundstrom and Sundstrom (1986), and Pejtersen et al. (2006).

4. See, for instance, Reagans (2011).

5. Granovetter (1973).

6. Zucker (1977) describes the role of institutionalization in cultural persistence and the resistance to change.

7. Bernstein (2012) writes of the "transparency paradox" wherein open work environments enable constant managerial surveillance, and he documents the sometimes counterproductive effects of surveillance on worker performance and motivation.

8. See Gilliom and Monahan (2013) for an incisive treatment of this issue.

9. Alsop (2008), and PWC (2011).

10. See, for instance, Oldham and Brass (1979), Hedge (1982), and Sundstrom and Sundstrom (1986).

11. Davis et al. (2011).

8. THE CONVERSATIONAL FIRM

1. https://www.google.com/about/company/facts/culture/

2. https://www.facebook.com/careers/; https://www.facebook.com/media/set/?set=a.1655178 611435493.1073741828.1633466236940064&type=3

3. http://www.slideshare.net/reed2001/culture-1798664/44-Why_Do_Most_Companies _Curtail; http://www.slideshare.net/reed2001/culture-1798664/42-Our_model_is_to_increase. From the Netflix culture document, http://www.slideshare.net/reed2001/culture-1798664 /netflix.

4. Examples of popular press coverage include Heller (2013), Silverman (2013), and Hardy (2014).

5. Both Talcott Parsons (1937) and Alvin Gouldner (1954) have criticized Weber for conflating these two distinct sources of authority. In *Patterns of Industrial Democracy*, Gouldner (1954) wrote, "Weber, then, thought of bureaucracy as a Janus-faced organization, looking two ways at once. One the one side, it was administration based on expertise; while on the other, it was administration based on discipline. In the first emphasis, obedience is involved as a means to an end; an individual obeys because the rule or order is felt to be the best-known method of realizing some goal. In his second conception, Weber held

that bureaucracy was a mode of administration in which obedience was an end in itself. The individual obeys the order, setting aside judgments either of its rationality or morality, primarily because of the position occupied by the person commanding" (22–23). According to Gouldner, conflating these two forms of authority led Weber to conflate two distinct forms of bureaucracy: a "representative" form in which the rules imposed were believed by workers to be the best means available, and a "punishment-centered" form in which the rules imposed were followed merely out of obedience. I argue that this conflation created another conceptual problem. Namely, it impeded a full understanding of the relationship between communication and hierarchical authority.

6. Weber (1978, 980). Endnote 32 of the introduction discusses a similar assumption made by Simon (1947).

7. See, for instance, Jackall (1988), Smith (1990), Kunda (1992), and Weeks (2004).

8. Rothschild and Russell (1986) review past attempts to build alternatives to bureaucracy, noting their common focus on the introduction of more democratic modes of decision making and control.

9. For analyses of specific attempts to build democratic organizations (typically in the form of cooperatives, collectives, or communes) as well as general reviews of this literature, see Zabolocki (1971), Kanter (1972), Fairfield (1972), Freeman (1973), Swidler (1976, 1979), Shey (1977), Rothschild-Whitt (1979), Rothschild and Russell (1986), Rothschild and Whitt (1986), Whyte and Whyte (1991), Handel (2003), Spiro (2004), and Chen (2009).

10. See Adler (1993, 2012) and Adler and Borys (1996). Also, Rothschild and Russell (1986) discuss this line of work.

11. For example, Vallas (2006).

12. For example, Heckscher and Donnellon (1994), Fulk and DeSanctis (1995), Volderba (1998), and Greenwood and Lawrence (2005). In his 2006 book, *From Counterculture to Cyberculture,* communications scholar and cultural historian Fred Turner argues that the anticorporate, antibureaucratic ambitions of some of these tech companies drew inspiration from the 1960s and 1970s countercultural experiments.

13. For example, Kunda (1992), Victor and Stephens (1994), and Courpasson and Reed (2004).

14. First Round Review (2014); https://medium.com/about-holacracy.

15. Shaer (2013), Silverman (2013, 2015), Warr (2013), Wohlsen (2014), and Useem (2015).

16. http://holacracy.org/how-it-works.

17. Weber (1978, 974).

18. Demsetz (1988), Conner and Prahalad (1996), and Hodgson (2004).

19. Freeland and Zuckerman (2014) provide an incisive discussion of this tension.

20. One way to understand the conversational firm is to see it as a model in which employee voice and conversation are harnessed to weave a procedural justice framework into the very fabric of the organization. As discussed in chapter 3, the procedural justice literature has documented how even when people disagree with outcomes, they care about the process by which the decisions were reached, and, furthermore, how having had a voice in that process is key to their sense of its fairness and legitimacy.

9. THE FUTURE OF THE CONVERSATIONAL FIRM

1. Meyer and Rowan (1977, 340).
2. Turkle (2011, 2015).
3. It is a classic finding in the social studies of technology that new technologies never really carry an inherent social or political outcome. Rather, their effects are always a function of how we choose to use them. Leonardi and Barley (2010) offer a review of this literature.
4. Leonardi and Barley (2010) also offer a thoughtful discussion of how we must not ignore the material affordances and constraints of new technologies even as we accept that social dynamics will shape the technologies' uses and consequences.
5. Some studies have noted the importance of deliberation for surfacing the tradeoffs of new organizational designs and practices in alternative organizations, collectives, and nonprofits (e.g., Rothschild and Russell 1986; Chen 2009). As noted, however, deliberations in these settings are often seen as a path to consensus decision making and nonhierarchical governance as well.
6. See, for example, Agan (2013), Belanger (2014), and Coughlin (2014).
7. In *Prometheus Wired: The Hope for Democracy in the Age of Networked Technology*, scholar Darin Barney (2000) warns against organizing for the sort of change we hope for, noting that this will only distract us from the hard work of harnessing the true potential of any cultural or technological change: "Hope enlightens, but it also blinds . . . [Hope] seduces human beings into overestimating and overreaching themselves, with tragic consequences" (5). Writing about organizations specifically, Azoulay, Repenning, and Zuckerman (2010) make a similar point about the importance of acknowledging the tradeoffs and limitations of any organizational action. They analyzed pharmaceutical firms' failure to manage their relationships with contract research organizations effectively. Because pharmaceutical firms failed to appreciate the nature of the tradeoffs they were making in these relationships, and instead hoped for the "first best" outcome they imagined was possible, they ended up mismanaging the situation and obtaining something worse than the "second best" option they would have achieved had they properly managed the situation at hand (474). The authors conclude, "Pathological practices result from a failure to accept the tradeoffs inherent in an organizational design" (474).

METHODOLOGICAL APPENDIX

1. Powdermaker (1966, 81).
2. See Coleman (2010) and Horst and Miller (2012).
3. My advice stems both from personal experience in the field and from Emerson, Fretz, and Shaw's (1995) superb book on the topic.
4. Jerolmack and Khan (2014).
5. Another group I specifically sought out were older (non-millennial) employees. See note 11 below.

6. Van Maanen (1988, 88).

7. Powdermaker (1966, 230).

8. Powdermaker (1966, 250).

9. Mitchell (1966, 56). See also Nader (1972) and Desmond (2014).

10. Invisible work refers to essential work that often goes unnoticed, either because it takes place behind the scenes or because it is simply not recognized or appreciated by others. See Nardi and Engestrom (1999) for an introduction to the subject and a special issue on it in the journal *Computer Supported Cooperative Work*.

11. Using my own experience as a guide, I made sure to include a number of employees older than the TechCo norm in my interview sample. I was curious to learn how their perspectives aligned with or differed from the perspectives of their younger colleagues. For the most part, they proved to be a self-selected group of individuals who had been attracted to TechCo precisely because of its proclaimed unconventionality and, as a result, not so different from their younger colleagues in most regards. It was impossible to enter the company's offices and not notice the hundreds of young workers, and everyone who interviewed for a job received a company tour; thus, by the time anyone accepted a job offer from TechCo, they had a good sense for the workforce's overall demographics and were choosing to work there knowing that. This is not to say there were no disgruntled employees, but I did not find age to be a primary correlate with employee disgruntledness. (Who one's manager was and how the individual got along with his or her manager were far more telling, for instance). Most important, on the issues profiled in this book the main division in perspectives that surfaced was between executives and workers (rather than among workers themselves), and this became my analytical focus. To be sure, I would not expect every individual who is older than TechCo's typical worker to be happy in a workplace like it; but given the self-selection dynamics at play, those I met and observed, with perhaps one or two exceptions, appeared to be just as happy and unhappy as other employees at the firm.

12. Geertz (1973, 14).

13. Kleinman (1996) includes a thoughtful discussion of this point.

14. Malcolm (1990, 3).

15. Geertz (1973, 10).

16. Geertz (1973, 27).

17. Burawoy (1991, 5).

18. In his 2008 book, *Coming of Age in Second Life*, Boeslstorff modified subjects' online comments so they would be difficult to look up by means of a simple search. Boellstorff et al.'s (2012) *Ethnography and Virtual Worlds* discusses the various methodological and ethical issues of online data collection.

19. Duneier (2000) originally discussed this issue, and it has become a topic of discussion again over the last year.

20. Khan (2011, 203).

REFERENCES

Adler, Paul. 1993. "The 'Learning Bureaucracy:' New United Motor Manufacturing, Inc." *Research in Organizational Behavior* 15: 111–194.

——. 2001. "Market, Hierarchy, and Trust: The Knowledge Economy and the Future of Capitalism." *Organization Science* 12(2): 215–234.

——. 2012. "The Sociological Ambivalence of Bureaucracy: From Weber via Gouldner to Marx." *Organization Science* 23(1): 244–266.

Adler, Paul and Bryan Borys. 1996. "Two Types of Bureaucracy: Enabling and Coercive." *Administrative Science Quarterly* 41: 61–89.

Adut, Ari. 2012. "Theory of the Public Sphere." *Sociological Theory* 30: 238–262.

Agan, Tom. 2013. "Embracing the Millennials' Mind-Set at Work." *New York Times,* November 10, 2013, *http://www.nytimes.com/2013/11/10/jobs/embracing-the-millennials-mind-set-at-work.html.*

Alexander, Jeffrey and Philip Smith. 2002. "The Strong Program in Cultural Theory: Elements of a Structural Hermeneutics." Pp. 135–150 in *Handbook of Sociological Theory,* edited by J. Turner. New York: Kluwer Academic.

Alsop, Ron. 2008. *The Trophy Kids Grow Up: How the Millennial Generation Is Shaking Up the Workplace.* San Francisco, CA: Jossey-Bass.

Anderson, Janna and Lee Rainie. 2012. "Millennials Will Benefit and Suffer Due to Their Hyperconnected Lives." Washington, DC: Pew Research Center, Internet and American Life Project.

Ashford, Susan, Kathleen Sutcliffe and Marlys Christianson. 2009. "Speaking Up and Speaking Out: The Leadership Dynamics of Voice in Organizations." Pp. 175–202 in *Voice and Silence in Organizations,* edited by Jerald Green and Marissa Edwards. Bingley, UK: Emerald Group Publishing.

Associated Press. 2013. "Techie Adria Richards Fired After Tweeting About Men's Comments." *cbsnews.com*, March 22, 2013, *http://www.cbsnews.com/news/techie-adria-richards-fired-after-tweeting-about-mens-comments/*.

Azoulay, Pierre, Nelson Repenning and Ezra Zuckerman. 2010. "Nasty, Brutish and Short: Embeddedness Failure in the Pharmaceutical Industry." *Administrative Science Quarterly* 55: 472–507.

Baker, George, Robert Gibbons and Kevin Murphy. 1999. "Informal Authority in Organizations." *Journal of Law, Economics, & Organization* 15: 56–73.

Banbury, Simon and Dianne Berry. 2005. "Office Noise and Employee Concentration: Identifying Causes of Disruption and Potential Improvements." *Ergonomics* 48(1): 25–37.

Barley, Stephen. 1986. "Technology as an Occasion for Structuring: Evidence from Observations of CT Scanners and the Social Order of Radiology Departments." *Administrative Science Quarterly* 31(1): 78–108.

Barnard, Chester. 1938. *Functions of the Executive.* Cambridge, MA: Harvard University Press.

Barney, Darin. 2000. *Prometheus Wired: The Hope for Democracy in the Age of Networked Technology.* Chicago, IL: University of Chicago Press.

Baron, James. 2004. "Employing Identities in Organizational Ecology." *Industrial and Corporate Change* 13(1): 3–32.

Baron, James, Diane Burton and Michael Hannan. 1996. "The Road Taken: Origins and Evolution of Employment Systems in Emerging Companies." *Industrial and Corporate Change* 5(2): 239–275.

Baron, James and Michael Hannan. 2005. "The Economic Sociology of Organizational Entrepreneurship: Lessons from the Stanford Project on Emerging Companies." Pp 168–203 in *The Economic Sociology of Capitalism*, edited by Victor Nee and Richard Swedberg. New York: Russell Sage.

Baron, James, Michael Hannan and Diane Burton. 2001. "Labor Pains: Change in Organizational Models and Employee Turnover in Young, High-Tech Firms." *American Journal of Sociology* 106(4): 960–1012.

Baron, James and David Kreps. 1999. *Strategic Human Resources: Frameworks for General Managers.* New York: Wiley.

Bauman, Zygmunt and David Lyon. 2012. *Liquid Surveillance: A Conversation.* Cambridge, UK: Polity Press.

Belanger, Lydia. 2014. "To Attract and Keep Millennials, Meet Their Demands: Here's What Generation Y Wants and Why You Should Hand It Over." *Inc.com*, January 27, 2014, *http://www.inc.com/lydia-belanger/to-attract-and-keep-millennials-meet-their-demands.html*.

Benkler, Yochai. 2006. *The Wealth of Networks: How Social Production Transforms Markets and Freedom.* New Haven, NJ: Yale University Press.

Bernstein, Ethan. 2012. "The Transparency Paradox: A Role for Privacy in Organizational Learning and Operational Control." *Administrative Science Quarterly* 57(2): 181–216.

Best, Joel. 2011. *Everyone's a Winner: Life in the Congratulatory Culture.* Berkeley, CA: University of California Press.

Bies, Robert and Debra Shapiro. 1988. "Voice and Justification: Their Influence on Procedural Fairness Judgments." *Academy of Management Journal* 31(3): 676–685.

Bies, Robert and Tom Tyler. 1993. "The 'Litigation Mentality' in Organizations: A Test of Alternative Psychological Explanations. *Organization Science* 4(3): 352–366.

Blau, Peter. 1955. *The Dynamics of Bureaucracy: A Study of Interpersonal Relations in Two Government Agencies.* Chicago, IL: University of Chicago Press.

Boellstorff, Tom. 2008. *Coming of Age in Second Life: An Anthropologist Explores the Virtually Human.* Princeton, NJ: Princeton University Press.

Boellstorff, Tom, Bonnie Nardi, Celia Pearce, and T. L. Taylor. 2012. *Ethnography and Virtual Worlds: A Handbook of Method.* Princeton, NJ: Princeton University Press.

Boyd, Danah. 2010. "Social Network Sites as Networked Publics: Affordances, Dynamics, and Implications. Pp. 39–58 in *A Networked Self: Identity, Community, and Culture on Social Network Sites,* edited by Zizi Papacharissi. New York: Routledge.

———. 2014. *It's Complicated: The Social Lives of Networked Teens.* New Haven, CT: Yale University Press.

Braverman, Harry. 1974. *Labor and Monopoly Capital.* New York: Monthly Review Press.

Brennan, Aoife, Jasdeep Chugh and Theresa Kline. 2002. "Traditional Versus Open Office Design: A Longitudinal Study." *Environment and Behavior* 34: 279–299.

Brockner, Joel, Grant Ackerman, Jerald Greenberg, Michele Gelfand, Ann Marie Francesco, Zhen Xiong Chen, Kwok Leung, Gunter Bierbrauer, Carolina Gomez, Bradley Kirkman and Debra Shapiro. 2001. "Culture and Procedural Justice: The Influence of Power and Distance on Reactions to Voice." *Journal of Experimental Social Psychology* 37: 300–315.

Brockner, Joel, Tom Tyler and Rochelle Cooper-Schneider. 1992. "The Influence of Prior Commitment to an Institution on Reactions to Perceived Unfairness: The Higher They Are, the Harder They Fall." *Administrative Science Quarterly* 37(2): 241–261.

Burawoy, Michael. 1979. *Manufacturing Consent.* Chicago, IL: University of Chicago Press.

———. 1991. *Ethnography Unbound: Power and Resistance in the Modern Metropolis.* Berkeley, CA: University of California Press.

Burris, Ethan. 2012. "The Risks and Rewards of Speaking Up: Managerial Responses to Employee Voice." *Academy of Management Journal* 55(4): 851–875.

Calhoun, Craig. 1992. *Habermas and the Public Sphere.* Cambridge, MA: MIT Press.

Carr, Nicholas. 2011. *The Shallows: What the Internet Is Doing to Our Brains.* New York: Norton.

Chen, Katherine. 2009. *Enabling Creative Chaos: The Organization Behind Burning Man.* Chicago, IL: University of Chicago Press.

Coleman, Gabriella. 2010. "Ethnographic Approaches to Digital Media." *Annual Review of Anthropology* 39: 487–505.

Conner, Kathleen and C. K. Prahalad. 1996. "A Resource-based Theory of the Firm: Knowledge Versus Opportunism." *Organization Science* 7(5): 477–501.

Coughlin, Joseph. 2014. "A Survival Guide to Working with Millennials." *WSJ.com,* January 13, 2014, *http://blogs.wsj.com/experts/2014/01/13/a-survival-guide-to-working-with-millennials/.*

Courpasson, David and Mike Reed. 2004. "Introduction: Bureaucracy in the Age of Enterprise." *Organization* 11(1): 5–12.

Cutler, Kim-Mai. 2013. "A Dongle Joke That Spiraled Way Out of Control." *TechCrunch*, March 21, 2013, *http://techcrunch.com/2013/03/21/a-dongle-joke-that-spiraled-way-out-of-control/*.

Danis, Catalina and David Singer. 2008. "A Wiki Instance in the Enterprise: Opportunities, Concerns and Reality." *Proceedings of the 2008 Conference on Computer Supported Cooperative Work:* 495–504. New York: ACM.

Davis, Gerald. 2014. "After the Corporation." *Politics and Society* 41(2): 283–308.

Davis, Matthew, Desmond Leach and Chris Clegg. 2011. "The Physical Environment of the Office: Contemporary and Emerging Issues." *International Review of Industrial and Organizational Psychology* 26: 193–237.

Dean, Jodi. 2005. "Communicative Capitalism: Circulation and the Foreclosure of Politics." *Cultural Politics* 1(1): 51–74.

De Croon, Einar, Judith Sluiter, P. Paul Kuijer and Monique Frings-Dresen. 2005. "The Effect of Office Concepts on Worker Health and Performance: A Systematic Review of the Literature." *Ergonomics* 48(2): 119–134.

Demsetz, Harold. 1988. "The Theory of the Firm Revisited." *Journal of Law, Economics and Organizations.* 4(1): 141–161.

Desmond, Matthew. 2007. *On the Fireline: Living and Dying with Wildland Firefighters.* Chicago, IL: University of Chicago Press.

——. 2014. "Relational Ethnography." *Theory and Society* 43: 547–579.

Detert, James and Ethan Burris. 2007. "Leadership Behavior and Employee Voice: Is the Door Really Open?" *Academy of Management Journal* 50(4): 869–884.

Detert, James and Amy Edmondson. 2011. "Implicit Voice Theories: An Emerging Understanding of Self-censorship at Work." *Academy of Management Journal* 54: 461–488.

Detert, James and Linda Trevino. 2010. "Speaking Up to Higher-Ups: How Supervisors and Skip-Level Leaders Influence Employee Voice." *Organization Science* 21(1): 249–270.

DiMaggio, Paul. (Editor). 2001. *The Twenty-First Century Firm: Changing Economic Organization in International Perspective.* Princeton, NJ: Princeton University Press.

DiMaggio, Paul and Walter Powell. 1983. "The Iron Cage Revisited: Institutional Isomorphism and Collective Rationality in Organizational Fields." *American Sociological Review* 48(2): 147–160.

DiMicco, Joan, Werner Geyer, David Millen, Casey Dugan and Beth Brownholtz. 2009. "People Sensemaking and Relationship Building on an Enterprise Social Networking Site." *Proceedings of the 42nd Annual Hawaii International Conference on System Sciences:* 1–10. Los Alamitos, CA: IEEE Computer Society Press.

DiMicco, Joan, David Millen, Werner Geyer, Casey Dugan, Beth Brownholtz and Michael Muller. 2008. "Motivations for Social Networking at Work." *Proceedings of the 2008 ACM Conference on Computer Supported Cooperative Work:* 711–720. New York: ACM.

Dishman, Lydia. 2010. "Corporate Social Media Policies: The Good, The Mediocre, and the Ugly." *Fast Company*, July 9, 2010, *http://www.fastcompany.com/1668368/corporate-social-media-policies-good-mediocre-and-ugly*.

Dundon, Tony, Adrian Wilkinson, Mick Marchington and Peter Ackers. 2004. "The Meanings and Purpose of Employee Voice." *International Journal of Human Resource Management* 15: 1149–1170.

Duneier, Mitchell. 2000. *Sidewalk.* New York: Farrar, Strauss, and Giroux.

Edelman, Lauren. 1992. "Legal Ambiguity and Symbolic Structures: Organizational Mediation of Civil Rights Law." *American Journal of Sociology* 97(6): 1531–1576.

Edmundson, Amy. 1999. "Psychological Safety and Learning Behavior in Work Teams." *Administrative Science Quarterly* 44(2): 350–383.

Edwards, Richard. 1979. *Contested Terrain: The Transformation of the Workplace in the Twentieth Century.* New York: Basic.

Emerson, Robert, Rachel Fretz, and Linda Shaw. 1995. *Writing Ethnographic Fieldnotes.* Chicago, IL: University of Chicago Press.

Fairfield, Richard. 1972. *Communes USA.* Baltimore, MD: Penguin.

Farzan, Rosta, Joan DiMicco and Beth Brownholtz. 2009. "Spreading the Honey: A System for Maintaining an Online Community." *Proceedings of the 2009 International Conference on Supporting Group Work*: 31–40. New York: ACM.

Ferenstein, Gregory. 2013. "Read What Facebook's Sandberg Calls Maybe 'The Most Important Document Ever to Come Out of the Valley." *TechCrunch,* January 31, 2013, *http://techcrunch .com/2013/01/31/read-what-facebooks-sandberg-calls-maybe-the-most-important-document-ever -to-come-out-of-the-valley/.*

First Found Review. 2014. "How Medium Is Building a New Kind of Company with No Managers." *First Round Review,* undated, *http://firstround.com/review/How-Medium-is-building-a -new-kind-of-company-with-no-managers/.* (Republished by *Fast Company,* July 15, 2014, *http://www.fastcompany.com/3032994/can-holacracy-work-how-medium-functions-without-managers.*)

Folger, Robert. 1977. "Distributive and Procedural Justice: Combined Impact of Voice and Improvement on Experienced Inequity." *Journal of Personality and Social Psychology* 35(2): 108–119.

Folger, Robert and Russell Cropanzano. 1998. *Organizational Justice and Human Resource Management.* Thousand Oaks, CA: Sage.

Foss, Nicolai. 2003. "Selective Intervention and Internal Hybrids: Interpreting and Learning from the Rise and Decline of the Oticon Spaghetti Organization." *Organization Science* 14(3): 331–349.

Fosse, Ethan. 2014. "Cultural Continuity and the Rise of the Millennials: Generational Trends in Politics, Religion and Economic Values." Unpublished dissertation. Department of Sociology, Harvard University.

Friedman, Hilary. 2013. *Playing to Win: Raising Kids in a Competitive Culture.* Berkeley, CA: University of California Press.

Freeland, Robert and Ezra Zuckerman. 2014. "The Problems and Promise of Hierarchy: A Sociological Theory of the Firm." Unpublished manuscript. University of Wisconsin and MIT Sloan School of Management.

Freeman, Jo. 1973. "The Tyranny of Structurelessness." Pp. 285–99 in *Radical Feminism,* edited by Anne Koedt, Ellen Levine and Anita Rapone. New York: Quadrangle.

Fuchs, Christian. 2012. "Dallas Smythe Today—The Audience Commodity, the Digital Labor Debate, Marxist Political Economy and Critical Theory: Prolegomena to a Digital Labor Theory of Value." *tripleC: Communication, Capitalism, and Critique: Journal for a Global Sustainable Information Society* 10(2): 692–740.

———. 2014. *Social Media: A Critical Introduction.* London, UK: Sage.

Fulk, Janet. 1993. "Social Construction of Communication Technology." *Academy of Management Journal* 36(5): 921–951.

Fulk, Janet and Gerardine DeSanctis. 1995. "Electronic Communication and Changing Organizational Forms." *Organization Science* 6(4): 337–349.

Fulk, Janet, Charles Steinfield, Joseph Schmitz and J. Gerard Power. 1987. "A Social Information Processing Model of Media Use in Organizations." *Communication Research* 14(5): 529–552.

Fung, Archon, Mary Graham and David Weil. 2008. *Full Disclosure: The Perils and Promise of Transparency.* Cambridge, UK: Cambridge University Press.

Geertz, Clifford. 1973. *The Interpretation of Cultures.* New York: Basic.

Gibbons, Robert and Rebecca Henderson. 2012. "Relational Contracts and Organizational Capabilities." *Organization Science* 23(5): 1350–1364.

———. 2013. "What Do Managers Do? Exploring Persistent Performance Differences Among Seemingly Similar Enterprises." Pp. 680–731 (Chapter 15) in *The Handbook of Organizational Economics*, edited by Robert Gibbons and John Roberts. Princeton, NJ: Princeton University Press.

Gilliom, John and Torin Monahan. 2013. *SuperVision: An Introduction to the Surveillance Society.* Chicago, IL: University of Chicago Press.

Giordano, Richard. 2007. "An Investigation of the Use of a Wiki to Support Knowledge Exchange in Public Health." *Proceedings of the 2007 International Conference on Supporting Group Work:* 269–272. New York: ACM.

Girard, Monique and David Stark. 2002. "Distributing Intelligence and Organizing Diversity in New Media Projects." *Environment and Planning A* 34: 1927–1949.

Gladwell, Malcolm. 2010. "Small Change: Why the Revolution Will Not be Tweeted." *The New Yorker*, October 4, 2010, *http://www.newyorker.com/magazine/2010/10/04/small-change-malcolm-gladwell*.

Goel, Vindu. 2014. "Facebook to Let Users Limit Data Revealed by Log-Ins." *New York Times*, May 1, 2014, *http://www.nytimes.com/2014/05/01/technology/facebook-to-let-users-limit-data-revealed-by-log-ins.html*.

Goffman, Erving. 1963. *Behavior in Public Places: Notes on the Social Organization of Gatherings.* New York: Free Press.

Gouldner, Alvin. 1954. *Patterns of Industrial Bureaucracy.* Glencoe, IL: Free Press.

Granovetter, Mark. 1973. "The Strength of Weak Ties." *American Journal of Sociology* 78(6): 1360–1380.

Greenhouse, Steven. 2013. "Even if It Enrages Your Boss, Social Net Speech Is Protected." *New York Times*, January 22, 2013, *http://www.nytimes.com/2013/01/22/technology/employers-social-media-policies-come-under-regulatory-scrutiny.html*.

Greenwood, Royson and Thomas Lawrence. 2005. "The Iron Cage in the Information Age: The Legacy and Relevance of Max Weber for Organization Studies." *Organization Studies* 26(4): 493–499.

Habermas, Jurgen. 1989. *The Structural Transformation of the Public Sphere.* Cambridge, MA: MIT Press.

Handel, Michael. 2003. "Democratic Alternatives to Capitalist Bureaucracy: Worker Ownership and Self-Management." In *The Sociology of Organizations: Classic, Contemporary and Critical Readings*, edited by Michael Handel. Thousand Oaks, CA: Sage.

Hannan, Michael, James Baron, Greta Hsu and Ozgecan Kocak. 2006. "Organizational Identities and the Hazard of Change." *Industrial and Corporate Change* 15(5): 755–784.

Hardy, Quentin. 2014. "The Monuments of Tech." *New York Times*, March 2, 2014, *http://www .nytimes.com/2014/03/02/technology/the-monuments-of-tech.html*.

Hargittai, Eszter. 2010. "Digital Na(t)ives? Variation in Internet Skills and Use Among the 'Net Generation.'" *Sociological Inquiry* 80(1): 92–113.

Hays, Sharon. 1996. *The Cultural Contradictions of Motherhood*. New Haven, CT: Yale University Press.

Heckscher, Charles and Anne Donnellon. 1994. *The Post-Bureaucratic Organization: New Perspectives on Organizational Change*. Thousand Oaks, CA: Sage.

Hedge, Alan. 1982. "The Open-Plan Office: A Systematic Investigation of Employee Reactions to Their Work Environment." *Environment and Behavior* 14: 519–542.

Heller, Nathan. 2013. "Naked Launch: What's Really New About the Big New Tech Companies?" *The New Yorker*, November 25, 2013, *http://www.newyorker.com/magazine/2013/11/25 /naked-launch*.

Hill, Kashmir. 2013. "'Sexism' Public-Shaming Via Twitter Leads to Two People Getting Fired (Including the Shamer)." *Forbes.com*, March 21, 2013, *http://www.forbes.com/sites /kashmirhill/2013/03/21/sexism-public-shaming-via-twitter-leads-to-two-people-getting-fired -including-the-shamer/*.

Hodgson, Geoffrey. 2004. "Opportunism Is Not the Only Reason Why Firms Exist: Why an Explanatory Emphasis on Opportunism May Mislead Management Strategy." *Industrial and Corporate Change* 13(2): 401–418.

Holt, Kris. 2013. "How a 'Big Dongle' Joke Brought Out the Worst of the Internet." *The Daily Dot*, March 21, 2013, *http://www.dailydot.com/society/pycon-dongle-joke-misogyny-sexism-adria-richards/*.

Holtzblatt, Lester, Laurie Damianos and Daniel Weiss. 2010. "Factors Impeding Wiki Use in the Enterprise: A Case Study." *Proceedings of the 28th International Conference Extended Abstracts on Human Factors in Computing Systems*: 4661–4676. New York: ACM.

Horst, Heather and Daniel Miller. (Editors). 2012. *Digital Anthropology*. London, UK: Berg.

Huh, Jina, Loretta Jones, Thomas Erickson, Wendy Kellogg, Rachel Bellamy and John Thomas. 2007. "BlogCentral: The Role of Internal Blogs at Work." *Proceedings of CHI '07 Extended Abstracts on Human Factors in Computing Systems*: 2113–2116. New York: ACM.

Jackall, Robert. 1988. *Moral Mazes: The World of Corporate Managers*. New York: Oxford University Press.

Jerolmack, Colin and Shamus Khan. 2014. "Talk Is Cheap: Ethnography and the Attitudinal Fallacy." *Sociological Methods and Research* 43(2): 178–209.

Kanter, Rosabeth. 1972. *Commitment and Community: Communes and Utopias in Sociological Perspective*. Cambridge, MA: Harvard University Press.

Kelly, Erin and Frank Dobbin. 1998. "How Affirmative Action Became Diversity Management." *American Behavioral Scientist* 41(7): 960–984.

Kellogg, Katherine. 2009. "Operating Room: Relational Spaces and Microinstitutional Change in Surgery." *American Journal of Sociology* 115(3): 657–711.

Khan, Shamus R. 2011. *Privilege: The Making of an Adolescent Elite at St. Paul's School.* Princeton, NJ: Princeton University Press.

Kish-Gephart, Jennifer, James Detert, Linda Trevino and Amy Edmundsom. 2009. "Silenced by Fear: The Nature, Sources and Consequences of Fear at Work." *Research in Organizational Behavior* 29: 163–193.

Klaas, Brian, Julie Olson-Buchanon and Anna-Katherine Ward. 2012. "The Determinants of Alternative Forms of Workplace Voice: An Integrative Perspective." *Journal of Management* 38: 314–345.

Kleinman, Sherryl. 1996. *Opposing Ambitions: Gender and Identity in an Alternative Organization.* Chicago, IL: University of Chicago Press.

Koetsier, John. 2013. "Breaking: Adria Richards Fired by SendGrid for Calling Out Developers on Twitter." *VentureBeat,* March 21, 2013, *http://venturebeat.com/2013/03/21/breaking-adria -richards-fired-by-sendgrid-for-outting-developers-on-twitter/.*

Kunda, Gideon. 1992. *Engineering Culture: Control and Commitment in a High-Tech Corporation.* Philadelphia, PA: Temple University Press.

Lamont, Michele. 2000. *The Dignity of Working Men.* Cambridge, MA: Harvard University Press.

Lauby, Sharlyn. 2009. "10 Must-Haves for Your Social Media Policy." *Mashable,* June 2, 2009, *http://mashable.com/2009/06/02/social-media-policy-musts/.*

Laureau, Annette. 2003. *Unequal Childhoods: Class, Race, and Family Life.* Berkeley, CA: University of California Press.

Leonardi, Paul and Stephen Barley. 2010. "What's Under Construction Here? Social Action, Materiality, and Power in Constructivist Studies of Technology and Organizing." *The Academy of Management Annals* 4(1): 1–51.

Leonardi, Paul and Jeffrey Treem. 2012. "Knowledge Management Technology as a Stage for Strategic Self-Presentation: Implications for Knowledge Sharing in Organizations." *Information and Organization* 22: 37–59.

Levine, Rick, Christopher Locke, Doc Searls and David Weinberger. 2009. *The Cluetrain Manifesto: The End of Business as Usual.* New York: Basic.

Lind, E. Allen, Jerald Greenberg, Kimberly Scott and Thomas Welchans. 2000. "The Winding Road from Employee to Complainant: Situational and Psychological Determinants of Wrongful-Termination Claims." *Administrative Science Quarterly* 45(3): 557–590.

Lind, E. Allen, Carol Kulik, Maureen Ambrose and Maria de Vera Park. 1993. "Individual and Corporate Dispute Resolution: Using Procedural Fairness as a Decision Heuristic." *Administrative Science Quarterly* 38(2): 224–251.

Lind, E. Allen and Tom Tyler. 1988. *The Social Psychology of Procedural Justice.* New York: Plenum.

Lindgren, Simon and Ragner Lundstrom. 2011. "Pirate Culture and Hacktivist Mobilization: The Cultural and Social Protocols of #WikiLeaks on Twitter." *New Media and Society* 13(6): 999–1018.

Mahler, Jonathan. 2014. "Cubicles Rise in Brave New World of Publishing." *New York Times*, November 10, 2014, *http://www.nytimes.com/2014/11/10/business/cubicles-rise-in-brave-new-world-of-publishing.html*.

Macoun, Robert. 2005. "Voice, Control, and Belonging: The Double-Edged Sword of Procedural Fairness." *Annual Review of Law and Social Science* 1: 171–201.

Malcolm, Janet. 1990. *The Journalist and the Murderer*. New York: Vintage.

Malone, Thomas. 2004. *The Future of Work: How the New Order of Business Will Shape Your Organization, Your Management Style, and Your Life*. Boston, MA: Harvard Business School Press.

March, James and Herbert Simon. 1958. *Organizations*. New York: Wiley.

Mayo, Elton. 1933. *The Human Problems of an Industrial Organization*. New York: McMillan.

Meister, Jeanne. 2013. "To Do: Update Company's Social Media Policy ASAP." *Forbes.com*, February 7, 2013, *http://www.forbes.com/sites/jeannemeister/2013/02/07/to-do-update-companys-social-media-policy-asap/*.

Merton, Robert. 1940. "Bureaucratic Structure and Personality." *Social Forces* 18(4): 560–568.

Meyer, John and Brian Rowan. 1977. "Institutionalized Organizations: Formal Structure as Myth and Ceremony." *American Journal of Sociology* 83(2): 340–363.

Michels, Robert. 1915. *Political Parties: A Sociological Study of the Oligrarchical Tendencies of Modern Democracy*. New York: Hearst.

Milgrom, Paul and John Roberts. 1990. "The Economics of Modern Manufacturing: Technology, Strategy and Organizations." *American Economic Review* 80: 511–528.

——. 1995. "Complementarities and Fit: Strategy, Structure and Organizational Change in Manufacturing." *Journal of Accounting and Economics* 19: 179–208.

Milliken, Frances, Elizabeth Morrison and Patricia Hewlin. 2003. "An Exploratory Study of Employee Silence: Issues That Employees Don't Communicate Upward and Why." *Journal of Management Studies* 40: 1453–1476.

Mills, C. Wright. 1951. *White Collar: The American Middle Classes*. New York: Oxford University Press.

Mitchell, J. Clyde. 1966. "Theoretical Orientations in African Urban Studies." Pp. 37–68 in *The Social Anthropology of Complex Societies*, edited by Michael Banton. Association of Social Anthropologists Monography No. 4. London, UK: Tavistock.

Morozov Evgeny. 2009. "How Dictators Watch Us on the Web." *Prospect*, November 18, 2009, *http://www.prospectmagazine.co.uk/2009/11/how-dictators-watch-us-on-the-web/*.

——. 2011. *The New Delusion: The Dark Side of Internet Freedom*. New York: Public Affairs.

Morrill, Calvin. 1995. *The Executive Way: Conflict Management in Corporations*. Chicago, IL: University of Chicago Press.

Morrison, Elizabeth. 2011. "Employee Voice Behavior: Integration and Directions for Future Research." *The Academy of Management Annals* 5(1): 373–412.

——. 2014. "Employee Voice and Silence." *Annual Review of Organizational Psychology and Organizational Behavior* 1: 173–197.

Morrison, Elizabeth and Frances Milliken. 2000. "Organizational Silence: A Barrier to Change and Development in a Pluralistic World. *Academy of Management Review* 25(4): 706–725.

Mowbray, Paula, Adrian Wilkinson and Herman Tse. 2015. "An Integrative Review of Employee Voice: Identifying a Common Conceptualization and Research Agenda." *International Journal of Management Reviews* 17: 382–400.

Muller, Michael, Kate Ehrlich and Stephen Farrell. 2006. "Social Tagging and Self-Tagging for Impression Management." Technical Report No. 06–02. Cambridge, MA: IBM Watson Research Center.

Musil, Steven. 2013. "Dongle Jokes and a Tweet Lead to Firings, Threats and DDoS Attacks." *CNET,* March 21, 2013, *http://www.cnet.com/news/dongle-jokes-and-a-tweet-lead-to-firings-threats-ddos-attacks/.*

Nader, Laura. 1972. "Up the Anthropologist: Perspectives Gained from Studying Up." Pp. 284–311 in *Reinventing Anthropology*, edited by Dell Hymes. New York: Pantheon.

Nardi, Bonnie and Yrjo Engestrom. 1999. "A Web on the Wind: The Structure of Invisible Work." *Computer Supported Cooperative Work* 8: 1–8.

Nohria, Nitin and James Berkeley. 1994. "The Virtual Organization: Bureaucracy, Technology and Implosion of Control." In *The Post-Bureaucratic Organization: New Perspectives on Organizational Change*, edited by Charles Heckscher and Anne Donnellon. Thousand Oaks, CA: Sage.

Oldham, Greg and Daniel Brass. 1979. "Employee Reactions to an Open-Plan Office: A Naturally Occurring Quasi-Experiment." *Administrative Science Quarterly* 24: 267–284.

O'Reilly, Tim. 2005. "What Is Web 2.0?" *oreilly.com*, September 30, 2005, *http://www.oreilly.com/pub/a//web2/archive/what-is-web-20.html.*

Orlikowski, Wanda. 1992. "The Duality of Technology: Rethinking the Concept of Technology in Organizations." *Organization Science* 3(3): 398–427.

Orlikowski, Wanda and JoAnne Yates. 1994. "Genre Repertoire: The Structuring of Communicative Practices in Organizations." *Administrative Science Quarterly* 39: 541–574.

Osterman, Paul. 2006. "Overcoming Oligarchy: Culture and Agency in Social Movement Organizations." *Administrative Science Quarterly* 51: 622–649.

Parsons, Talcott. 1937. *The Structure of Social Action.* New York: McGraw-Hill.

Patterson, Orlando. 2014. "Making Sense of Culture." *Annual Review of Sociology* 40: 1–30.

Pejtersen, Jan, Leila Allermann, Tage Kristensen and O. M. Poulsen. 2006. "Indoor Climate, Psychosocial Work Environment and Symptoms in Open-Plan Offices." *Indoor Air* 16: 392–401.

Pejtersen, Jan, Helene Feveile, Karl Christensen and Hermann Burr. 2011. "Sickness Absence Associated with Shared and Open-Plan Offices: A National Cross-Sectional Questionnaire Survey." *Scandinavian Journal of Work, Environment & Health* 37(5): 376–382.

Perrow, Charles. 1967. "A Framework for the Comparative Analysis of Organizations." *American Sociological Review* 32: 194–208.

——. 1986. *Complex Organizations: A Critical Essay* (3rd Edition). New York: Random House.

Pew Research Center. 2010. "Millennials: A Portrait of Generation Next. Confident. Connected. Open to Change." (February 2010).

——. 2014. "Millennials in Adulthood: Detached from Institutions, Networked with Friends." (March 2014).

Powdermaker, Hortense. 1966. *Stranger and Friend: The Way of the Anthropologist.* New York: Norton.

Powell, Walter. 1990. "Neither Markets nor Hierarchy: Network Forms of Organization." *Research in Organizational Behavior* 12: 295–336.

———. 2001. "The Capitalist Firm in the 21st Century: Emerging Patterns." Pp. 33–68 in *The Twenty-First Century Firm: Changing Economic Organization in International Perspective,* edited by Paul DiMaggio. Princeton, NJ: Princeton University Press.

Power, Brad. 2014a. "How GE Applies Lean Startup Practices." *HBR Blog,* April 23, 2014, *https://hbr.org/2014/04/how-ge-applies-lean-startup-practices.*

———. 2014b. "How GE Stays Young." *HBR Blog,* May 13, 2014, *https://hbr.org/2014/05/how-ge-stays-young.*

Prensky, Mark. 2001. "Digital Natives, Digital Immigrants." *On the Horizon* 9(5): 1–6.

PWC. 2011. "Millennials at Work: Reshaping the Workplace." London, UK: PWC, *https://www.pwc.com/m1/en/services/consulting/documents/millennials-at-work.pdf.*

Reagans, Ray. 2011. "Close Encounters: Analyzing How Social Similarity and Propinquity Contribute to Strong Network Connections." *Organization Science* 22(4): 835–849.

Rainie, Lee and Barry Wellman. 2012. *Networked: The New Social Operating System.* Cambridge, MA: MIT Press.

Rivera, Lauren. 2012. "Hiring as Cultural Matching: The Case of Elite Professional Service Firms." *American Sociological Review* 77(6): 999–1022.

Ronson, Jon. 2015. "How One Stupid Tweet Blew Up Justine Sacco's Life." *New York Times,* February 15, 2015, *http://www.nytimes.com/2015/02/15/magazine/how-one-stupid-tweet-ruined-justine-saccos-life.html.*

Rothschild, Joyce. 2000. "Creating a Just and Democratic Workplace: More Engagement, Less Hierarchy." *Contemporary Sociology* 29(1): 195–213.

Rothschild, Joyce and J. Allen Whitt. 1986. *The Cooperative Workplace: Potentials and Dilemmas of Organizational Democracy and Participation.* Cambridge, UK: Cambridge University Press.

Rothschild, Joyce and Raymond Russell. 1986. "Alternatives to Bureaucracy: Democratic Participation in the Economy." *Annual Review of Sociology* 12: 307–328.

Rothschild-Whitt, Joyce. 1979. "The Collectivist Organization: An Alternative to Rational-Bureaucratic Models." *American Sociological Review* 44(4): 509–527.

Scholz, Trebor. 2012. *Digital Labor: The Internet as Playground and Factory.* New York: Routledge.

Schweitzer, Tamara. 2010. "Does Your Company Need a Social Media Policy?" *Inc.com,* January 25, 2010, *http://www.inc.com/articles/2010/01/need-a-social-media-policy.html.*

Scott, Richard. 1992. *Organizations: Rational, Natural and Open Systems* (3rd Edition). Englewood Cliffs, NJ: Prentice Hall.

Selznick, Philip. 1949. *TVA and the Grass Roots.* Berkeley, CA: University of California Press.

———. 1957. *Leadership in Administration: A Sociological Interpretation.* New York: Harper & Row.

Sewell, Graham. 1998 "The Discipline of Teams: The Control of Team-based Industrial Work Through Electronic and Peer Surveillance." *Administrative Science Quarterly* 43: 397–428.

Shaer, Matthew. 2013. "The Boss Stops Here." *New York Magazine,* June 16, 2013, *http://nymag.com/news/features/bossless-jobs-2013-6/.*

Shaw, Aaron and Benjamin Mako Hill. 2014. "Laboratories of Oligarchy? How The Iron Law Extends to Peer Production." *The Journal of Communication* 64(2): 215–238.

Shey, Thomas. 1977. "Why Communes Fail: A Comparative Analysis of the Viability of Danish and American Communes." *Journal of Marriage and Family* 39: 605–613.

Shirky, Clay. 2008. *Here Comes Everybody: The Power of Organizing Without Organizations.* New York: Penguin.

——. 2011. "The Political Power of Social Media: Technology, the Public Sphere, and Political Change." *Foreign Affairs,* January/February 2011 Issue, *https://www.foreignaffairs.com /articles/2010–12–20/political-power-social-media.*

Shontell, Alyson. 2013. "Sheryl Sandberg: 'The Most Important Document Ever to Come Out of the Valley.'" *Business Insider,* February 4, 2013, *http://www.businessinsider.com /netflixs-management-and-culture-presentation-2013–2.*

Silverman, Rachel. 2013. "Some Tech Firms Ask: Who Needs Managers?" *Wall Street Journal,* August 6, 2013, *http://www.wsj.com/articles/SB10001424127887323420604578652051466314748.*

——. 2015. "At Zappos, Banishing the Bosses Brings Confusion." *Wall Street Journal,* May 20, 2015, *http://www.wsj.com/articles/at-zappos-banishing-the-bosses-brings-confusion-1432175402.*

Simon, Herbert. 1947. *Administrative Behavior.* New York: MacMillan. (Page references refer to 1997, 4th Edition).

Smith, Victoria. 1990. *Managing in the Corporate Interest: Control and Resistance in an American Bank.* Berkeley, CA: University of California Press.

Spector, Robert and Patrick McCarthy. 2012. *The Nordstrom Way to Customer Service* (2nd Edition). Hoboken, NJ: Wiley.

Spencer, Daniel. 1986. "Employee Voice and Employee Retention." *Academy of Management Journal* 49: 488–502.

Spiro, Melford. 2004. "Utopia and Its Discontents: The Kibbutz and Its Historical Vicissitudes." *American Anthropologist* 106: 556–568.

Stark, David. 2001. "Ambiguous Assets for Uncertain Environments: Heterarchy in Postsocialist Firms." Pp. 69–104 in *The Twenty-First Century Firm: Changing Economic Organization in International Perspective,* edited by Paul DiMaggio. Princeton, NJ: Princeton University Press.

Sundstrom, Eric and Mary Graehl Sundstrom. 1986. *Work Places: The Psychology of the Physical Environment in Offices and Factories.* New York: Cambridge University Press.

Swidler, Ann. 1976. "What Free Schools Teach." *Social Problems* 24: 214–227.

——. 1979. *Organization Without Authority.* Cambridge, MA: Harvard University Press.

——. 1986. "Culture in Action". *American Sociological Review* 51(2): 273–286.

Taylor, Frederick. 1911. *The Principles of Scientific Management.* University of Wisconsin Madison, WI: Harper & Brothers.

Thibaut, John and Laurens Walker. 1978. "A Theory of Procedure." *California Law Review* 66(3): 541–566.

Treem, Jeffrey and Paul Leaonardi. 2012. "Social Media Use in Organizations: Exploring the Affordances of Visibility, Editability, Persistence, and Association." *Communication Yearbook* 36: 143–189.

Turco, Catherine. 2010. "Cultural Foundations of Tokenism: Evidence from the Leveraged Buy-out Industry." *American Sociological Review* 75(6): 894–913.

——. 2012. "Difficult Decoupling: Employee Resistance to the Commercialization of Personal Settings." *American Journal of Sociology* 118(2): 380–419.

Turco, Catherine and Ezra Zuckerman. 2014. "So You Think You Can Dance? Lessons from the US Private Equity Bubble." *Sociological Science* 1: 81–101.

Turkle, Sherry. 2011. *Alone Together: Why We Expect More from Technology and Less from Each Other.* New York: Basic.

——. 2015. *Reclaiming Conversation: The Power of Talk in a Digital Age.* New York: Penguin.

Turner, Fred. 2006. *From Counterculture to Cyberculture: Stewart Brand, the Whole Earth Network, and the Rise of Digital Utopianism.* Chicago, IL: University of Chicago Press.

Twenge, J. M. (2006). *Generation Me: Why Today's Young Americans Are More Confident, Assertive, Entitled—and More Miserable Than Ever Before.* New York: Free Press.

Tyler, Tom and E. Allen Lind. 1992. "A Relational Model of Authority in Groups." *Advances in Experimental Social Psychology* 25:115–192.

Tyler, Tom, E. Allen Lind and Yuen Huo. 2000. "Cultural Values and Authority Relations: The Psychology of Conflict Resolution Across Culture." *Psychology, Public Policy and Law* 6(4):1138–1163.

Useem, Jerry. 2015. "Are Bosses Necessary?" *The Atlantic,* October 2015, *http://www.theatlantic.com/magazine/archive/2015/10/are-bosses-necessary/403216/.*

Vallas, Steven. 2003. "The Adventures of Managerial Hegemony: Teamwork, Ideology, and Worker Resistance." *Social Problems* 50(2): 204–225.

——. 2006. "Empowerment Redux: Structure, Agency, and the Remaking of Managerial Authority." *American Journal of Sociology* 111(6): 1677–1717.

Van Dijck, Jose. 2013. *The Culture of Connectivity: A Critical History of Social Media.* Oxford, UK: Oxford University Press.

Van Maanen, John. 1988. *Tales of the Field: On Writing Ethnography.* Chicago, IL: University of Chicago Press.

Verma, Anil and Thomas Kochan. 2004. *Unions in the 21st Century.* New York: Palgrave.

Victor, Bart and Carroll Stephens. 1994. "The Dark Side of the New Organizational Forms: An Editorial Essay." *Organization Science* 5(4): 479–482.

Volberda, Henk. 1998. *Building the Flexible Firm: How to Remain Competitive.* New York: Oxford University Press.

Warr, Philippa. 2013. "Former Valve Employee: 'It Felt a Lot Like High School.'" *Wired UK,* July 9, 2013, *http://www.wired.com/2013/07/wireduk-valve-jeri-ellsworth/.*

Wattal, Sunil, Pradeep Racherla and Munir Mandviwalla. 2009. "Employee Adoption of Corporate Blogs: A Quantitative Analysis." *Proceedings of the 42nd Hawaii International Conference on Systems Sciences*: 1–10.

Weber, Max. 1978[1922]. *Economy and Society* (Vol. 2), edited by Guenther Roth and Claus Wittich. Berkeley, CA: University of California Press.

Weeks, John. 2004. *Unpopular Culture: The Ritual of Complaint in a British Bank.* Chicago, IL: University of Chicago Press.

Whyte, William H. 1956. *The Organization Man.* New York: Simon and Schuster.

Whyte, William F. and Kathleen King Whyte. 1991. *Making Mondragon: The Growth and Dynamics of the Worker Cooperative Complex.* Ithaca, NY: Cornell University Press.

WikiLeaks. 2011. "What Is WikiLeaks?" *wikileaks.org,* April 7, 2011, *https://wikileaks.org/About.html.*

Williamson, Oliver. 1996. *The Mechanisms of Governance.* New York: Oxford University Press.

Wilson, Sloan. 1955. *The Man in the Gray Flannel Suit.* New York: Simon and Schuster.

Wohlsen, Marcus. 2014. "The Next Big Thing You Missed: Companies That Work Better Without Bosses." *Wired,* January 7, 2014, *http://www.wired.com/2014/01/holacracy-at-zappos/.*

Wood, Stephen and Toby Wall. 2007. "Work Enrichment and Employee Voice in Human Resource Management-Performance Studies." *The International Journal of Human Resource Management* 18: 1335–1372.

Woodward, Joan. 1965. *Industrial Organization: Theory and Practice.* New York: Oxford University Press.

Yardi, Sarita, Scott Golder and Michael Brzozowski. 2009. "Blogging at Work and the Corporate Attention Economy." *Proceedings of the 27th International Conference on Human Factor in Computing Systems*: 2071–2080.

Zablocki, David. 1971. *The Joyful Community: An Account of the Bruderhoff, a Communal Movement Now in Its Third Generation.* New York: Penguin.

Zandt, Deanna. 2013. "Why Asking What Adria Richards Could Have Done Differently Is the Wrong Question." *Forbes.com,* March 22, 2013, *http://www.forbes.com/sites/deannazandt/2013/03/22/why-asking-what-adria-richards-could-have-done-differently-is-the-wrong-question/.*

Zucker, Lynne. 1977. "The Role of Institutionalization in Cultural Persistence." *American Sociological Review* 42(5): 726–743.

Zuckerman, Ezra. 2010. "Speaking with One Voice: A 'Stanford School' Approach to Organizational Hierarchy." *Research in the Sociology of Organizations* 28: 289–307.

INDEX